Yetminster High Street looking east. Petty's Farm on left.

# YETMINSTER
# and
# BEYOND

### Nina Hayward

*"To the people who made the history
which it has been my pleasure
to discover"*

ISBN 0-9512700-36

*Author:*   Mrs Nina Hayward, 22 St Osmond Close,
            Yetminster, Sherborne, Dorset, DT9 6LU

*Maps*:     Dennis R. Seaward

*Drawings*: Samantha Chaffey and the late Isobel Walker
            Modern photography: Hazel Rogers

*Cover:*    The shaft of the Saxon Cross,
            Drawing by Isobel Walker

*Printed by Henry Ling Ltd., The Dorset Press*

# Acknowledgements

I wish to thank Mr. Hugh Jaques and the Staff of Dorset Record Office and the Archivist and Staff of Wiltshire Record Office for their assistance.

Also, Sherborne Museum and all those who have kindly given me information, especially the following: Mr. John Andrews, Miss Lois Greenwood (U.S.A), Mr Cameron Hayward (U.S.A), Mr Ken Hayward (N.Z), Mrs Anne Leahy (N.Z), Mrs Carole Olding, Mr. Stuart Thompson and Mr. Vivian Warry.

Also, Mr. David Andrews for permission to include the letter from Benjamin Watts.

## References

D.R.O.  Parish Registers of Yetminster, Leigh and Chetnole.
Parish Registers of Ryme Intrinseca, Melbury Bubb and Melbury Osmond.
Vestry Minute Books Yetminster
Vestry Minute Books Leigh
D.R.O.  Manor Court Books: Yetminster Prima 1797–1834.
Manor Court Books: Yetminster Secunda 1769–1855.
Manor Court Records: Digby Manor: 1653–1749.
W.R.O.  Manor Court Books: Yetminster Secunda 1686–1768.
D.R.O.  D375/1 Diary of Thomas Oldfield Bartlett of Wareham.

## Bibliography

John Hutchins  The History and Antiquities of the County of Dorset
R. Machin  The House of Yetminster
R. Machin  Probate Inventories and Manor Court Excepts of Yetminster, Leigh and Chetnole.
The Case-book of Sir Francis Ashley, J.P., Recorder of Dorset 1614–35. Edited J. H. Bettey.
Peter Clarke  The English Ale-house.
Patrick Cowley  Church Houses, their religious and social significance.
Leslie Brook  The Book of Yeovil.
Norman Wymer  English County Crafts.

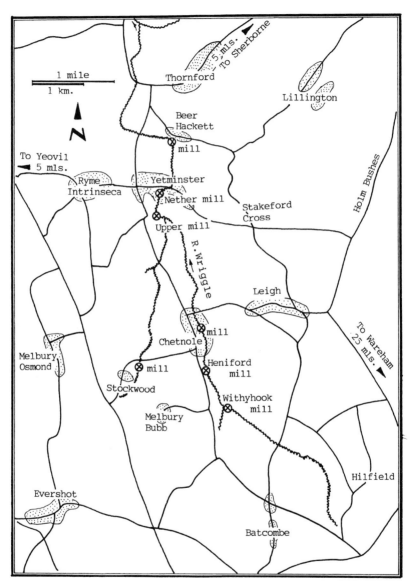

Yetminster and Beyond

vi

# Contents

1. Manor and Parish . . . . . . . . . . . . . . . . . . . . . . . . . . . . . . . . . . . . . . . . 1

2. Roads . . . . . . . . . . . . . . . . . . . . . . . . . . . . . . . . . . . . . . . . . . . . . . . . . 17

3. Law and Order . . . . . . . . . . . . . . . . . . . . . . . . . . . . . . . . . . . . . . . . 23

4. The Mills on the Wriggle . . . . . . . . . . . . . . . . . . . . . . . . . . . . . 35

5. Alehouses . . . . . . . . . . . . . . . . . . . . . . . . . . . . . . . . . . . . . . . . . . . . 47

6. The Hayward family of Ryme Intrinseca and Yetminster . . . . . 66

7. The High Street . . . . . . . . . . . . . . . . . . . . . . . . . . . . . . . . . . . . . . 89

8. Manor House . . . . . . . . . . . . . . . . . . . . . . . . . . . . . . . . . . . . . . . 107

9. The Church House . . . . . . . . . . . . . . . . . . . . . . . . . . . . . . . . . . . 117

10. Tanners . . . . . . . . . . . . . . . . . . . . . . . . . . . . . . . . . . . . . . . . . . . . . 126

11. Church Street . . . . . . . . . . . . . . . . . . . . . . . . . . . . . . . . . . . . . . . 137

12. Gable Court . . . . . . . . . . . . . . . . . . . . . . . . . . . . . . . . . . . . . . . . 163

13. Queen Street . . . . . . . . . . . . . . . . . . . . . . . . . . . . . . . . . . . . . . . . 175

14. The Ryall Family . . . . . . . . . . . . . . . . . . . . . . . . . . . . . . . . . . . 186

15. Chapel Lane . . . . . . . . . . . . . . . . . . . . . . . . . . . . . . . . . . . . . . . . 197

16. The Brake Family . . . . . . . . . . . . . . . . . . . . . . . . . . . . . . . . . . . 212

17. Sieve and Basket makers . . . . . . . . . . . . . . . . . . . . . . . . . . . . . 229

18. The Anne and Mary Charity . . . . . . . . . . . . . . . . . . . . . . . . . . 237

19. Tailors and Tape . . . . . . . . . . . . . . . . . . . . . . . . . . . . . . . . . . . . 243

20. Here and There . . . . . . . . . . . . . . . . . . . . . . . . . . . . . . . . . . . . . 256

Glossary . . . . . . . . . . . . . . . . . . . . . . . . . . . . . . . . . . . . . . . . . . . . . . . . . 256

# Manor and Parish

Most probably, the oldest object to be found in Yetminster is the shaft of the Saxon Cross now in St. Andrew's Church. In 1938, it was discovered, buried in undergrowth, in the churchyard. Originally, it may have stood on the triangle by Cross Farm. But, its presence is an indication that, by the 10th century, Christianity had reached the area. There was probably a settlement long before that. The situation above the little River Wriggle was, doubtless, a consideration in the choice of site and the area abounds in springs so providing an abundant supply of water for man and beast.

The Church is dedicated to St. Andrew. 'Minster' was the old English form of 'monasterium' and suggests a date after the year 600 when Celtic Christianity in England submitted to Rome and Latin was adopted. A 'Minster' was an important church probably the 'mother church' of an area.

'Yet', spelt variously 'Yet', 'Yat', 'Yate', 'Gat', 'Gate', may have referred to a person - - - - - named 'Eata', possibly, who may have built the church. Nothing is known of the appearance of the early church, the first building was probably of wood.

Towards the end of the 13th century, it was re-built, but it was not consecrated until 1326. The Bishop's excuse for this neglect was "preoccupation with national affairs."

The year 1326 must have been a busy one for him: as well as Yetminster, he consecrated fifty churches, including Ryme and Batcombe. Note the rare Consecration Crosses *outside* the Church, ten large ones and two smaller ones over the door.

The nave was re-built in the 15th century by the parishioners whose responsibility it was. Sadly, the Chancel, for which the Prebend was responsible, was often neglected and in need of repair.

It is not known exactly what was lost at the Reformation, but there were two side altars, a Rood Screen and painted decoration, vestiges of

1

which remain. At the east end of the North aisle may be seen a small alabaster angel, probably part of an altar torn out at this time.

What became of the stained glass windows? A faint rumour says the glass was thrown out in the church-yard and there it remains!

The Church is situated on high ground to the south of the village. Most of the dwellings are to be found along the High Street at the foot of the hill with a few in Queen Street to the west and Church Street to the east. Only a handful of cottages were built to the south of the Church in Birch Lane and Mill Lane. The land is not particularly fertile and somewhat stoney. The stoniness was to prove an advantage in later years when men began to build in stone for they were able to open several quarries and extract the good building material which we see in so many of the houses today.

There were also a number of lime-kilns. One interesting example, intact but for the loss of the top of its chimney, has survived near the old quarry off Tarks Hill. Another kiln may be seen in the bank in Melbury Road and a third in Downs Lane. Much lime was spread in an attempt to improve soil fertility, it was also in demand for building work and was essential to the tanning process.

At the time of Domesday, the Bishop of Sarum held Yetminster.

Domesday Book records Yetminster as follows:

*Before 1066 it paid tax for 15 hides. There is land for 20 ploughs. Besides this there is land for 6 ploughs which never paid tax before 1066. 4 ploughs in lordship, 6 slaves, 25 villagers and 25 small-holders with 8 ploughs. A mill which pays 5s; meadow 30 acres; pasture 2 furlongs long and 1 furlong wide; woodland 1 league long and another wide. The value was, and is, £22. William holds 6 hides of this land from the Bishop. He has 4 ploughs there and 4 slaves and 6 villagers and 10 smallholders with 2 ploughs. A mill, meadow 12 acres, woodland 3 furlongs long and 1 furlong wide. Value £4.*

The Bishop was Osmund de Seaz, Bishop of Sarum and nephew of William the Conqueror.

Soon after the Conquest, the Bishop wished to make financial provision for some of the Prebends or Canons of his Cathedral. He divided his Manor of Yetminster (which included Leigh and Chetnole) into four Manors.

2

*Yetminster Ecclesia or Rectory Manor.* He includes Grimston with this but it has no bearing on the history of Yetminster. The Prebend who held this Manor was the Rector of Yetminster. He was entitled to the Greater Tithes of the parish and he appointed the Vicar who took the Lesser Tithes. The principal house of this Manor was probably the house which stood by the Church gate. It was known as the Old Rectory and was demolished in the 1920s to make room for the Church Hall.

*Yetminster Prima or Upbury.* The Mansion House was probably the present Upbury Farm on the south side of the Church. It was built in the 15th century as an open hall house and, perhaps replaced an earlier dwelling since there must have been a house to this Manor during the previous three hundred years.

*Yetminster Secunda or Netherbury.* The capital messuage of this Manor was the present Gable Court.

*Yetminster Episcopi* was the part the Bishop retained for himself. The location of the principal dwelling is not known but it may have been across the river at Brister End. Documents refer to Bishop's Farm which included a close called "Downs" adjacent to Downs Lane in that area. Many hundreds of years later, whilst the See of Sarum was vacant, Queen Elizabeth managed to get her hands on this fourth part and she bestowed it upon her favourite, Raleigh. From him, it devolved to the Digbys of Sherborne and became known as Digby Manor.

In the Chapter House of Salisbury Cathedral may be seen the stalls of the Canons. Over each stall is inscribed the name of the Manor held by that particular Canon. Two are inscribed Yetminster Prima and Yetminster Secunda.

The Prebends, having been granted their Manors, were, of course, interested in income. Just what arrangements were made in earlier centuries is not known, but, after the Reformation, the Manors were leased out. We know that from 1576 to 1729 Upbury Manor was leased to the FitzJames family of Leweston, it may have provided a home and income for younger sons. In 1729 the Manor passed to Lord Broke at which time there were 55 copyhold tenements, 203 acres of land and an annual income of £111 10s 6d. By the next century it was held by the Rev. Thomas Lydiat who was the incumbent of a parish near Kettering. From 1622 to 1706 the Minternes of Batcome leased Yetminster Secunda. The lessee became Lord of the Manor. He appointed a

St. Andrew's Church, early 19 c. From a water-colour by G. F. Cooper, curate.
After his death in 1842, his family emigrated to New Zealand. Note the steps
in church-yard wall.

Steward to conduct affairs, to receive rents and the fines and heriots
imposed when property changed hands.

Twice a year, the Court Baron was held, presided over by the Lord's
Steward. At this Court all changes of tenancy were recorded whether
by inheritance or by purchase. The granting of a mortgage was also
recorded, since, until the debt was paid, the property was held by the
lender. The customs of the Manor required that all who held property
of the Manor should attend the Court or be fined and early records give
lists of absentees and of those attending, the latter known as the
Homage or Jury. In effect, they were witnesses to the transactions and
decided the fines or heriots to be paid when a new tenant was admitted
to a property.

At the commencement of the Court the Jury was sworn in. Those relinquishing property appeared as did those wishing to take it over, or, if unable to appear in person, they might appoint an 'attorney' to act for them. Sometimes, of course, the Jury had to declare that, since the last Court, a lessee or copyholder had died, the Court then waited for someone to come forward and prove their right to succeed. If the deceased had left a Will, there was no problem. Sometimes, witnesses had to declare on oath the last wishes of the deceased as expressed in their presence. Each time a property changed hands a 'Fine' became payable. In the case of a widow succeeding to her late husband's cottage, this might be as little as 6d but for a large tenement, it might be £20 or more.

If the late tenant had died a heriot also became due. This derived from Saxon times and it was an obligation on an heir to return to the Lord the war apparel of the deceased tenant which the Lord had supplied. At about the time of the Norman Conquest the custom was superseded by the Lord receiving the best beast of the deceased. By the 17th/18th century it became simply a money payment.

By the customs of the Manor, a man did not have to wait for a Court to meet, he could pass on his property at any time as long as he did it before witnesses, the change was then recorded at the next Court on the oaths of the witnesses.

Yetminster also had a system of "excepts". A person might pass on part of his property to another whilst retaining certain specified rooms, or ground or even apple trees for his own use. It was not uncommon for a father to make this arrangement when he felt he was getting too old to run the farm and his son, perhaps, had married, needed a home and was ready to take over responsibility.

On 14 December 1603 Roger Ball of Yetminster excepted to John, his son:

*"The east hall of the said tenement with the butterie and the two chambers over them, with free use of the entry with the tenant, the barne, the stable with the tallett over the stable, the kytchine, the hemplands next adjoining conteininge half an acre bee it more or lesse, the wester garden, the wester orchard and five closes totalling 16½ acres. Also the east orcharde from the greate elme unto the*

*greate garlande tree, the piggestye, the cartehouse at the weste end of the kytchine and the barton. Allowing the tenante to have free ingresse and egresse over and through the said barton and a little house without the backdoore."*

On 20 September 1586 Thomas Kete senior of Leigh excepting to John his son, mentioned specified fruit trees: "a pere emperor, a warden, and two apple trees called coxe apple and best pippin tree."

The Court elected a Reeve and a Hayward. In early days, the Reeve organised the daily business of the Manor, he received a monetary payment and certain priviledges during his term of office. The Hayward was responsible for seeing that hedges and fences were kept in good repair so that cattle did not stray onto the common fields. He also impounded stray animals, putting them into the care of the pinder, if there was one.

For some years in the latter part of the 18 c Fooks, the Sherborne solicitors, had acted as stewards of both Yetminster Prima and Secunda. They were, thus, in a good position to see how lucrative Lordship of these Manors could be. Thomas Fooks, himself, took over as Lord of the Manors. By the middle of the 19 c, as property changed hands, he was granting enfranchisement, at a price! The Digby Manor was also selling off its Yetminster property. Yetminster Ecclesia had devolved to the Church Commissioners and they, too, sold their property. By the 1920s the Manors were no more.

## The Parish

The Parish Vestry had for long existed to deal with Church affairs, but in the 16 c and 17 c Parliament gave it responsibilities in the secular field particularly in regard to provision for the poor and the upkeep of the roads.

The Vestry was an unelected body responsible to the local Magistrates. It consisted of "We, the principal inhabitants of the parish of . . ." as they invariably styled themselves. The Vestry ordered almost every aspect of Parish life. Each year, at the annual Easter Vestry Meeting, Officers for the ensuing year were appointed and the names sent to the Magistrate for approval. These were: 2 Overseers of the Poor, 2 Surveyors of the Highway or Waywardens and a Constable.

If you ever wondered why our financial year ends in April and not December, here is the reason. The Gregorian Calendar was not introduced into the United Kingdom until 1752 (known as New Style) and henceforth January 1st was New Year's Day. Previously, March 25th was New Year's Day. Parishes did not change, throughout the land, Easter Vestries were held. All parishioners were free to attend and the Officers presented their accounts for the year. These accounts were of great interest to the parishioners for they showed how the money contributed by them in Poor Rates had been disbursed.

The Parish Officers were unpaid, receiving only out-of-pocket expenses incurred on Parish business.

Finance came from the Parish Rate levied on every household except those of the very poor. In Yetminster in the 18 c the rate varied from 1s to ¼d. But the amount collected depended upon the cash needed to meet expenditure. The Vestry might order the collection of, for example, 20 rates, twenty times each individual's assessment. And this collection might be made more than once in a year, according to need. A bad epidemic of smallpox could bear heavily on the rate-payers.

The greater part of the Parish expenditure was on the poor. The dissolution of the monasteries had caused a tremendous increase in the number of poor people, tramping from place to place begging for sustenance where they could. This became intolerable. The great Elizabethan Poor Law Act of 1601 put the care of the poor squarely in the hands of the Parish, where it remained until, in 1834, the New Poor Law replaced the Old. Responsibility was then removed to Poor Law Unions administered by Boards of Guardians on which each Parish had a representative. Groups of Parishes made up a Union and a Workhouse was built for each Union to house the Poor of those Parishes. Yetminster was part of Sherborne Union, the Workhouse was situated in Acreman Street but has now been demolished.

For over two hundred years every need of the Poor was fulfilled by the Parish. They needed housing. Every Parish owned a Poor House. The Poor House of Yetminster has survived, standing well outside the village on the Chetnole road, it was, and is, known as "Holbrook" possibly from a small stream nearby. It followed the usual pattern of a parish Poor House, a row of tiny cottages, one up and one down, each with a fireplace, but, small as they were, people were still required to

7

share. Arriving at compatible occupants must have been a headache for the Overseers, human nature being what it is, there were always some who could not agree under the same roof. Other Poor Houses have survived at Batcombe, Leigh, Chetnole and Hilfield. These cottages were poorly built and needed constant repair, especially to the thatched roofs. Yetminster Parish owned other cottages for the use of the Poor or sometimes paid a person's rent.

The needy poor received weekly amounts of money, and, every Saturday night, the Overseer sat in the Church porch distributing these payments. Clothing was purchased and bedding for the sick. From time to time, Elizabeth Hayes, inn-keeper of the White Hart, was paid for making shirts and shifts. The children of the Poor were apprenticed and the putative fathers of bastard infants compelled to contribute towards the cost of keeping them. Medical attention for the sick was provided, usually the Parish contracted with a Doctor to attend the Poor for, perhaps, £10 per annum. But they also paid out for specific cases, on occasion becoming so exasperated because the patient did not recover, that they paid only part of the Doctor's fee, promising the remainder when the cure was complete!

Sometimes, the sick were sent to what might be regarded as a 'specialist' as when, in 1767, blind John Cheesman was sent, expenses paid, to Salisbury to consult Dr. Goldwine. Women were paid to nurse the sick, the midwife, if needed, was paid, and, finally, when a poor person died, the Parish met the expenses of the funeral. These amounted to around fifteen shillings.

In 1763, Edward Harris died, he was laid to rest at a cost of 16s:

*shroud 2s 10d*
*coffin & laying out 7s 6d*
*bell, grave & cloth 3s*
*bread, cheese & cyder 2s 8d*

In 1770, Jane Bartlett followed:

*shroud 2s 8d*
*coffin 6s*
*cloth 1s*
*gave two women for laying her out 1s 2d*

*for putting her in the coffin 6d*
*liquor when she was buried 1s*
*bell & grave 2s*

There were two classes of Poor, the First Poor, more or less permanently in need through age or infirmity and the Second Poor, only temporarily in want, usually through sickness, accident or the loss of the bread-winner. Many people leaving legacies for the poor in their Wills, would specify that the money was to go to the "Second Poor".

It fell to the Overseers and the Vestry to decide which applicants were eligible for relief and to what extent. If refused, the applicant could appeal to the Magistrate who might, if he thought fit, order relief to be given. Only those settled in a parish were entitled to relief from that parish and doubtful cases were referred to the Magistrate who would determine their place of settlement by examination. If he considered this to be in another parish, he would issue a Removal Order. This system of removing those who had no right of settlement in a parish and who were unable to maintain themselves, gave rise to much litigation between parishes. If the receiving parish disagreed with the Magistrate's decision, the Order would be contested at Court. Such litigation involved both parishes in much expense, attorneys were engaged and journeys were undertaken to Quarter Sessions by the Overseers, these could be as far as Bridport. Quarter Sessions were notorious for adjourning cases, so the whole process might be repeated at a later date. But great was the satisfaction if a parish won its case! No doubt, the cost of the action was balanced against the cost of providing for a pauper and his family for many years to come.

An Order could be made removing an individual to a parish many, many miles away. There is the case of the Bere Regis man who joined the army. His regiment was posted further and further north, until, finally, it arrived in the Newcastle area. Here the soldier married a local girl. The regiment was sent overseas and no more was heard of him. Meanwhile, the wife had borne a child and she was compelled by circumstances to seek help from the local parish. The Overseer promptly sent her off to the Magistrate to be examined as to her place of settlement. A wife took the settlement of her husband, so, having heard her story, the Magistrate decided she should be sent to Bere

Regis. The Order was made, detailing the route to be taken and she was passed from parish to parish each a day's journey from one to the next. Each parish was obliged to provide her with board and lodging and sent her on the following day, with an escort, to the next place on the route. It was not until a year later that she finally arrived at her destination. Parishes situated on main roads were frequently required to assist with such journeys.

During his year of Office, the Overseer's life was a busy one. Apart from attending Vestry meetings, he collected the Poor Rate, paid the Poor, arranged housing and the purchase of clothing. He made arrangements for the apprenticing of poor children, went in search of putative fathers of bastard children, arranged for medical attention and nursing and the burial of the dead. Much time must have been spent in the saddle as he made frequent visits to the Magistrate, carried out Removal Orders and attended Quarter Sessions. In order to carry out his duties, he required a good knowledge of the Law – yet he was completely untrained. The Overseers appear as compassionate men carrying out a difficult task to the best of their ability. If some treatment appears harsh, the times were harsh, many laws were harsh and so were punishments. How many people today would be willing to take on, voluntarily, such a vast and wide-ranging commitment?

## A Rental for the Manor of Yetminster Episcopi made and taken the 25 of March 1703

*Per annum*

*Freeholders*

| | | |
|---|---|---|
| The Master and Brethren of the Almshouse at Sherborne | 6s | 10d |
| Bathshua Fisher widow | | 4d |
| Luttrells Farm William Hewlett | 20s | 00d |
| now dividend ⎰ Joseph Watts, Sarah Watts wid. (erased) <br> ⎱ Master Abraham Miller, gent. (sub.) | 19s | 00d |
| William Taunton | 10s | 4d |
| John Reynolds | 6s | 6d |
| Edward Harris | 6s | 6d |
| Richard Miller | 1s | 00d |

10

| | | | |
|---|---|---|---|
| Yetminster | George Welsh | | 4d |
| Leaseholders | Richard Lillington (William sub.) | 1s | 4d |
| | Abraham Miller | 1s | 4d |
| Customary | Martin Strange clerk | 7s | 8d |
| Tenants | John Mintern (Clapcott Esq. sub.) | 6s | 1d |
| | Thomas Allambridge | 6s | 8d |
| | John Munden | 3s | 8d |
| | William Hewlett (William erased) | 7s | 9d |
| | Edward Wheadon | 7s | 8d |
| Tenant at Will | John Blaydon for a water course | 1s | 2d |
| Leigh | William Goldring | 2s | 0d |
| Leaseholders | Thomas Goldring | | 8d |
| | John Bishop | 1s | 4d |
| | John Winter | 1s | 4d |
| | Richard Miller | 10s | 0d |
| Customary | Richard Miller | | 2d |
| Tenants | Joan Caffe wid. | 6s | 1½d |
| | Richard Miller | | 7d |
| | Oliver Hayward | 6s | 1½d |
| | Magdalen Justy wid. (erased) James Illary | 1s | 3d |
| | Robert Gundry | 2s | 0d |
| | William Miller | 1s | 3d |
| | William Taunton | 3s | 5½d |
| | Damaris Miller (erased) John Deering | 3s | 3½d |
| | William Whiffen | 1s | 2d |
| | Thomas Downton | 2s | 6d |
| | Mary Williams wid. | 6s | 9d |
| | John Gast | 7s | 10d |
| | The same for a cottage | | 4d |
| | Thomas Miller | | 7d |
| | Samuel Michell (Saml. erased, sub. illeg.) | 8s | 9d |
| | Sarah Gast wid. | 3s | 6d |
| | Thomas Cooper | 4s | 0d |
| Tenants at | John Caffe | | 8d |
| Will | Moses Lacy & Matthew Lacy | | 8d |
| | Elizabeth Cafe & William Cafe | | 8d |
| | Thomas Read | | 8d |

11

| Chetnoll | Thomas Cooper Esq. | 7s | 6d |
|---|---|---|---|
| Customary | Thomas Meech | 10s 11½d | |
| Tenants | Dorothy Burd wid. | | 1d |
| | Andrew Middleton | 8s | 6d |
| | Thomas Meech | 3s | 7d |
| | Mary ?Conway erased (sub. William ?) | 1s | 0d |

## Pounds and Commons

One of the responsibilities of the Lord of the Manor was the provision and upkeep of a parish Pound. The location of a pound may often be traced from the existence of a "Pound Farm" or "Pound Lane".

The Yetminster Pound was the small stone enclosure on the north side of Ryme Road just past the modern estate of Uplands. It is believed that the cottage overlooking the Pound was the pinder's house. The pinder was responsible for the care of impounded animals, or, in the absence of a pinder, the duty fell to the hayward. In the days when strip cultivation of arable fields was practised, it was essential that stray animals were not permitted to damage the crops. Similarly, where tenants had grazing rights on the Common, these rights were jealously guarded and subject to strict rules to prevent over-grazing. Stray beasts were promptly impounded and any owner claiming an animal in the Pound was required to pay a fine before it would be released.

The customs of the manor laid down the number and type of beast each tenant might graze and what time of the year. In Leigh, tenants might only put in beasts normally held on their holdings, animals from land rented elsewhere could not be brought in and turned onto the common. Sheep might be put in at All Saints (1 November) but must be removed by St. Mark's Day (25 April). No ale-house keeper or baker could cut furze on the common and no one might cut furze in order to sell it. Bakers and Ale-house keepers, of course, used a tremendous quantity of fuel all the year round and furze was much in demand.

*On 18 April 1655 Walter Hunt was presented for cutting furze on the Common and ten years later, William Payne was presented.*

As the open field system fell into disuse, so, too, gradually, the commons were enclosed. The earliest Enclosure Acts were passed privately through Parliament. But these private Enclosure Acts were expensive, and, by 1801 a General Enclosure Act was passed which enabled the process to be speeded up. There is no evidence as to when enclosure took place in Yetminster, probably in the 16 c. In Leigh, it was considerably later, not until 1804. When a common was enclosed, every man with rights thereon was granted a parcel of land, the size depended upon the size of his tenement and the number of beasts he was entitled to graze. Roads had to be constructed for access and each allotment fenced or hedged. In effect, this proved too costly for the smaller man, and, frequently, he sold out to his wealthier neighbour. By this, of course, a man with only one or two animals was deprived of the grazing he had previously enjoyed. At this time, the Manor Court records are full of instances where small portions of the former Leigh Common change hands.

In 1750, the parishioners of Leigh, ever ready to defend their rights, had taken and impounded cattle belonging to the people of Batcombe found trespassing upon Leigh Common. In response, the inhabitants of Batcombe brought an action against Leigh. The Leigh Vestrymen resolved to appoint Mr. Loder, Attorney, of Dorchester to defend the action "all charges to be paid by parishioners and owners of land respectively within the said Parish in proportion to their several lands, as they are respectively charged in the Poor Rates."

There was a good turn-out for this Meeting on 19 November 1750. The following were signatories:

| | | |
|---|---|---|
| William Taunton | Robert Jennings | Thomas Stone |
| John Isles | John Willsher | William Gray |
| John Read | Peter Perrott | John Allambridge |
| John Humber | July Jenkins | Joseph Harris |
| Thomas Hunt | James Hillary | John Guyer |

Unfortunately, the outcome is not known, maybe the parties were advised to settle their differences out of Court when tempers had cooled down somewhat! Over the years, a vast amount of Ratepayers' money was wasted by parishes going to law against each other, usually over Removal Orders.

The Pounds of both Yetminster and Leigh were part of the Manor of Yetminster Episcopi, later Digby Manor, probably that of Chetnole, too, though no records have survived. Ryme Intrinseca formed part of the Duchy of Cornwall.

Here are some extracts from the Digby Manor Courts respecting the Pound at Leigh:

1679    A brown mare impounded and prised at £2 13s 4d.

1688    We present 2 ewes and a lamb strayed and cried and valued at 4s and handed over to the Lord's bailiff.

1690    5 Sheep impounded, cried and strayed and delivered to the Lord.

1694    We present 1 black heifer 2 years, pounded, cried and prized at 40s and delivered to the Lord's use. Also 2 black colts prized at £2 10s 9d.

1695    We continue the presentment against the Lord to repair the Pound at Leigh. We present 2 sheep pounded, cried and strayed and prised at 10s and delivered to the Lord's use.

1699    The Lady of the Manor should repair the Pound at Leigh.

When stray animals were impounded, they were first 'cried', probably at the nearest market, in the hope that the owner would come forward. To get his animals out, he had to pay a fine.

In 1632, life in Ryme must have been quite lively. Amongst the inhabitants were the Husday family, who, between them, caused quite a bit of trouble. It is recorded that:

*George and Nicholas Husday were fined 1s apiece for retaking their horses from James Kellway, he driving them towards the pound.*

*Robert Husday was fined 12d for that his wife and son made a rescue and took away his cow from the hayward when he was driving him to the pound.*

*George and Nicholas Husday were also fined 11s 2d for assaulting Anthony Wood and "drawing blood of him with batts".*

*Anthony was staunchly supported by his wife, Armirell, she was fined 9d for assaulting Robert Husday and drawing blood of him.*

and, finally, they even carried their quarrels into the Church:

*Susan, the wief of Robert Husday and Agnes, the wief of John Plowman be contendinge and stewinge in the church, the one thrustinge and pulling out the other.*

The Pound in Leigh has recently been re-built, it is situated next to Pound Farm. The location of Chetnole Pound is also known, it is next to Pound Lane at the Hamlet end of the village, but, alas, in ruins.

## Moles or wants

Was Yetminster Parish unusual in giving so much attention to the eradication of moles?

In 1749, the Parish agreed to pay Joseph Watts 2 rates yearly for 7 years for catching all the wants or moles throughout the Parish. "If he do not keep the ground clean, he is not to be paid his money and he is to receive it half-yearly."

1770    Thomas Baker paid £2 12s 9d for half-year's mole-catching.

1777    At the Easter Vestry it is agreed between the principal inhabitants of the Parish of Yetminster and John Chant of the Parish of Odcombe in Somerset, the said Chant doth hereby agree to ketch and kill all the wants or moles in all the fields belonging to the said Parish of Yetminster for the term of eight years viz. the first four years at 4 gns. yearly, the other four years at 3 gns. yearly and the said Chant doth engage to keep all the hills clean occasioned by the wants or moles, and if it appears to the said inhabitants, that they are not killed or destroyed, according to this agreement, the money is not then to be paid. N.B. The money to be paid one half at Michaelmas and the other half at Easter next following from the date hereof. And, in case the said Chant should die before the expiration of the said eight years, his son, Robert Chant, is to succeed him in the said agreement.

Wm. Warry, J. Jenkins, Thomas Allambridge, John Deering, mark of Wm. Coombes, Edward Hayes.

John Chant    Robert Chant

15

It would be interesting to know the method used and how many hours a week were devoted to the task. Were the farmers crying, 'Me first!' And did the moles play fair or did they invade from neighbouring parishes?

1792   We whose names are subscribed have agreed with George Edmunds to destroy the moles at £4 4s 0d per year to be paid out of the Poor Stock.

      J. Vincent Esq., N. Galpin, Hugh Andrews, Wm. Warry, J. Jenkins, Wm. Watts, Wm. Edwards, E. Hayes, B. Jesty.

1855   A rate, not exceeding 1d per acre shall be collected with the Church Rate and assessed on land alone, for the purpose of destroying moles.

1872   The Vestry resolved to levy a rate of £3 per year and that the work of catching the moles be offered to Thomas of Coker or to Robert Jesty or Robert Bugler or any of the older men of the Parish

1875   Uriah and George Thomas agree to catch the moles on the several farms in the Parish at 1d per acre, except for such lands as the occupiers object to paying on their acreage for catching moles.

No more is recorded of mole destruction.

# Roads

The office of Waywarden or Surveyor of the Highways was the most disliked of the Offices which members of the Vestry could be called upon to fill. Without proper resources and with little co-operation, the man was expected to keep the roads of the Parish in a state of repair.

In 1715 William Warry, the tanner, actually refused to act as Waywarden. The Vestry book records:

*19 March 1715. The Churchwardens and Overseers shall discharge Benjamin Coombes, Constable, Joseph Hodges, bailiff and John Symes Surveyor of the Highways from all known costs and damages which shall, or may, happen to them by reason of them taking distress on William Warry for his refusing to execute the office of Surveyor of the Highways.*

For the next couple of years, records are missing, so the result is unknown, but for the next one hundred and fifty years, through four generations, the Warry family continued to play a part in the proceedings of the Vestry.

Until the mid 16 c roads, as we know them, did not exist. The highway was only a right of way along a customary course, which, if much frequented, became a beaten track. The holder of the land, secular or religious, had the obligation of keeping the way open and, in his own interests, there were constant attempts at repair. If the highway became impassable, for whatever reason, travellers had a right to find a better passage over the adjoining fields.

The Highways Act of 1555 laid down that the roads of each parish should be maintained for six days per year by the unpaid labour of every householder, cottager and labourer of the parish able to work. The burden invariably fell upon the farmers because they had horses, carts and men available, but the Surveyor had a difficult task trying to persuade them into action. When one considers the magnitude of the task, amounts of money expended upon the highways were modest in the extreme.

1705  William Snook received £3 13s 2d "for full payment of all labour and cost by me laid out about the highways of this Parish of Yetminster".

1729  £1 2s 0d for repairing the highways for the year past.

1732  William Warry and William Watts paid 18s 1d for highways, bridges and chain-well.

1733  £3 19s 5½d paid for highways.

10 May 1736 A Memo. from the Magistrates reads:

> *As it appears to us to have been customary for some years for your Parish in a Vestry to allow the expences of your Surveyors of your Highways out of the Poor Stock, on that consideration (of the custom) we do recommend it to you, to allow Mr Thomas Allambridge reasonable expences towards repairing the Highways for the year past, but for the future (if the six days labour are not sufficient) you may apply to the General Sessions for a rate not exceeding sixpence in the pound.*

1751  Paid £7 11s 0d.

1761  Paid £3 8s 8d

1762  Mr Vincent to collect £30 for Highways.

1765  £5 to pay labourers for work on Highway, statute labour not being sufficient.

1770  Paid George Bartlett's bill for stone to repair highway £8 14s 1d.

1729  A Memo stated: Mr King, Farmer Harris and Jonas Vincent for not going out with their plows last year do promise to make it up the next year. Mr King 2 days, the others 1 day each.

The year 1715 brought a confrontation with Chetnole. Yetminster had made preparation for its road-mending by laying in a stock of gravel.

*"And whereas Robert Williams alias Barbe, John Elford, John Hunt, George Kellow and William Symes, all of Chetnole, did, on the 8th October 1715 come into our Parish of Yetminster and carried away four loads of gravel to amend the highways in their parish of Chetnole contrary to law and justice and for which they refuse to make reasonable satisfaction though they have been thereunto*

*required. Therefore, we do, as much as lyeth in us, order Mr T. Allambridge, Joseph Hodges and James Little or William Hunt who were witnesses thereunto, or any of them, to indict the said offenders at the next Quarter Sessions unless they do in the meantime make satisfaction and do promise to pay all reasonable expences for so doing."*

*Signed: Abraham Miller, John Richardson, John Warr, William Warry, Thomas Allambridge, Arthur Cosens, Abraham Miller jun.*

In 1835 the Highway Act abolished statutory labour and empowered the levy of a Highway Rate. It provided for the unification of parishes into a Highway District and allowed the payment of a District Surveyor.

The following year, the Vestry agreed as follows:

*". . . namely, that it being very difficult to get stone for the repair of the Highways carried at the price directed by the Magistrates, we agree to pay the sum of six shillings per day for seven hours for each put drawn by 3 horses and 1 man attending same, and, if the same person shall have 2 puts employed on the same day, he shall send 2 men and 1 boy with the same and that each person having a team shall be employed such a number of days as shall be proportionate to his rate. And, in case any such person shall refuse or neglect to do the same, the Surveyors shall be at liberty to employ some other person to do it."*

In 1848 this resolution was repeated with the further agreement that the road scrapings be got together and sold.

By this time, the state of the roads was causing more concern than ever, doubtless wheeled traffic was increasing and the roads were not fit to cope. The Vestry was clearly at its wits' end. The Magistrates, too, were taking much more interest and demanding action.

For centuries, Yetminster had muddled along, trying to keep its footpaths unobstructed and the highways more or less in a state of repair. But now, a momentous event was coming its way and things would never be quite the same again. The Wilts, Somerset and Weymouth Railway was extending its line from Yeovil to Weymouth. To this end, young Mr. William Penistone with his wife and four small children had taken up residence in the village as Surveyor to the

19

Railway Company. In December 1848, a Vestry was once more considering the state of the Parish roads when someone had a splendid idea! Why not confer with Mr. Penistone on the subject? This was done and Mr. Penistone kindly offered his expertise. At the Easter Vestry of 1849 Mr. William Penistone and Mr. John Andrews were appointed Waywardens for the year. A Committee consisting of Messrs Andrews, Groves, Langdon and Brake was appointed to consider the advisability of alterations at the Mill and the ford where the road would cross the railway. Most probably, there had always been a bridge at the Mill for this was a road to Chetnole, albeit narrow and awkward since the ground rises steeply either side of the river. At Brister end, there was only a foot-bridge, wheeled traffic using the ford, now obliterated, it was situated below Ford House.

In May, the Vestry met to consider Penistone's recommendations:

*(1) the advisability of contracting with the Railway Co. for metalling and fencing any new roads over the railway;*
*(2) that employment for the Poor should be provided in works connected with the Parish roads.*

A new Committee was appointed to deal with any contract with the Railway Co. George Brake, John Andrews, James Langdon and Daniel Ring.

At the beginning of 1851, the Parish was offering to co-operate with the Railway Co. by agreeing to level crossings instead of bridges at Yetminster Ford and Winterhayes.

In August 1853, the roads were still a matter of concern and it was decided to have them repaired by contract. Mr. Penistone wrote expressing his willingness to undertake the repair and maintenance of the Parish roads for £60 per annum for five years from March last. This offer was accepted but for a term of three years which Penistone agreed. Six months later, nothing had been done and it was decided to apply to the Magistrates for advice on how to proceed, Mr Penistone having failed to fulfil the contract. The Magistrates were not sympathetic. They ordered the Surveyors to have the highways repaired immediately. Also, the old footpath from Yetminster to Beer Hackett was to be restored. This had been the subject of complaint by the Rev. Hugh Helyar of Beer Hackett. Mr. Daniel Sampson, the remaining

Waywarden, after being summoned to meet the Magistrates, reported that he had been imperatively instructed to repair the highway and restore the foot-path under penalty of £5. Clearly, the patience of the Magistrates was running out. Perhaps things were moving too fast for them as well. They had always been able to control the Vestries, and, now, here was Yetminster getting itself in a tangle just because it was about to get a new-fangled railway and a station.

The deterioration of the foot-path to Beer Hackett was largely the fault of the Railway Co., since, when acting as Engineer to the Company, Penistone had removed bridges without the consent of the Parish. Maybe Beer Hackett was just a little piqued because, although the line would run right beside the village, it was not to get a station. It was resolved to apply to the Railway Co., to restore these bridges. Penistone was to be informed of the situation and asked what he proposed to do about his contract. Nothing more is recorded of Mr. Penistone.

The Vestry advertised in the local press for someone to repair the roads by contract. The tender of John Vincent of Thornford was accepted. The Magistrates, however, were giving the Parish no respite. In October 1854, they ordered the widening of Back Lane (now Melbury Road). This was extremely narrow with high banks on either side. On the lane, to the south of the present garage, were two cottages, since demolished, one occupied by Mr James Arnold, shoemaker and organist at the Church for 47 years. Exact instructions were given for the building of a 3 ft. wall around Mr. Arnold's barton and the planting of a quickset hedge. A rate of 9d was to be levied to meet the expence of repairs to the highway and the widening of the lane. Two years later, in 1856, Common Lane was to be widened to 13 ft. and Lord Ilchester thanked for paying one moiety of the cost, the remaining sum defrayed by the rates. The cost was £26.

1857 and the Vestry met to consider the assessment of the Railway to the Poor Rate. Clearly, much damage to the roads had been caused by the Railway contractors. The Vestry now demanded that this should be rectified: roads were to be properly repaired, cleansed, the sides dropped, drains cleared out and the scrapings removed. The Railway Co. was to re-fix the stones and parapet at the culvert at Winterhayes and the approaches to the bridge at Yetminster Ford to be metalled to the extent of 30 cubic yards of gravel.

The skill shown by the Railway Engineers in laying the permanent way would not have passed unnoticed by the Vestrymen. No doubt, much time was spent walking along the track to study the work in progress. And even longer afterwards discussing the matter in the local Inns. Much comparison must have been made between the level and beautifully aligned track and the appalling roads which they were expected to keep in a state of repair.

In 1858, Mr Charles Harris of Ilchester was approached and asked if he would be willing to undertake the repair of the main parish roads, the Waywardens seeing to the minor lanes. Or, would he be willing to survey the roads at the end of each quarter before payment was made under any contract? He replied that he would be willing to inspect the roads four times a year at a charge of 4 guineas a year.

Nothing more is recorded about the roads until 1872 when the Waywarden is John Brake. He is requested by the Vestry to report to the Highway Board that Church Lane (Queen Street) has not been repaired. The years pass and John Brake is succeeded by George Brake who continues in the Office until 1885 when Robert Holloway is appointed. From 1890–1894 George Loder and William White alternate in holding Office and, after that date, no further mention is made of a Waywarden. It would appear that George Loder has the distinction of being the last Waywarden appointed in the Parish of Yetminster, the last of a long succession of men who tried against the odds, to bring to the highways of the parish some semblance of order.

The first known Waywarden was Lionel Brown in 1705.

# Law and Order

The Constable, working with the Vestry, was responsible for maintaining law and order in the parish. He had the support of the local Magistrates to whom recourse would be made for warrants of arrest. Some parishes had a small lock-up where suspected miscreants could be held overnight or until they could be taken before the Magistrate. There is no evidence for such a building in the Yetminster area, but there are records of payment having been made to various people for holding prisoners. It is most likely that these were Inn-keepers, certainly, Elizabeth Hayes was land-lady of the White Hart in Yetminster and Elizabeth Perrott kept an ale-house in Leigh.

1700　Leigh ". . . pay Martha Allwood her hire for keeping Sarah Stickland and the gard that waited upon her part of 4 days £1 1s 0d".

1714　Leigh ". . . allow the charges of taking & keeping in hold one night and carrying of John Long to prison 4s".

1721　Leigh ". . . pay 5s charge for keeping Thomas Paine at Elizabeth Perrott".

1766　Yetminster "Paid guard & expences at Mrs Hayes with Peter Wheadon 14s 6d".

Much expence was incurred in obtaining warrants for arrests from Magistrates and escorting prisoners to gaol.

1707　Leigh. Nicholas Daggle was paid 3s 6d for carrying Catherine Goldring and John Paine to the house of correction.

1711　Leigh. Paid the bill for carrying Thomas Bucey to prison 13s 8d.

1728　Leigh. paid 2s 10d for expences for 5 men for going to Dorchester with Andrew Hunt and Peter Whiffen.

1722 Leigh. "Pay Mr Allambridge for riding to Dorchester about Robert Maber, for a copy of the Warrant and exps. at Dorchester 3s 4d. For his horse and self 2s 6d".

A watch was kept for crime of any description. Theft of timber appears to have been a particular problem. Fires were a necessity all the year round, since they provided the only means of cooking and heating water. In consequence, there was a constant demand for wood. Sometimes, the poor would be provided with firing by the parish but much theft went on. Doubtless, some of the stolen wood was sold.

In the year 1710 Yetminster Vestry recorded:

*"In order to prevent, as much as lyeth in us, the grave mishap that hath too often happened by lewd wood-stealers, we do order that a search be shortly made in the Houses of Suspicious persons for stolen wood and other things and that all suspected persons be prosecuted at the Parish charge."*

In 1714, their resolve was reiterated:

*"We do, as much as in us lyeth, for the prevention of further and future mischiefs and disorders done and committed daily by lewd, thieving people, order that a reward shall be paid at a public parish charge to all and every person that shall discover and make known to two or three of the Principal Inhabitants of the Parish the name or names of any persons whom they shall at any time discover stealing of any trees, breaking or cutting of any hedge or fences or carrying in the Highway any bundles of greenwood, first, for the Information and also a good satisfaction for his or her time & labour appearing before a Justice of the Peace to give evidence which shall be paid upon conviction of the accused.*

*For every conviction of any person who shall steal any Gates, bars, styles, rails, posts or iron, the informer shall have a reward of half a crown for the discovery and will be paid for attending Court to give evidence. To be paid after the conviction and not otherwise by the Overseer of the Poor & shall be allowed in passing his accounts."*

24

1717 ". . . to pay out of the Poor Stock (i.e. rates) such reasonable costs as John Willis shall be put to in prosecuting Joseph Cheeseman for feloniously taking away his Iron Bar."

1753 The practice of throwing timber trees & breaking hedges having become very common an informer will receive 1s reward and the guilty individual be prosecuted.

1791 The Vestry repeated its determination to prosecute all people caught cutting trees or hedges or stealing rails or any other thing.

The Parish Officers, paid expences only, were constantly making journeys to Magistrates or to Quarter Sessions. The latter might entail a journey as far as Bridport and an overnight stay and the man would have to leave his farm or business in order to undertake it, for few were gentry who might not have such commitments. But, no doubt they enjoyed the sense of importance it gave them! And, at Quarter Sessions, officers from other parishes would be encountered, gossip exchanged and useful information passed on. Quarter Sessions was a Court of Magistrates for the whole County. It took place four times a year at Blandford, Sherborne, Bridport or Shaston, and, occasionally, Dorchester. Each Session lasted three days so it is, perhaps, not surprising that cases were constantly adjourned, entailing another journey three months hence for the unfortunate parish officers.

As well as dealing with wrong-doers of every kind, from time to time, the Vestry would round up 'Masterless persons', unemployed young men and girls wandering about the parish making a nuisance of themselves. Such youngsters who had "nothing to support themselves but their hired labour" could be warned to find themselves masters, and, if they failed to heed the warning, could be taken before the Magistrate and ordered so to do. If they still failed to heed this warning, they could be taken before Petty Sessions.

In the Spring of the year 1710, Yetminster Vestry ordered the Constable to get Warrants for a group of such persons: Joan Hayward, Rachel Harris, Barbara Lumber, Anne Harris and Eleanor Curtis. At the same time, Thomas Fudge, Christopher Curtis, Walter Shave, George Harrison and Thomas Maidman were to be warned to appear to answer for stealing from the woods.

Two years later, another group were in similar trouble as 'masterless persons': Mary Welsh, Elizabeth Comb, Mary Stevens, Christian Bartlett, the daughter of Thomas Lumbard, Mary Sherry alias Buck and James Shave.

In 1720, it is recorded that Abraham and Isaac Brake refused to put themselves in service according to the Justice's order. These two young men were 20 and 18 years old respectively and the sons of Richard Brake, a 'poor man' as the Register records.

The Parish system certainly had the advantage that the parish Officers were known to all and those misbehaving were usually well-known to the Parish Officers!

## The Court Leet

This usually refers to a Manorial Court, but it applied to some Hundred Courts and this seems to have been the case in Yetminster, no doubt, because of the several manors. The Hundred of Yetminster included Yetminster, Leigh, Chetnole, Melbury Osmond, Melbury Bubb, Clifton Maybank, Newland and Batcombe.

Whilst the Court Baron dealt with transfer of property, the Court Leet concerned itself with petty offences such as obstruction of the highway, failure to cut back hedges and trees or to clean out ditches. Illegally taking in parts of the common or having a house in a dangerous state of repair or a mantel in decay were also matters for the Court Leet. In a village of thatched roofs, it was vital that every precaution should be taken against fire. Larger, substantial houses had stone-built chimneys, but poorly-built cottages had 'mantels', baulks of timber standing on end, rather in the shape of a tent which was then plastered over. Inevitably, as time went on, the fire in the hearth started to burn the timber, thus creating a dangerous fire-hazard, not only for the occupier, but also for neighbouring properties. From this, incidentally, comes our word 'mantelpiece', the shelf fixed to the mantel above the fire.

The Court Leet also dealt with minor offences such as attacks on the person, fights and quarrels because such were 'contrary to the peace! In an attack, the value of the weapon used was always stated.

Illicit gaming, brewing and baking without a licence and overcharging as a miller were also matters for the Court Leet.

## From Yetminster Hundred Court Leet 1599/1600

*No inhabitant shall put manure in the streets or other places of the same village sub pena 11d.*

*Thomas Maie is in mercy for permitting his pigs to go at large . . .*

*Thomas Witch of Leigh in mercy in that he permitted divers persons to play illicit games in his house contrary to statute. And the same Thomas for brewing and baking without a licence, fine 20s.*

*Edward Taunton of Leigh in mercy for attacking John Munden with a stick of no value and drawing blood contrary to the peace 14d.*

*Tythingman of Melbury Bubb presents William Miller in mercy, with a mattock worth 2d he attacked Henry Devonish and drew blood contrary to the peace. 11d.*

*Melbury Bubb. Andrew Cole in mercy for overcharging as a miller. 3d. William Hodges ditto. 6d.*

*Yetminster. William Loope and Alexander Everod in mercy for overcharging as millers. 6d each.*

## From the Courts Leet held 1680–1689

*Yetminster, 26 Apr 1680. Bowlebridge Lane is in decay from the ends of the parish unto Bowlebridge and the bay in the highway over against William Combe's gate. To be sufficiently repaired by the Surveyors of the Highway by midsummer. s.p. 20d,*

*William Conway's chimney in the end of his house against Benjamin Oldis is dangerous for fire. To be amended within a fortnight. s.p. 5d.*

*Robert Bartlett's chimney in his brew-house is dangerous in relation to fire and the said house is in decay. To be repaired in a fortnight's time. s.p. 4d.*

*Yetminster. 11 Oct 1682. Joseph Hodges and John French to plash their hedges and scour their ditches at their grounds against Coles Lane by the next Court. s.p. 5d each.*

*Gabriel Trasker for watering 2 roads of flax in the common river, forfeited according to the statute.*

Leigh. *11 Oct 1682. Richard Keate to dike his ditch and plash his hedge against Altonmead Lane at his ground called Leehay by 1 Dec. s.p. 6s 8d.*

Leigh. *26 Apr 1680 Richard Andrews alias Miller to remove his hog-sty that stands against the street which is an offence to the inhabitants. To be removed by 1 June. s.p. 20d.*

*11 Apr 1683* Newland. *Joan Dicker and Agnes Dicker for keeping a suspicious house of bawdery. 10p.*

Chetnole. *26 Oct 1683 Thomas Downton and Thomas Byrt to dike their ditches and plash their hedges and Thomas Byrt to lay a bridge against Hole Lane. To be done by Christmas. s.p. 3s 4d each.*

Chetnole. *6 May 1685. John Bishop for laying cinders in the highway, it being stoppage to the water and causing of pools in the upper side of it. To remove in a week's time s.p. 5d.*

*Amos Warren jun. to be a common alehouse haunter.*

Leigh. *7 Apr 1686. Upon the testimony of Thomas Gast, Richard Andrews alias Miller hath not put away his dog according to last presentment. To be put away within a week. s.p. 20d.*

Chetnole. *20 Oct 1686. John Prankard and his wife for suspicion of a felony, for, since the last Court Leet, Jane Cooper, having lost a smock from her master's hedge, found him 3 weeks later upon the garden hedge of the house where John Prankard do live. Jane then fetched her master's daughter and they both swore it to be Jane's smock and she did carry it away and hath it yet.*

*The Surveyors of the Highway for the neglect of their office in not proceeding according to law against those of the Tything which ought to have worked on the highway and did not perform their six days of labour.*

Yetminster. *7 Oct 1687. Mr John Minterne, Mr John Blackdon, Mr John Gollop, Thomas King and William Barber to plash their hedges and repair their banks on both sides of Watery Lane from Will Barber's gate unto Mr Minterne's gate leading into Marmead. To be done by 1 May. s.p. 3s 4d each.*

Clifton. *The Surveyors of the Highway to lay broader and higher stepping stones at Trill Lane behind Mr - - - -'s ground and Moses Leas.*

Yetminster. *5 Apr 1689. The Tything of Yetminster to set up posts and rails to keep off horses that they may not annoy the well in the said Tything called Pool Well and likewise to repair the well at the end of Church Lane. To be done by midsummer. s.p. 10p.*

These Presentments had the intention of making the environment a safer and more pleasant place for the inhabitants generally. If trees and hedges were left uncut, passage along the highways and byways was impeded, choked up ditches allowed the roads and foot-paths to become flooded. Foot-paths were of great importance, not for recreational purposes, but for everyday use in getting as easily as possible from one place to another. A flooded or obstructed path might mean a long detour for someone almost certainly on foot, for only the gentry and better-off owned horses. The bridges mentioned were probably modest affairs to allow pedestrians to cross wet stretches of land or ditches. There is frequent mention of Moses Leas (wet to this day!) and Watery Lane at Brister End running from the Ford near the right bank of the river, also wet until the present. Many lived in tumbledown hovels, but, at least an effort was made to keep them in repair for the safety of the community. Dangerous dogs must be destroyed and public wells kept in good repair. The animal which Richard Andrews failed to put down is a rare mention of a dog. Before it could be spun and woven, flax had to be "retted" or soaked to extract the fibres. A pond was normally constructed for this purpose, retting in the river was strictly prohibited since it polluted the water.

The mention of William Conway's chimney against the house of Benjamin Oldis in 1680 reveals that Oldis occupied the cottage adjoining the "Swan" William Conway's ale-house in High Street.

The exact location of the Pool Well is not known for certain, there must have been two public wells since two are referred to in the same presentment and one was certainly at the bottom of Church Lane nearly opposite the "White Hart". There is a clue, however, in two Excepts made 13 Aug 1622 between Robert Cooth and John, his son and Joan, his daughter, respectively. Two tenements are involved, that excepted to John is described as ". . . in Yetminster over against the Cross sometime the tenement of Thomas Strode, gent." and that given to Joan as ". . . tenement between the well and the bridge in which the said Robert Cooth did, and yet, dwelleth."

The 'Cross' was the area opposite Oak House and Cross Farm, with, possibly, the Preaching Cross in situ thereabouts. The well, also, must have been a landmark. At the beginning of the 18 c Arthur Cosens took possession of two adjacent properties known as Hardings and Grimsteads – Hardings named probably from a Captain Harding and Grimsteads from Henry Grimstead, the latter was the present Gable Court and Hardings was below it and demolished in the late 19 c when it had fallen into disrepair. We know that Cosens occupied these two properties because it was upon this occupation that a later Arthur Cosens based his claim to erect two pews in the chancel of the Parish Church. They were gentry property and Cosens refers to them in his Will. So, we may assume that the Pool Well was situated between these two properties. At the present time, there is a high bank above the road, but, with the coming of the railway in the mid 19 c, this road was altered considerably the Railway Co. buying land to the north from Sherborne Almshouse to provide access to the new bridge. The bridge referred to by Cooth was the foot-bridge which crossed the river beside the ford.

The Pool Well was obviously a well of some importance, the Vestry was frequently ordering repairs and cleansing of the bays, and, here in 1689, we find the order to set up posts and rails to keep the horses out, from which one might suppose a pool of some size, fed by a spring possibly.

In the earlier Court Leet of Elizabeth 1599/1600 there is a requirement for the 'waterspitt' in the common ground of Francis Hardie, gent. to be made good. s.p. 11d. Could Hardie be synonymous with Harding? A 1649 Survey of Yetminster Secunda shows Thomas Hardie, gent, holding a customary tenement.

On 2 November 1635 a great meeting was held of all the Tythings in the Hundred of Yetminster, its purpose the raising of £124 towards the building of a ship of war for the King's Majesty's service. Every man and a few widows, was assessed for the rate he was expected to pay. Robert Cooth was assessed on £30, one of the highest assessments. For three hundred and fifty years this document lay in the Parish Chest of Yetminster and is remarkably well preserved.

In the Tudor Subsidy of 1524 Robert Cooth is assessed on goods of £10, only five men have a higher assessment and, in 1543 it has doubled to £20 and he is in top position with William Shere and William Winterhay. This could not have been the Robert of 1622 and 1635, his father, perhaps, but both are of a status to have occupied one of the principal properties in the parish.

The Court Leet included the View of Frankpledge or Lawday. In Saxon times, each area was divided into Tythings of ten men who were bound to stand security for the good behavior of all. This was known as 'Frankpledge' and the View of Frankpledge was an inspection to make sure it was in place.


## Quarter sessions

These were meetings of the Magistrates of the County held four times a year in Blandford, Sherborne, Shaftesbury or Bridport and, sometimes, Dorchester. Each session lasted three days and dealt with a multitude of matters such as crime, upkeep of roads and bridges, licensing, the administration of the Poor Law, Returns of Aliens, lunacy and Land Tax and much else.

We know from the Vestry Books how often parishes had recourse to Quarter Sessions over Bastardy or confronted one another over contested Removal Orders. Surveyors of the Highway could be brought before Quarter Sessions if they failed in their duty to have roads and bridges repaired. But, we know little of crimes committed in the Yetminster area. Two local incidents are recorded in 'The Casebook of Sir Francis Ashley, Recorder of Dorchester, 1614–1635.'

The first, in January 1623/4 concerns Margaret Baine, wife of Lawrence Baine of Chetnole. She complained that she had been many times threatened by one Walter Peirce, labourer, of Clapton, Somerset. He said he would "winde her necke and pull her out of doors". Her sons, too, had seen a man hearkening at her window at night, who, as

31

soon as they opened the door, ran away. Margaret was in fear of her life. The outcome is not known: was the fellow, perhaps deranged or did he have some grudge against her? The Baines appear to have been quite prosperous yeomen, in 1627, Lawrence Bayne, the elder, made an Except of half his tenement to John, his son. In 1688, the Inventory of Lawrewnce Bayne of Chetnole, yeoman, shows him to have been worth £151. £24 10s 0d was the value put on his animals, and, he had no less than £70 in ready money and due upon bond and desperate debts of £20. Like many, in the days before Banks, he made his money work by lending it out at interest.

The second case, in 1633, concerns William Coombes, the elder, of Yetminster and his wife, Joan, who were the victims of a piece of trickery perpetrated by one Gregory Hillary.

The Coombes stated that, about a week after Candlemas, Gregory Hillary, servant to their son, Mr. William Combe, Minister of Belchalwell, came from his master to ask for 'Pitchers of red withie' which they willingly granted. Hillary also said that his master wished them to lend him £10. They gave Hillary the £10 and saw him put it into a purse and put the purse into a bag of apples which they were sending to their son's children. Hillary, however, did not deliver the money but ran away with it.

William Coombe of Belchalwell, clerk, was bound over to the next Sessions at Sherborne to bring a Bill of Indictment against Gregory Hillary. William Coombe of Yetminster, yeoman, and his wife were bound over to give evidence.

In April, Robert Carter alias Browne of Woolland, husbandman, made a statement: On 15 February, Gregory Hillary, late servant to William Coombe of Belchalwell, clerk, came to his house 'with a packe of cloathes under his arme'. His wife was the mother of the said Hillary and demanded why he had left his master's service. He answered that she should 'not take no care for that' and that he was going to Blandford to make provision for his speedy departure to sea. The next day, Hillary came again to their house, wearing new clothes but refused to say where he had got them. He said that he had lately been at Yetminster with Mr. Coombe's father and mother and was by them well entertained. He also told his mother that he had been with an old woman, a friend of his, that had lent him ten pounds without a Bond which she put into a linen bag amongst apples because her husband should not know it.

The County Police Act of 1839 was a permissive measure by which Justices were enabled to set up a paid County Police Force. A later Act of 1856 required the Justices to set up a force for any parts of the County not covered. This was the year in which a County Force was set up for Dorset. And, this was the year when certain local people signed a Petition for the establishment of a Force.

The signatories were:

| | |
|---|---|
| Thomas Hayward, grocer | John Andrews, maltster |
| James Langdon, schoolmaster | Thomas Read, yeoman, Ryme |
| George Southwell, clerk | George Brake, yeoman |
| William Ring, carpenter | Richard Andrews, saddler |
| John Read, baker | Henry Jeffrey, yeoman |
| W. C. Richardson, contractor | John Curtis, miller |
| John Stevens, cooper | S. Jeffrey, yeoman |
| Henry Collins | James Chadwick, retired major, Chetnole |

At one time, Yetminster had two resident Police Constables. It is recalled that, lacking transport, the Constable had to hire a pony and trap to convey any suspect to Sherborne.

# 1798 MILITIA LIST

## Men aged between 18 and 45 liable to serve in the Militia

Robert LANGDON schoolmaster
George RING carpenter, wife 5 ch. 5' 6"
Thomas BARTLETT lab. 5' 7"
Edward HAYES currier
Peter EDWARDS carpenter
James EDWARDS yeoman
Richard ANDREWS tyler
John WINTER lab. 5' 8"
Robert JESTY lab. 5' 8"
James BISHOP lab. 5' 9"
John MITCHEL weaver wife, 3 ch. 5' 8"
Charles TOMPKINS Yeoman
Philip BARRETT servant 5' 8"
Daniel BEAZANT attorney at law
Thomas BEAZANT servant 5' 8"
John BUCKLAND yeoman
John GUPPY yeoman
William WATTS farmer
Samuel WATTS yeoman
Benjamin WATTS yeoman
Thomas GINER lab. 5' 8"
Barnes BANGER lab. 5' 9"
Mr. Robert SHIRLEY gent.
Mr. William VINCENT gent.
Thomas WHEADON lab. 5' 6"
William WHEADON lab. 5' 6"
John BLAKE gardener 5' 8"
Boise RICHARDSON servant 5' 10"
William NEAL lab. 5' 8"
James NEAL lab. 5' 7"
Samuel EASTMENT farmer
Edmund LAVER yeoman 5' 8"

William GORING mason 5' 9"
Thomas CUPPER miller 5' 9"
William DAWE yeoman
Thomas PAINTER lab. 5' 5"
Thomas COOMB dairyman, wife 4 ch.
Hugh ANDREWS jun. farmer
Stephen BARTER
Charles CHEESMAN lab. 5' 9"
William BRAKE lab. 5' 8"
John GALPIN yeoman
William ANDREWS yeoman
Francis BARTLETT substitute prov. cavalry
Edward GRANGER cooper 5' 7" drawn
Samuel STROUD lab. wife, 2 ch., 5' 6"
James REYNOLDS lab. 5' 8" one eye
Samuel BISHOP servant 5' 5"
John MOORE shoemaker 5' 4"
David FUDGE shoemaker 5' 8"
William BARTLETT collar maker 5' 8"
John WALBRIDGE lab. wife, 5' 7"
Abraham DONNE cooper 5' 8"
William RICHARDSON lab. 5' 8"
John RICHARDSON carpenter 5' 9"
William HILLYAR mason 5' 7"
Robert HULL lab. wife, 3 ch. 5' 8"
Thomas RICHARDSON lab. 5' 8"
William PITCHER servant 5' 0"
Richard OLIVER lab. 5' 8" one eye
James REYNOLDS lab. 5' 8"

D.R.O. LA: 3/9/14/8

# The Mills on the Wriggle

Once man ceased to be nomadic and settled down to the growing of crops, it was necessary to process the grain produced before it could be utilised for food. In early days, the quern was used for grinding grain, this was time-consuming. Man began to look for other ways of grinding.

It is generally accepted that the earliest reference to a water-mill in England was made in a charter dated A.D. 762 granting the use of a mill near Dover to the Monastery of Sts. Peter and Paul.

Mills were not always constructed actually on the river bank, care had to be taken not to obstruct the waterway. A suitable site having been selected for the building, a leat would be dug to bring the water to the mill and a sluice or weir constructed across the river to divert the water from the mainstream along the leat, as and when, it was required. Wheels were either external or internal, and, after it had passed over the wheel, the leat took the water back to the river downstream. When milling was finished for the day, the miller opened the sluice gate and the water continued on its normal course.

Briefly, wheels were of three types: undershot, breastshot and overshot. The first was equipped with paddles and the water hit the wheel at its lowest point. The latter two were driven by the weight of water and had buckets, in the breastshot, the water struck the wheel at axle height and in the overshot at the top. The latter usually required a mill-pond so that a good head of water could be built up.

Inside the mill were the mill-stones. The best stones obtainable were French burr stones found only in the Paris basin. They were quarried in small pieces and then bonded together. They were so much in demand, that, in 1809, despite the Napoleonic war, a special licence was granted for their importation for a period of three months.

Also used were Peak stones, mainly from the Millstone Grit areas of Derbyshire/Yorkshire. Peak stones were suitable for grinding cattle food, but could be used for barley, oats, beans and peas. They were far inferior to French burr.

Before they could be used, the stones had to be dressed. The grinding process depended upon the sharp edges of one stone meeting the sharp edges reversed on the other. Some millers carried out their own stone-dressing, others employed itinerant craftsmen, known as the 'tramping millers', who would call at the Mill asking for work. If unknown to him, the miller would ask the man to 'show his metal'. Judging by the small, black particles embedded in his skin, the miller could tell how experienced he was at stone-dressing.

Dressing a stone involved putting in the furrows or lands in a pre-arranged pattern. A common way was to divide the stone into ten divisions or 'harps'.

With use, there was a build-up of meal in the grooves and the edges had to be re-sharpened. In time, the stone became too thin for further use and was discarded, to be used as a door-step, perhaps, or, in the case of a deceased miller at Sydling St. Nicholas, as a gravestone!

For many hundreds of years, the miller was entitled to pay himself for his work by keeping back a proportion of the flour he ground, usually about one sixteenth, but he was invariably regarded with suspicion of having taken more than his due.

> *"One hand in his pocket*
> *And the other in his bag*
> *As the wheel went round*
> *He made his grab."*

John Stow, in his Survey of London 1558, writes that the miller shall have no hogs, geese nor ducks and no poultry save a cock and three hens. Infringement of this law might mean that, after two warnings, the miller found himself in the pillory. With so much grain about, to indulge in a little profitable side-line must have been a great temptation.

The little River Wriggle rises in hills to the south of Yetminster. In earlier times, doubtless, it carried a greater volume of water than is the case today. It held trout, gudgeon and eels and would have had a bearing on the choice of site for the various settlements in and around Yetminster.

A tributary served two grist mills and a power mill in the tiny parish of Stockwood. In 1576 John Bartlet was a miller there, and, in 1592, a mill owned by William Stroude was granted to his son, Thomas, John Foy of Bubdown, gent. and John Elford of Chetnole, chandler. The property is described as "all that Powder mill, messuage, lands etc. called Southpark or Upper Stockwood, and also those two mills and the dwelling-house wherin the said William Stroude now lives."

In 1625, there is another reference to a powder-mill and two mills, one a grist-mill and the other a malt mill. In 1648, the Minute Book of the Dorset Standing Committee records the theft of powder from Parks Mill.

In 1851 there were twenty-three adults living in Stockwood in nine families, but only four of those adults were born in Stockwood.

The first mill on the Wriggle was Withyhook. Actually in Leigh parish it occupies a remote situation off the Chetnole-Batcome road. It first appears as 'Stones Mill' on a map of c 1560 and it was probably connected with the Stone family for the next three hundred years.

There is a Will and Probate Inventory for Thomas Stone, dated 1696 in which he is styled 'gentleman', the Inventory gives no indication of any milling activity, but, possibly, the Mill had already been handed over to his son, Thomas. His assets are valued at £126 10s 0d, of this amount £74 was accounted for by livestock, £5 10s 0d by oats and plow-tackling, £15 by debts and the remainder covered his household goods.

He owned:

| | | | |
|---|---|---|---|
| two tester bedsteads and three truckell bedsteads & all yt belongs to them | 12 | 00 | 00 |
| 2 trunks, 2 tableboards 2 forms 4 half hogsheads & other small barrells a churne six toobs 4 pailes 2 chairs | | | |
| & other lumber ware in all roomes too | 3 | 10 | 00 |
| one dossen of pewter dishes | 1 | 10 | 00 |
| three crocks 4 kittles 2 skillets and warming pan | 3 | 00 | 00 |
| 3 spits one jacke one iron driping pan a pair of andirons & divers other small things | 1 | 10 | 00 |
| three fletches of bacon | 2 | 10 | 00 |
| two silver cups & two silver spoons | 3 | 00 | 00 |

As may be seen, his household goods were sparse, typical, perhaps, of a yeoman but hardly those of a gentleman.

In his Will, he bequeathed £100 each to his son, John, an apprentice in Bristol and to each of his three daughters. The remainder of his estate, he left to his wife, Elizabeth and then to his son, Thomas.

Were Thomas and Elizabeth to return today, they would certainly recognise their old home. They would find the hall with its great fire-place, to one side the spiral stair-case, to the other, the bread-oven. Adjoining, behind the fire-place, to the west, is the old Mill building and, today, there is a way through by a very low doorway beside the hearth. To the east of the hall is a further heated room and a straight flight of stairs. The R.C.H.M. Survey reads:

*". . .turned balusters, c 1700 with moulded handrail, square newels with ball finials (now missing) and a portion of it hinged on a dog-gate with contemporary hinges and wrought-iron bolt."*

Outside, on the East gable, is a date-stone, "ES TS 1702", which must refer to building work by Thomas's widow and her son, Thomas. Perhaps, the Stone family had, at last, tired of negotiating the spiral stair-case. Perhaps, too, Thomas senior had left money or property elsewhere and there were funds sufficient to fulfil his bequests and allow his widow and son to embark upon building work.

No trace of the Mill machinery remains, the wheel would have been at the back, on the south, the leat coming in across the fields and out to the front returning to the river below the sluice, traces of which may be seen by the bridge giving access to the property.

The Mill was mentioned in the Proceedings for the Defence of Dorset and appears on the 1811 O.S. map.

In 1871, there was another Thomas Stone. He took the Yeovil Water Co. to Court. The Company was extracting water from the Wriggle for the use of Yeovil town, this meant that there was insufficient water to run the Mill. Stone called as witnesses several of the previous millers to determine the worth of the Mill. The Water Co. lost the case, lost again on appeal and Stone received his full damages of £1,687.

There are records of the Stone name as early as 1524.

The Dorset Tudor Subsidy lists:

| 1524 | Christopher Stone | Melbury Bubb |
|------|-------------------|--------------|
| 1543 | Richard Stone | Melbury Bubb |
| 1543 | John Stone | Yetminster |
| 1544 | Beatrice Stone | Yetminster |
| 1598 | Andrew Stone | Chetnole |

On the 20 April 1578, the Court Roll of Upbury or Yetminster Prima records an Except from John Stone to Andrew, his son:

*"all the hall howse wth all the chambers and edifices under the roof of the same hall howse, all the barne wth the leninge under the south end of the sayd barnes roofe, one chamber without the hay doore in the north end of the sayd barnes roofe with the loft over the same. Item: the occupac'on of the ketchin to bake, brue, washe and make malt with the tenante, the occupac'on of halfe the stable wth halfe the loft over the same stable being the north end. Item: one pigge howse. Item: two part of the orchard in the west side. Item: the occupac'on of all the barton, saving free coming and going for the tenant to his howses reserved. Item: the west halfe of the great garden and all that little garden and the barton without the street doore."* Plus four closes.

The location of this property is not known, though probably in Chetnole. On the 1635 Ship Money, Mr. Thomas Stone of Leigh had an income recorded of £60 per annum and Andrew Stone of Chetnole £36.

Memorial Inscriptions in Yetminster Churchyard include Henry Stone in 1614, Alice in 1649, Mrs Jane Stone of Chetnole in 1691 and Thomas Stone in 1696. All buried under fine table tombs.

## Henneford Mill

Proceeding downstream, the next mill is Henneford. In 1667, John Foy of Melbury Bubb leased the mill to Thomas Bartlett upon surrender of a previous lease. The fine paid was £80, the yearly rent 18s and the heriot 40s. In a Conveyance of the Manor dated 1670, it is referred to as 'all that water grist mill with appurtenances lying in Hynnerford, now in the tenure of Roger Bartlett.

The Mill is listed in the 1799 Proceedings for the Defence of Dorset.

In 1814, it was surveyed on an Estate map which depicted the wheel on the west of the building with the leat running from a pond to the south, whilst the overflow followed the present route of the river to the east.

In 1819, the Mill was leased to Fred Forward and it is described as 'a flour or grist mill, bake-house, stable and outhouses adjacent ... with gardens, three orchards, one meadow called Lower Hams and one called Bailiffs Meadow. The bakehouse and stable lay across the road. Lower Hams was between the leat and spillway, while the orchard and garden approximate with the present garden. The wheel was 'overshot'.

In 1839, the Tithe Map lists the miller as Benjamin Watts although he had died in 1837.

In 1871, the mill was referred to in the Court Case Stone v. Yeovil Water Co. Henneford appears to have survived the reduction in water capacity although alterations made in 1881 may have been made necessary by the fall in water level. The accounts of Henry Owen, carpenter, show how the wheel-bearings and cog-teeth were renovated with the grindstone at a cost of £67.00.11.

In 1890, the mill suffered damage in one of the most severe spells of freak weather ever recorded in Dorset. A waterspout dug holes eight to nine feet deep and heavy rain caused extensive flooding. Today, the mill has been converted into a dwelling and nothing remains of the mill machinery.

### Chetnole Mill

Continuing downstream, the next mill is that at Chetnole. Situated at the end of a narrow lane, until about four years ago (1992), the 17 c building appeared much as it must have done when the last miller closed the door for the last time. The leat had dried up but the dilapidated overshot wheel was in position. It drove two sets of stones. It is known that the mill produced both animal feed and flour. Inside, much of the machinery was still intact and the French burr stones and grit stones were still in place. The Mill has now been modernised and turned into holiday cottages, though some of the features, such as the stones, have been retained. Just inside one of the doors, there is an interesting carved stone, it depicts the torsos of two figures, one in floor-length robes, the other in a short tunic, possibly a Roman soldier. It may have come from the Church, ended up in a builder's yard and been used at some time to repair the wall in the Mill.

In the mid 19 c Levi Symes was miller and baker at Chetnole. He was born, illegitimate, in Ryme Intrinseca and died intestate in 1866 leaving a widow, Harriet and six adult children. Harriet, born Harriet Wilton in Stockwood, was the young widow of William Jeanes a Chetnole shoemaker when she married Levi in St. Thomas's Church, Salisbury on 27 December 1826. Just how they came to be in Salisbury in mid-winter is not known, but they were in Chetnole for the birth of their first child nine months later. Levi died intestate, there appears to have been some disagreement over the estate and the eldest son took his mother to Court. Honour may have been satisfied but a large portion of the small estate went in costs!

| Plaintiff's costs: | £43. | 2s. | 7d |
| Defendant's costs: | £23. | 17s. | 6d. |

The remainder, £146. 5s. 9d. was distributed, three-ninths to the widow, Harriet Symes and one-ninth to each child. Amongst the papers relating to the case is the Bill for Mourning submitted by W. Leeman, draper, of Yeovil. It is interesting as revealing the purchases deemed necessary by a tradesman's widow in 1866 in order that her late husband might be mourned with due solemnity and respect. Three of Harriet's four daughters were married, so, presumably, these purchases were made for herself and Ann, the unmarried one. Somewhere, no doubt, a little dressmaker was hastily running up dresses in time for the funeral, lining the bodices and sewing on all those buttons, yards of crape, ribbons and jet trimming.

Mr. Leeman also furnished funerals and the Bill includes 7s 6d for a shroud, although 'use of pall' has been crossed out.

A short letter from Harriet to the Court has survived. She wrote an excellent hand, neat and decisive, where, one wonders, had she learned to write? Harriet was born in 1803, in Stockwood, could she, perhaps, have attended the Girls' School known to have existed in Yetminster, but, as yet, unidentified as to situation. Four girls who attended this school

## 19 June 1866

Mrs Symes bought of W. Leeman, linen & woolen draper, Hatter & Hosier, Millinery & Mantle Rooms.
Funerals furnished.

| | | | |
|---|---|---:|---:|
| Caps 1s 6d, 2s 9d | | 4s | 3d |
| Front 1s | | 1s | 0d |
| Fale (veil ?) | | 2s | 0d |
| 4 Moreen @ 1s 4½d | | 5s | 6d |
| 2 handkerchiefs @ 1s 2d | | 2s | 4d |
| 2 Ties @ 1s 3d | | 2s | 6d |
| Gloves 2s 5d, 2s 11d | | 5s | 4d |
| 4 doz buttons @ 3½d | | 1s | 2d |
| Pins | | | 3d |
| 12 linning @ 5½d | | 5s | 6d |
| Collar | | | 6d |
| 3 crape @ 2s | | 6s | 0d |
| Flower 2½d, Top 4½d | | | 7d |
| 3 casbin 1s, 2½ Victoria lawn 7½d | | 4s | 7d |
| 18 French Toile @ 1s 6d | £1 | 7s | 0d |
| 8 Henrietta cloth @ 3s 9d | £1 | 10s | 0d |
| Shirt | | 6s | 0d |
| 2 prs. silk hose @ 3s 9d | | 7s | 6d |
| 1 pr. cashmere | | 2s | 0d |
| ? | | 7s | 0d |
| 4½ crape @ 1s 4d, 1½ ribbon @ 2½d | | 6s | 4d |
| 5 yds crape @ 3s, Buckle 1s 9d | | 16s | 9d |
| Buttons, Waist ribbon | | | 11d |
| Use of Pall (crossed out) | | | |
| Top 6½d    Flower 4½d | | | 11d |
| Button | | | 2d |
| 3 bonnets @ 8s 4d | £1 | 5s | 0d |
| 3 veils | | 8s | 3d |
| 1 bonnet @ 8s 9d   box 4d | | 9s | 1d |
| Gloves 2s 10d    Veil 2s 3d | | 5s | 1d |
| 5 crape @ 5s 6d | £1 | 7s | 6d |
| 4 jet trimming @ 1½d | | | 6d |
| 3 yds mule muslin @ 8½d | | 2s | 1½d |
| | £10 | 14s | 1½d |
| Credit | | 6s | 1d |
| | £10 | 8s | 0½d |

are known to have made Samplers. One, made by Martha Sampson, daughter of the Rector of Thornford, is in Dorchester Museum.

## Upper Mill, Yetminster and Nether Mill

Upper Mill is mentioned in Domesday as taxed at 5s. It is situated at the bottom of Mill Lane, a narrow way leading from Church Street. Before the coming of the Railway, this lane continued past the Mill as a road to Chetnole. For part of its way, it followed Herbury Lane, now a pleasant and intriguing "Green Lane" with verges and gates into adjacent fields – only the tarmacadam is missing. This road is now a foot-path only with access by a bridge over the river and a level-crossing. Between the two Yetminster Mills, the Railway followed the river along the valley.

Upper Mill is shown on Isaac Taylor's map of 1765. It is situated just below the confluence of the Wriggle River from Chetnole and the stream from Stockwood. At this point, there was a hatch which diverted the water to the leat, the dry bed of which may still be seen together with the bricked-up arches where the water went through the Mill and out to re-join the river. The wheel was 10 ft. diameter and undershot. The building has now been converted into a dwelling.

In the late 18 c William Dawe leased Upper Mill. He had two sons, Ellis and William, and, in 1795, Ellis Dawe took over from his father as Miller and Baker.

Less than a quarter of a mile downstream was the site of Nether Mill. Until the coming of the Railway in the mid 19 c, there was no bridge where the road from Yetminster to Brister End crosses the river, just a foot-bridge and a ford. Nether Mill was situated on the Left bank of the river a few yards before the river reached the ford. The long, narrow meadows either side of the river were also known as Nether Mills.

One hundred years earlier, the Courts Leet had been ordering various lease-holders to scour the water-course in this area. In 1682, Joseph Hodges was ordered to "cleanse the water-course in his ground called Nether Mill from the river to Robert Bartlett's backside" s.p. 6s 8d. It is likely that Hodges was the occupier of the present Bridge House.

About 1800, one John Barrett arrived in Yetminster. He leased Nether Mill, it is doubtful if a building was still in situ and more likely that he erected a Water Mill to weave sail-cloth. But things soon began to go wrong. Barrett recruited a work-force to work regular hours but he was totally dependent upon Dawe for water. He soon found that working regular hours was impossible because Dawe let the water down only when it suited him.

Instead of employing a regular grinder, Dawe did the work himself with the assistance of two men who also helped in the bakery. He might bake once, twice or three times a day and the Mill would work to suit at 10 a.m., 3 p.m. and 10 p.m. Sometimes Dawe might be out searching for a supply of wheat which was particularly scarce and dear in 1801. Sometimes the millwrights might be working on repairs at the Mill or the stones needed dressing. All this contributed to the irregular hours worked by Dawe . . . so he said! But the truth was, probably, that he had worked the Mill for years with no one to consider but himself, and, now, along came Barrett demanding water at regular hours. Furthermore, Barrett's overshot wheel required more water than Dawe's undershot.

Barrett sent his foreman up to complain, Dawe answered: "You shall have it when I have done with it and not before, I shall not let it down to please Mr. Barrett."

Barrett, exasperated, commenced a Court case against Dawe claiming £1,000 damages. In support of his case, William Jennings, Land Surveyor of Evershot, made a splendid plan, showing the two mills and the system of sluices whereby the water was controlled. In order to draw up the plan, Jennings needed access to Dawe's land, and, this too annoyed Dawe. He wrote Barrett a terse note threatening to bring a case of trespass if either he or his agent came onto his land.

The decision of the Court was that the Defendant "shall not use, pound or let down water in any way to prejudice the Plaintiff". Each party was ordered to pay his own costs, the total was £10 1s 6d with an additional charge to Daw of £1 1s 0d. Nevertheless, Barrett gave up and went out of business. The premises were sold and came to be known Padbury's or the Spinning Factory, later still, the building was converted to dwellings. With the arrival of the Railway, they were demolished and no trace remains.

The Dawe family was widespread but the first mention in Yetminster is the marriage in 1777 of William Dawe and Sarah Baker of Chetnole.

He was, possibly, the first Dawe miller, though it could have been another William Dawe, buried in 1806 aged 82. Families were very small and they were singularly unlucky in the number of children who died in infancy.

On 24 May 1813, Ellis Dawe married Judith, daughter of Charles and Ann Brake, she was 26, he 60 years old. Four months later, their son, Ellis, was born, followed by Judith who died, and, in 1817 Judith herself was carried up the hill to the church-yard. The son, Ellis, grew up to succeed his father at the Mill.

Both Ellis and his younger brother, William, appeared regularly at the bi-annual Manor Courts, no doubt keeping an eye on what property was changing hands. From time to time, like many yeomen and suchlike, before the banking era, they sometimes had spare cash to lend. At some time, prior to 1819, Ellis Dawe had loaned £130 to the widow, Catherine Hutchings. On 5 January 1819, her father, William Bishop, carpenter of Yetminster, died, leaving his property to Catherine and his other daughter, Elizabeth, wife of Thomas Wright, cooper, of Locksfield, Walworth, London. Thomas and Elizabeth passed their share to Catherine and she used it to repay her debt. The property is described as "customary cottage, orchard and premises late William Bishop". Its location has not been identified.

By his Will dated 31 May 1831, Ellis Dawe set up a Trust under the Trusteeship of John Travers Burt Read and James Langdon (Master of Boyle's School) for his son, Ellis, not yet of age, his daughter, Ann, by an earlier marriage, who, in 1810, had married Nathaniel Bartlett of East Chinnock, described as gentleman, and Elizabeth Stephens, his natural daughter by Mary Stephens. Ellis Dawe, the younger, married Ann, daughter of Jacob Osment, they had two children, Ellis and Ann, still very young when their father died in 1849. In 1853, the widowed Ann married Benjamin Legg Bagg, yeoman, of Cattistock.

There was one more Mill on the Wriggle, at Beer Hackett. Little is known of this. The 1840 Tithe Map showws an oval field called Mill Mead (near the present Railway bridge). The field appears surrounded by a stream with a small bridge across but there is no sign of buildings.

However, in 1617 Simon Kente, miller of Beer Hackett and his wife were presented by the Churchwardens for absenting themselves from

Church on Sundays and Holidays. Could it have been that the unfortunate Simon, with six mills upstream, received water only on those days when his fellow millers were resting?

---

**Extracts from the Account Book of Yetminster Mill**
**1849–1866**

*Ellis Dawe*    Miller

| | | | | |
|---|---|---|---|---|
| George Frampton | mason's bill | £2 | 1s | 4d |
| „ | „ | | 9s | 10½d |
| A. Barnwell | plumber | 1 | 8s | 1d |
| W. Painter | repairing Mill dam | | 10s | 6d |
| Robert Jesty | „ | | 6s | 9d |
| Bill for lime | | | 5s | 3d |
| William Andrews | thatcher | 2 | 3s | 6d |
| George Frampton | mason | 1 | 5s | 4d |
| Cutting fuel for draining | | | 19s | 6d |
| Mr G. Brake | fuel for draining | 1 | 0s | 0d |
| William Vardy | for draining | 9 | 9s | 4d |
| Isaac Chipp | for stone | 1 | 0s | 2d |
| Solomon Brake | draining 15 days | | 15s | 0d |
| Robert Jesty | „ | | 18s | 9d |
| Robert Bugler | „    12 days | | 15s | 0d |
| John Ring | carpenter | | 19s | 10½d |
| Mr Coombes | millwright | 13 | 16s | 6d |
| Mr Vining | for tiles | | 8s | 0d |
| William Painter | repairing mill dam | | 9s | 0d |
| John Bishop | blacksmith | | 8s | 8d |
| „ | „ | 2 | 15s | 4d |
| John Hutchings | blacksmith | | 18s | 0d |
| P. Ridout | lime | | 10s | 8d |
| Mr Whitby | for paper-hanging | | 13s | 10d |
| Mr Corfield | cement | | 1s | 9d |
| Mr Sheppard | blacksmith | 1 | 11s | 8d |

DCRO D148/14/26

# Alehouses

The origins of ale-houses are lost in the mists of time! Quite early, the necessity for some kind of control became apparent. Licensing was first sanctioned by Statute in 1495. It was not until the late 17 c or early 18 c that licensing records become more abundant. In 1753, Parliament passed a law requiring all Clerks of the Peace to keep a Register of Licensed Victuallers, so, little is known of ale-houses in the Yetminster area before the 18 c. Each ale-house keeper applying for a licence required two sureties of £10 each. In practice, the applicants in any one area stood surety for one another. Thus, we know the names of the Yetminster inn-keepers for the greater part of the 18 c. However, forging a firm link between the inn-keeper and the name and location of his or her premises is far from easy and needs a cross-reference from some other documentation or source.

Generally speaking, an Inn probably sold spirits as well as beer and might provide accommodation, whereas an ale-house sold only beer. In early days, ale-houses came and went. Ale would often be sold from a cottage only immediately after a brewing and sales would continue until supplies were exhausted. Poor people, unable to work from age or infirmity, would frequently make a little money in this way. Traditionally, the ale-stake, a pole with a bush on the end, would be displayed when a brew had taken place. Sometimes, this caused complaints, particularly in the narrow streets of towns, that the poles were too low and inconveniencing passers-by. Later, Magistrates insisted that ale-houses should display a sign, making it easier to identify a house should the landlord permit any disorderly behaviour. Just as the ale-stake came and went, so the names of Inns were often of short duration. A landlord might give up and the house revert to being a private dwelling or a new landlord might prefer a different name.

The internal fittings of a small Inn or Ale-house were similar to the spartan furnishings to be found in the house of any small yeoman or craftsman. Basically, one or more trestle tables, some forms and stools

47

and pots for serving the drink, earthernware and later, pewter. The floor, stone-flagged or strewn with rushes. Until the days of Tarmacadam, roads were filthy, churned-up mud and dung from the horses and cattle which constantly passed to and fro. The landlord must have been hard-pressed to keep his place clean, even by the standards of the day. But his customers were the local labourers and artisans with the occasional traveller, and no one could keep his boots clean.

A vital feature of the ale-house was the fire, kept going all the year round, as it was needed for both cooking and water-heating. But, in winter, both travellers and locals went to the Inn to warm themselves. Lighting was by candles or rush-lights, or, possibly, oil-lamps. Candles were expensive and had to be snuffed frequently to obtain the maximum light. Rushes were gathered in high summer, soaked, to facilitate the removal of the peel, and then dipped in tallow. They did not require snuffing, but burned out more quickly. Oil lamps were liable to give out an unpleasant smell as the oil used was fish-oil.

Accommodation, if available, was often spartan, travellers bedding down by the fire or even in the landlord's own bed. Even in large Inns, travellers often had to share a bed with strangers. It should be remembered, that, it is only in comparitively modern times that people have come to expect to spend their nights in privacy.

From Vestry Book records we know that Parish Poor were sometimes boarded out with an Inn-keeper.

The Inn-keeper often had a secondary occupation and the day to day running of the Inn was frequently in the hands of his wife, so, it is not surprising that many women, upon the death of the husband, carried on alone.

## The White Hart

The White Hart is the only Inn in the Yetminster area to have survived, at least, from the early 18 c to the present day. Well placed in the High Street, formerly known as Front Street, it stands opposite Queen Street, an ancient thoroughfare known as Church Lane. At the lower end of Church Lane, on High Street, was a public well, and, beside that, it is believed, stood the stocks.

For many, many years, the White Hart was run by the Hayes family.

In January, 1730, Edward Hayes of Yetminster rode over to Glanvilles Wootton to claim his bride, Elizabeth Young. They returned to Yetminster, and, over the next twelve years, Elizabeth was kept busy. Eight times the midwife was called, and, on three occasions, a sad little procession made its way to the church-yard. What they were doing during these twelve years is not known, for, it was not until 1742 that Edward's name appears for the first and only time, as a licensee. On 15 August 1742, he too was carried to the grave.

However, the Court Book for the Manor of Yetminster Secunda throws some light into what was going on prior to the death of Edward Hayes. But, really, they are pieces of a jig-saw and nothing is conclusive. In 1728, Nathaniel Tilley and Benjamin Coombes surrendered a property to Henry Bishop. Nathaniel Tilley was a wealthy man living in Lillington and Benjamin Coombes held what is now known as Pettys Farm to the east of The White Hart. It is very probable that Tilley had granted a mortgage to Coombes and, now, possibly, the property was being re-mortgaged to Bishop. In 1729 Robert Bartlett surrendered to Henry Bishop, land 10 ft.×2 ft. adjacent to his cottage for a similar piece at the end of Bishop's orchard. The property to the west of the White Hart was formerly known as Bartletts.

In 1733 Elizabeth Bishop succeeded to the cottage of her late husband, Henry Bishop. Only three years later, it is recorded that Elizabeth Bishop, widow, deceased, had appointed her kinsman, Edward Hayes, Lord's next tenant to her customary held cottage in Yetminster. It might, therefore, be supposed that Henry and Elizabeth Bishop were occupying the White Hart. But no Bishop is mentioned as a Licensee. We have here an intriguing puzzle: Who was licensee of the White Hart before 1742?

At the Court held on 27 October 1742, the first since her husband's death, Elizabeth Hayes was admitted to her late husband's customary cottage, paying a Fine of 1d and a heriot of 6d. She was to remain there for the next thirty years, appearing regularly on the annual Ale-house Recognances. We can be sure it was the White Hart, for that is where she was in 1753 when the premises are named.

Elizabeth must have been kept busy, as well as having the Inn to run, she had been left to bring up 10 year old Elizabeth and the toddlers, Mary, Edward, Sarah and Eleanor.

From Elizabeth's Will, we know that she sold Spirits as well as ale. The White Hart was also the venue for Meetings and for Auction Sales of Property. It is very likely that the Vestry met there, and that Elizabeth, overhearing the discussions of the Vestrymen, which centred largely on provision for the Poor, was moved to put forward some practical suggestions of her own. For, in 1765, she was appointed an Overseer of the Poor. It was, no doubt, with relief that the male Overseer writing up his book, inscribed:

*". . . provide 3 shirts and 2 shifts for Thomas Jean's children such as Mrs Hayes shall think convenient not exceeding fifteen shillings for the five."*

Elizabeth was one of only four women recorded as serving as Overseers of the Poor in Yetminster. The others were:

1697   Joan Grimstead;
1763   Elizabeth Jenkins;
1766   Edith Jesty

In her spare time, Elizabeth made shirts and shifts for the Poor for which she was paid, we know this from the records of Dame Dorothy Gorge's Charity.

The Inn had some kind of secure lock-up, for there are also records of payments being made to Mrs Hayes for holding prisoners overnight pending their removal to Sherborne gaol.

It is likely that very little happened in the village without Elizabeth being aware of it.

She was to see all her children married.

*Elianor to John Browne.*
*Betty to Edward Quilton of Yeovil in 1759.*
*Mary to Robert Holt of Batcombe in 1766.*
*Sarah to Robert Granger of Yetminster in 1769. Sarah died in 1781 after bearing seven children, but Robert lived to 1827, dying aged 84 after spending 44 years as Parish Clerk. He is commemorated by a plaque in Yetminster Church. Edward Hayes and his wife, Mary, had two children, Edward and Mary.*

50

The "White Hart", Yetminster. Drawing by Isobel Walker

On 19 October 1769, Elizabeth Hayes made her Will. She had certainly prospered during her years at the White Hart. To her four daughters, she left £40 each, to be paid in two years, less any money she might already have advanced to them. To Sarah, she bequeathed half her household goods (except her stock of liquor) to be handed over at the end of 3 months. To her other three daughters, £2. 2s 0d at the end of 3 months, half the legacy to be paid by Sarah.

Her grand-children, Elianor Browne, George Quilton and Edward Hayes were also to receive £2. 2s. 0d each, the sum to be paid to their respective parents until they reached the age of twenty-one. Elizabeth's only son, Edward Hayes, cooper, was appointed Lord's next tenant of the White Hart held of the Manor of Yetminster Secunda plus the remainder of her goods and chattels and her stock of liquor.

Elizabeth signed her Will very legibly. She died just two years later.

Edward Hayes duly succeeded to the Inn and ran it for thirty years. He died in 1804 aged 65 and, his wife, Mary, died in 1812 aged 75.

The cottage adjoining the White Hart to the west certainly came into the hands of Edward Hayes. In 1776, it passed from Martha

Bartlett, widow, to her daughter, Mary Hunt. In 1779, to John Jenkins, probably a mortage, then to John Bartlett, Mary Hunt's brother, perhaps, and, from him, in 1782 to Edward Hayes.

Edward and Mary Hayes had only two children. Edward inherited but died unmarried in 1811. In 1793, his sister, Mary, married Richard Andrews and he inherited from the last Edward Hayes both Inn and Bartletts. The latter, Hayes described as "my newly-erected dwelling-house", so, he had, possibly, re-built the cottage his father bought from John Bartlett. An unexpected entry in the Court Book for 1835, states that Richard Andrews has paid William Barrett of Leigh, £400 for "that customary cottage etc. in Yetminster, for many years used as an Inn known as the White Hart, formerly Elizabeth Hayes, widow, deceased." William Barrett of Leigh was a wealthy yeoman, and, the most likely explanation is that he had granted Andrews a mortgage. Mortgages were entered in the Court Book just as though the property had actually changed hands, but, the fact that it is a mortgage is not always stated. In this case, there is no record of the granting of a mortgage but this is not all that unusual, sometimes papers were lost, or clerks failed to make entries.

Richard and Mary Andrews had eight children. She died in 1835, aged 66, and Richard in 1846 aged 86. By his Will, Richard bequeathed the White Hart to his son, William Andrews and Bartletts to his son Charles. However, Richard appeared to be considerably worried by the question of access. Bartletts had been squeezed in between the Inn and the neighbouring property, Higher Farm. To the east of the White Hart there was, as now, only a fairly narrow way between the Inn and the back of Petty's Farm. Bartletts had a garden at the back but the only access thereto was through the White Hart yard. Andrews was adamant that, whoever owned the Inn should allow access to the rear of Bartletts.

However, the brothers solved the problem. In 1847, Charles Andrews yeoman, of Hummer, Trent, sold Bartletts to William for £348 with a small piece of land used as a garden with Bartletts but part of the White Hart, together with the roadway for £27.

William Andrews remained at the White Hart until about 1870 when Joseph Morey took over and he was landlord for another twenty years.

## The Five Bells

An Inn with a sign embracing the word "Bells" is nearly always to be found near the Church. From 1727 to his death in 1744, John Batt held the Five Bells. He probably succeeded John Hodges who died in 1727. After the death of John Batt, his widow, Mary, married Benjamin Coombes and the property passed to him. Opposite the Church, stands the Old Vicarage. Originally, this was two cottages, the Vicar occupied that to the south, the other was the Five Bells. Eventually, the Vicar acquired both cottages and made them into one house. The cellar and the rolling- way for the barrels, part of the Five Bells, remain to this day.

## The New Inn

Situated at the west end of the High Street, the New Inn was the property now known as Sunnyside. Thomas Bartlett first appears as a Licensee in 1735, and, in 1753 when the names of premises are given, he is landlord of the New Inn. He was buried on 31 July 1756 and his widow, Elizabeth, carried on until 1760. From the Account Book of Dame Dorothy Gorge's Charity we have this entry:

> 1746 "Spent at Thomas Bartlett's making up Mr Read's Account 1s 6d".

## The Swan

Travelling east along the High Street, passing the Post Office on the left, then a drive to a new property, Field House, lying well back from the road, one comes next to a row of cottages. The first two, thatched, comprised The Swan. One has a nice Tudor doorway.

Joseph Conway appears on the list of Licences granted for Christmas 1727, but not on the annual lists until 1732. He was born in 1692, the son of William Conway, Inn-holder, who died in 1696. During the period, 1696 to 1727 no Conway is recorded as an Inn-keeper. Perhaps a relative of another name was running it.

The Inventory made at William Conway's death, shows that his house contained a parlour, a hall, a buttery with 3 hogsheads, 6½ hogsheads

Clare Cottage, formerly "The Swan". Kept by the Conway family

and 2½ hogsheads of beer and a kitchen with a furnace-pan, a mashing vat and "other lumber for the brewing".

Upstairs, were three chambers. His furniture was that normally to be found in a modest dwelling of the time, but, he owned 12 pewter dishes and 8 pewter flagons, 2 table boards and frames, a form and 10 chairs. All consistent with the calling of an Inn-keeper. He also possessed 2 table-cloths, ½ dozen napkins and 3 pairs of sheets. The whole valued at £16. 19s. 0d.

Joseph Conway ran the "Swan" for nearly twenty years. He was also a cordwainer. In 1717, the Trustees of Dame Dorothy Gorge's Charity apprenticed George Chisman of Leigh to Joseph Conway as a shoe-maker.

Joseph Conway was a Churchwarden, his name "Joseph Conaway" appears on the front cover of the Parish Register. He also attended Vestry Meetings and served his turn as both Overseer of the Poor and Surveyor of the Highways.

On 20 September 1750, he made his Will, signing with a neat and firm hand. He describes himself as "cordwainer", this is not unusual, many inn-keepers had a second occupation.

He bequeathed his customary-held cottage with backside, orchard and a piece of ground of 3 acres called Common Close, together with his household goods, to his wife Susannah Conway, and, after her decease, to his daughter, Mary Conway.

To his son, William, he left one shilling and all his working tools and leather with "my best and worst suits of cloathes and all my wearing-apparel (except my middle or second-best suit of cloathes which I give and bequeath to my journeyman, Richard Walbridge)".

He left 1s to his daughter, Susanna Ayers and 1s to his daughter Elizabeth Conway. He also requested that his wife and daughter, Mary should take an Inventory of his goods the day after his burial "to prevent disputes that may arise and for the better securing of the said household goods unto my daughter, Mary". The residue of his estate he left to his wife, Susanna whom he appointed executor.

Joseph was buried on 7 June 1751.

In 1756 Mary Conway married John Maidment. Susanna carried on business at the "Swan" until her death in June 1760. There is no further mention of the "Swan". A 19 c Manorial Survey shows the property as "Conways" so the name must have persisted.

## The Half Moon

The location of this Inn has not been established. Susannah Buckland ran it from 1751–1754. Before that, it is possible that it was held by Andrew Dodge.

## The Bell

Again, the location is unknown. It was kept by Thomas Chinnock from 1747–1758.

Between 1738 and 1753, Thomas and Elizabeth Chinnock had eight children: William, Eleanor, Ann=James Richardson in 1763, Mary=William Jesty in 1765, Thomas=Margaret Shepherd in 1771, Grace=George Cooper in 1775, James and Sarah.

Elizabeth Chinnock died in 1766 and Thomas in 1771. Their son, James, died in 1781, their daughter, Sarah in 1784 and daughter-in-law, Margaret in 1790, the last two of consumption.

## The Fleur de Lys

Location unknown. It was, probably, first in the hands of Margaret Brake in 1749. Margaret was born Margaret Douglas and was the widow of John Brake. She married Henry Fox and the premises passed to him until his death in 1761 when the licence reverted to Margaret Fox, who was still there in 1768. She was buried in 1772.

Henry Fox was the widower of Constance by whom he had several children. He had two daughters, Margaret and Lettice by Margaret.

## The Blackamoor's Head

The Blackamoor's Head was the building on the east side of Church Lane (Queen Street), set end-on to the road with the cottage behind facing the lane. Today, the only house beyond it to the south, is the Red House, the former Methodist Manse built only in the early twentieth century.

From 1730–1768 and possibly longer, it was kept by James Hayward. He was born in 1699, son of Peter Hayward and Eleanor Wright, daughter of blacksmith William Wright. In 1720, James married Mary Shepherd. The couple had six children, all of whom grew up and married. He first appears as a Licensed Victualler in 1727 when he is granted a Licence for Christmas of that year. But, he first appears on the regular lists in 1730 and may have succeeded John Hodges, last mentioned in 1728.

The marriages of their children cover a span of twenty years.

1742   James Hayward=Ann Read
      It is possible that they moved to Sherborne
1746   Elizabeth Hayward=Richard Bishop
      After his death, she re-married
1758   Elizabeth Bishop=Azariah Burbidge of Sherborne
1755   Peter Hayward=Susannah Tomkins

1755   Jane Hayward=George Edmonds
1757   Mary Hayward=Isaac Russell
1763   Judith Hayward=William Edwards

Edwards was also an Inn-keeper, the location of his premises is not known but, it is very likely that he succeeded his father-in-law at the Blackamoor's Head.

On 8 June 1770, James Hayward made his Will. He described himself as "victualler and baker" and appointed his daughter, Judith, wife of William Edwards, as executrix.

His bequests were:

> *To son, Peter Hayward, £5 and wearing apparel both linen and woollen.*
>
> *To daughter, Mary, wife of Isaac Russell, £5.*
>
> *To daughter, Jane, wife of George Edmonds, £5.*
>
> *To grand-children:*
> *Edward, son of James Hayward, jun.*
> *Richard Bishop*
> *Mary, wife of John Winter*
> *Lettice, wife of James Penny  5s each*
>
> *To son-in-law, Azariah Burbidge 10s*
>
> *Witnesses: Henry Shepherd sen.    The testator made his mark*
> *           Ann Shepherd*

James Hayward was buried 10 February 1785, aged 86 years. He died of 'Natural decay'. No burial is recorded for his wife, Mary, presumably, she pre-deceased him.

It might be noted, that his daughter, Judith, received nothing, neither did any of her children, which makes it all the more likely, that Judith and her husband were running the Blackamoor's Head. It is strange, however, that James did not appoint "the Lord's next tenant" to his property. He is not mentioned in the Court Book of Yetminster Secunda, neither at his death nor when he first became licensee of the Inn.

The former "Blackamoor's Head" kept by James Hayward. The date-stone reads:
*Abraham and Mary Donne    1821*
Probably considerably altered by Donne. He succeeded Hayward and William
Edwards who m. Hayward's daughter, Judith

The Court Book does, however, tell us that brothers, William and
Benjamin Coombes, were, in some way implicated in the property. In
1811, it is recorded, that, a property described as "customary copyhold
dwelling-house, garden and orchard situated in Church Lane,
Yetminster" passed from the Coombes, both deceased, to William
Miller of Holwell, from him to William Jeffrey and thence to Abraham
Donne.

The building bears a date-stone $A^D M$ 1821. Abraham and Mary
Donne. They were incomers to Yetminster, in 1803 they had a daughter,
also Mary, who married Peter Brake a son of Charles Brake and his
wife Ann, daughter of William and Judith Edwards. Abraham Donne
died in 1845 leaving the property to his brothers-in-law, Edmund Laver,
yeoman, of Sutton Bingham and James Lemon yeoman, of Over

Compton. Donne's wife, Mary had died in 1832 aged 59 years. Abraham lived to the age of 81 years.

The identification of the Blackamoor's Head came about in a quite remarkable manner. From Tasmania, came a copy of a letter written in 1839!

William Edwards and Judith Hayward married in 1763.

Their surviving children were:

*Ann who m. Charles Brake in 1786. She died in 1845 aged 78.*

*William unmarried, migrated to London, died 1856.*

*Mary who m. John Eyears in 1795. At one time, kept the Royal Oak.*

*James who m. ? He emigrated to Tasmania where he called his farm "Yetminster".*

*Jane who m. Robert Brake of Ryme Intrinseca in 1801.*

*Peter who m. ?. He was a carpenter and migrated to Wincanton. He was buried in Yetminster in 1845, 'from Sherborne' so, very likely, died in the Workhouse.*

*Judith who m. William Watts in 1792. He farmed at Upbury and, their only surviving child, Mary Watts m. Thomas Hayward.*

Peter Edwards wrote the following letter to his brother James in Tasmania. Peter was 63 year old, for that era, an old man.

*Wincanton February 24 1839.*

*Dear Brother and Sister,*

*I received your kind letter and am glad to hear of your well doing, which I wish I could say the same. But I am sorry to inform you that I have lost my poor wife. She have bin dead this 3 years. She was ill for 2 years which drove me to every distress. I was blidged to sell everything I had to pay (for) the death, which I had no friend to help me to a penny. But, thank God, I have paid everyone their due.*

*Dear brother, you said in your letter to send you Particklars of the family which I will inform you to the best of my power. William Watts is liven at the same place. Thomas Hayward is living at Yetminster at the same place. Sister Eyears liven at Yetminster and keep the Inn of the Royal Oak. Sister Brake is liven in the old hous where she yusst to and your words be come to truth, you said before you went away that David oud be bankrupt, which he has, and cost William £549 17s (? £59 17s) to settle the affair. Sister Jane is liven at Closworth, the Blackamoor's Head is Donne and one of the Smith of Chetnole married with Mr. Jenkins (?) daughter of Chilthorne and they rent the farm. I was at Yetminster 2 years ago and they were all well.*

*Dear Brother, you said in your letter to inform you how my brother William did behave to me. But I am sorry to inform you that I have no friend in he. I have two sons in London which I went to see them & call on William, which I have not seen him for four years, nor heard from him, and he kep me in the shop for 2 ours before he ask me (to) try any refreshment, which I took as kind of him. But he never ask me of my welfare, how I was, nor where I lived, nor how I was off in the world. Dear Brother, I should of come to see you had I but money to pay my passage, but I am sorry to inform you this (not in my power).*

*I work at Gillingham, near Tisbury, 3 days a week and some days at 2 shillings, so I leave you to guess my situation in life is grim. I find lodging and washing, I have but little to spare.*

*Dear Brother, I should be thankful to you if you could help me to five pounds, if it in your power, but if not, not to hurt yourself, but if you could pay my carridge out, I will come, for I oud sooner die in a foreign country than to live in poverty in my own, for at this time, I don't see anything but . . . as I have no friend but my own hands.*

*I remain, your ever loven brother, Peter Edwards.*

*Direct to me, Peter Edwards, at William Edwards, saddler, Wincanton, and he will send to me.*

Poor Peter, here we have a tradesman who had always paid his way, reduced to penury through the unfortunate circumstance of his wife's last illness. Yet, he had three sons, presumably working, and all his siblings prospered, he had nephews and nieces, but none prepared to give him any help.

In particular, William Edwards seems to have prospered in London. He died in 1865 and, in his Will describes himself as 'gentleman' though

Peter refers to a 'shop', this could have been a shop selling goods or a work-shop. Be that as it may, he owned four freehold properties, Nos. 1, 2, 3, and 4 Globe Terrace, Devonshire Street, Mile End. He, himself, was living at 2, Peel Terrace, Bethnal Green. He left two of these houses to his sister, Mary Eyears, and two to his sister Jane Brake.

After their deaths, the four properties were to go to his nephews, James and David Brake, sons of Jane. The nephews also received his shares in the East London Waterworks Co. and the Eastern Counties Railway Co., subject to the payment by them of £30 to his friend Charles Roper of 1, Peel Terrace and £100 to the Deaf and Dumb Asylum in the Old Kent Road. The remainder of his estate he left 'to the use of my friend, William Samuel Eastman of Bethnal Green, butcher' subject to the payment for her life of 10s per week to his housekeeper, Sarah Colley Duris.

The David mentioned in the letter as having gone bankrupt, was, probably, David Brake son of Peter's sister Ann. A David Brake of St. John's Street, Smithfield, beer dealer, was made bankrupt in 1833.

We know of another David Brake who died in 1867. In his Will, he describes himself as 'formerly of Ruscombe, Nr. Twyford, Berks. and now of 101, Devonshire Street, Mile End, saddler. To his brother, John Brake, he left £19 19s and the remainder of his estate to Sarah Neal and Mary Neal spinsters, of 142, Haningford Road, Islington, executrices.

The most momentous piece of information included in Peter Edward's letter was that Donne had the Blackamoor's Head, thus making it possible to tie this up with the date-stone and establish the location of the property which was the Inn for so many years.

Nearly opposite, at the top of Church Lane on the west side, stands Everards, now, unfortunately, renamed The Muntins. Prior to 1749 this property was aquired by John Allambridge, he died un-married and it passed to kinsmen, the Feavers. In 1803, William Edwards bought it, presumably for retirement, the Court Book refers to him as 'Innkeeper'. William died in 1817 aged 75 and left it to his wife, Judith. She died the following year and left it to the son, William Edwards, in Bethnal Green, together with some land known as Woodlands Gate.

In 1826, William Edwards sold Woodlands Gate to David Brake, saddler of St. Sepulchre for £180. In 1839, he sold Everards to Daniel

Penny of Sherborne for £200. William was then described as 'gentleman' of 5, Globe Terrace, Mile End. It was rented by the Penny family for very many years, primarily to Peter Brake, son of William Edward's sister Ann. In 1823, Peter had married Mary, only child of Abraham Donne at the Blackamoor's Head.

Walking through Yetminster Church-yard one remembers Peter Edwards in his unmarked grave, little did he know, that his letter, passed around the world one hundred and fifty years after he wrote it, would solve one mystery for which a solution had long been sought. Thank you, Peter!

---

# Ale-Houses

Here are the Licences granted for Christmas 1727.

A is probably for brandy and D ale. But what are B and C? One could be cider,s the other, perhaps, wine or rum.

| | | |
|---|---|---|
| William Fudge | Chetnole | ABCD |
| John Hussey | ,, | ,, |
| James Dunsford | Ryme | ,, |
| John Glyde | ,, | ,, |
| Thomas Taylor | ,, | ,, |
| Thomas Soper | ,, | D |
| Bryan Shear | Batcombe | ABD |
| John Sturmey | Hilfield | ABD |
| Elizabeth Perrott | Leigh | ABD |
| Nathaniel Allambridge | Yetminster | brandy CD |
| Elinor Lillington | ,, | D |
| Joseph Conway | ,, | ACD |
| John Coombes | ,, | ACD |
| John Batt | ,, | ABCD |
| James Hayward | ,, | ABCD |
| Hester Miller | ,, | brandy BCD |

*Crossed out* for Yetminster were: John Hodge, John Beaty, John Cooke, Thomas Cheesman.

*Crossed out* for Leigh: James Ellary, Thomas Bridle, Peter Whiffen.

# Ale-Houses

Records of Ale-house licensing commence in 1715 and continue until 1768, but it is only for the years 1753, 1755 and 1768 that the names of premises are given. In 1853, there were no fewer than eight Inns in Yetminster.

| | |
|---|---|
| The Five Bells | Benjamin Coombes |
| The Half Moon | Susannah Buckland |
| The Fleur de Lys | Henry Fox |
| The New Inn | Thomas Bartlett |
| The Bell | Thomas Chinnock |
| The Swan | Susannah Conway |
| The White Hart | Elizabeth Hayes |
| The Blackamoor's Head | James Hayward |

If none of these suited, the thirsty could go further afield, to . . .

## Leigh

| | |
|---|---|
| The Crown | William Spencer |
| The White Hart | William Bastable |

## Batcombe

| | |
|---|---|
| The Greyhound | Bryant Shear |
| The White Hart | William Hooper |

## Chetnole

| | |
|---|---|
| Huntsman & Hounds | Bernard Winch |
| The Boot | John Meech |
| The Royal Oak | Edward Cave |

## Holnest

| | |
|---|---|
| The Rose & Crown | John Hutchings |
| The Sawpit | William Hare |
| The Crown | Elizabeth Miller |
| The Black Lyon | William Chaffey |

## Melbury Bubb

| | |
|---|---|
| Three Horseshoes | Henry Durden |

## Ryme Intrinseca

| | |
|---|---|
| The Greyhound | William Bartlett |
| The New Inn | Andrew Lovelace |

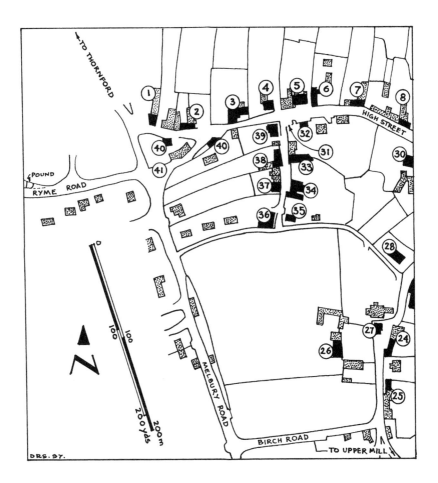

1. Sunnyside
2. Boyle's School
3. Court House
4. Higher Farm
5. The White Hart
6. Petty's Farm
7. Manor House
8. Devon House
9. Swan Inn
10. The Church House

11. Manor Farm
12. Hill View
13. Gable Cottage
14. Lower Farm
15. Forrd House
16. Sussex House
17. Willow Farm
18. Approx. site of Nether Mill
19. Bridge House
20. Site of Pool-well

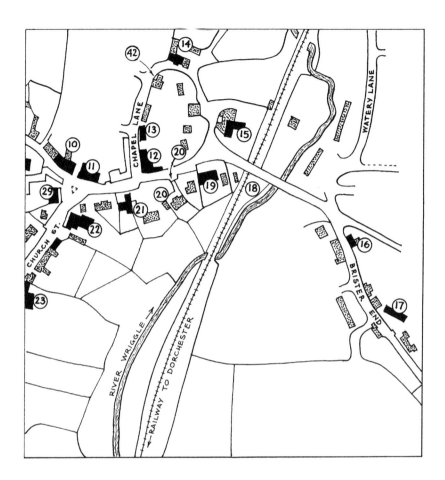

| | | |
|---|---|---|
| 21. Gable Court | 31. Site of pump/well | 41. Site of |
| 22. Hill House | 32. The Laurels | former |
| 23. Old Vicarage | 33. Ryalls (Briar House) | cottages |
| 24. Stone House | 34. Blackamoor's Head | |
| 25. Greystones | 35. Red House | |
| 26. Upbury | 36. Muntins (Everards) | |
| 27. Sexton's Cottage | 37. Spring Cottage | |
| 28. Church Hall | 38. Fairings | |
| 29. Cross Farm | 39. Rock House | |
| 30. Prior's Cleve | 40. Smithy (2 sites) | |

# The Hayward family of Ryme Intrinseca and Yetminster

The name Hayward derives from the office of 'hayward', the man responsible for the boundaries of the common fields and the impounding of stray animals. There was a hayward in every parish and numbers of Hayward families arose in different parts of the country, all unrelated.

Ryme Intrinseca is a small village to the west of Yetminster. For several centuries, it belonged to the Duchy of Cornwall. The little church is dedicated to St. Hippolytus, and is one of only two such dedications in the whole country.

In the year 1645, Thomas Hayward of Ryme Intrinseca married Bazill Masters. He is described as "servant to William Strode" and was, possibly, a bailiff living at Frankham Farm which lies a good $^1/_2$ mile to the west of Ryme, very near to the present A37 Yeovil–Dorchester road.

Thomas and Bazill Hayward had issue:

i. *Thomas=Mary – – –. He set up as a shoe-maker in Yetminster and died in 1680. No issue.*

ii. *Bazill=Giles Miller of Yetminster. She died 1699. Issue: Bazill 1678; Joan 1680; Elizabeth 1686; Giles b. & d. 1688 and Mary d. 1690.*

iii. *Joan b. 1656=Henry Chilcott in 1695.*

iv. *Giles b. 1658. Of whom late.*

v. *Agnes b. 1662=Richard Taylor. 4 children.*

vi. *John. d. 1671.*

vii. *William= – – –. Issue: Thomas, Mary and 4 others.*

Thomas Hayward was buried in Ryme in 1676. One might suppose that Thomas died somewhat unexpectedly, on 17 September, he executed a non-cupative Will before his wife, Bazill, his son, Thomas and John Russell, Rector of Ryme.

Thomas left everything to his wife to pay his debts and to distribute what was left amongst his children.

On 30 September, 1676 John Munden the elder, Thomas Glyde and John Munden the younger, took an Inventory of the goods of the deceased. From this, we know that his house consisted of a hall, buttery, kitchen, old chamber, new chamber, chamber over the kitchen and a cheese loft.

His household goods were valued at £31 2s 4d, his wearing apparel at £2. His furniture was what one might expect of a 17 c farmer, extremely sparse by modern standards, but accepted as the norm by thousands of families throughout the land. He possessed 5 bedsteads, 1 feather bed, 3 dust beds with bed-clothes, a chest, a trunk, 2 coffers, 2 boxes. These last items served for the storage of clothing, bed and table linen, spare cash and any documents that might be held.

In the hall were one table-board, frame, form and benches and 1 chair. In the kitchen, 1 table-board, frame, form and benches.

At this period, the table-top was separate from the frame on which it was supported and, all but the very wealthy sat on benches. Thomas owned one chair, for himself, maybe.

His household utensils were few: 1 small silver bowl and two silver spoons, some pewter, 9 porringers, four saucers (receptacles for sauce and not the pieces of china we place under cups!), 3 candlesticks, 1 flagon, 1 dish, 2 salts, a little bottle, and 2 brass candlesticks.

In the kitchen were 3 brass pots, 1 skillet and 1 furnace pan. He also owned a musket valued at 13s 4d.

There were timber vessels in the dairy, a vat and a cheese press. Nine dozen of butter and 1 butter barrel were worth £2 8s 4d. In the cheese loft were 900 cheeses valued at £9 0s 0d, a cheese rack, frame and scales and wool £1 2s 4d. Unfortunately, we do not know the weight of the butter and cheese. The space needed to store 900 cheeses must have been considerable.

The appraisors moved outside and here lay Thomas's wealth:

| | |
|---|---|
| *20 cows    1 bull* | *£80.00.00* |
| *1 mare and colt* | *10.00.00* |
| *10 wendling calves* | *10.00.00* |
| *4 plough steers* | *17.00.00* |
| *70 sheep* | *18.10.00* |
| *6 yearling heifers* | *12.00.00* |
| *2 yearling bulls* | *3.00.00.* |
| *4 swine* | *6.00.00* |

A total of £156 10s 0d in livestock.

He was bringing on young heifers and calves to replenish his herd of milking cows and two young bulls, perhaps to sell or to replace the one he had. The mare would have been the family saddle-horse, Thomas used oxen for ploughing. His flock of sheep provided wool and lambs for market and were probably folded at night on the arable to manure the land.

In crops, he had:

| | |
|---|---|
| *15 acres of wheat* | *£30  00s  00d* |
| *4½ acres of barley* | *£6  15s  00d* |
| *3 acres of oats* | *£4  00s  00d* |
| *2 acres of beans* | *£3  00s  00d* |
| *and 4 mow-staddles in the field £2.* | |

It is somewhat surprising that, at the end of September, these crops had not been harvested. Or, maybe they were safely in the barn, the appraisors knowing full well how many acres their neighbour had under each crop.

The farm implements were those usually to be found: wain and wheels, putt and draught, 2 zulls, 1 drag, 2 harrows, 4 iron chains, yokes, wain rope, a winnowing-sheet, bags, peck and seed-lipp.

The total value of Thomas's goods came to £263 4s 5d.

The widowed Bazill Hayward was to live for another 24 years, she died in 1700. It is probable that her son, Giles, had been living with her and running the farm.

On 7 July 1700, Bazill made her Will, witnessed by Samuel Strode, John Munden and Elizabeth Masters. Bazill and Elizabeth made their marks. She bequeathed:

*£20 to her son, William*
*40s to each of his 6 children*
*her gold ring to his son, Thomas*
*her best holland apron to his daughter, Mary.*

*£10 to her daughter, Joan Chilcott & my best coverlet.*
*40s to daughter, Agnes Taylor and 40s to each of her 4 children on this consideration: 'that their father, Richard, doth purchase his own life and his eldest son's life, in consideration of the tenement that his mother, Elinor Taylor, now holdeth by her widowhood in Ryme Intrinseca.' If this were not done within 8 months of her decease, then her Executor was to detain the children's legacies until he thought fit to pay them to the best benefit of the children.*

*to daughter, Agnes, 'my large red whittle and my best serge coat', all the rest of her apparel to Joan and Agnes.*
*40s to grand-daughter, Bazill Miller.*
*40s to grandson, John son of Giles, at 12 years of age.*
*The residue of goods and chattels to son, Giles, whom she made executor.*

On 27 July, John Munden and Samuel Strode arrived to take an Inventory of her goods. The household goods are much the same as in Thomas's Inventory. The silver bowl and spoons are missing and she has acquired 7 barrels. The butter and cheese is valued at only £5, but this is not significant, since a large quantity may have recently been sent to market. The farm implements are the same and the farm stock, except that there are no sheep and 6 plough steers instead of 4. The value of the livestock has dropped to £99 13s 4d, nearly £57 less than in Thomas's Inventory. Nearly every animal has a decreased value, and, of course, the sheep have gone. No crops are included and the total value of all Bazill's possessions was £130 13s 4d.

*2. Giles Hayward 1658–1735. = 1) Katharine – – – 1 child, John,*
*bp. 1698 Katharine d. 1698.*

69

= *2) Mary Stickland of Melbury Bubb*
*m. Sherborne 22 June 1700.*

Giles and Mary had issue:

i. *Giles b. & d. 1710.*

ii. *Thomas bp. 1702 = Elizabeth – – – Issue: Giles 1727, Mary 1729, Ann 1730, William 1738.*

iii. Giles *of whom later.*

iv. *William bp. 1709 = Sara – – –. Issue: Mary 1735, Hannah 1736, Sara 1740, Oliver 1746, William 1749.*

v. *Basill = William Andrews.*

vi. *Mary bp. 1713.*

No Will has survived for Giles.

*3. Giles Hayward 1703–1780. = Elizabeth Stone 1732 at Yetminster. She was bp. 1706, eldest of the nine children of Thomas & Elizabeth Stone of Withyhook Mill. She was buried in 1776.*

Giles and Elizabeth had issue:

i. *Susanna = George Vincent, fuller of Fontmell Magna. m. 1759 she died in childbirth after only a year of marriage.*

ii. *Margaret bp. 1740 = Thomas Clarke 8 Dec 1766. Issue: Mary, Elizabeth and Ann.*

iii. Giles *Of whom later.*

iv. ⎰ *Betty* ⎱ *Both pre-deceased their father & one m. a Mr. Turner*

v. ⎱ *Mary* ⎰

Giles was Churchwarden of Ryme and his name, appears on the treble bell, cast in Closworth in 1753. It bears the inscription:

*Thomas Beere, Giles Hayward C.W.*

*'T.R.B.F.' (Thomas Roskelly, Bell Founder).*

At Lady-day, 1751, Giles Hayward gave up the tenancy of Frankham Farm with 100 acres of pasture, 27 acres of meadow and 32 acres of arable. After over one hundred years, the Hayward family left Frankham and moved into Ryme, probably to a tenement known as

'Mundens' of which more in the next generation. Great must have been the excitement as the 25 March dawned, the waggons were loaded and everyone set out on the short journey into Ryme. Giles and his wife were not yet fifty and, Giles, the son and heir, but nine years old.

On 15 July 1780 Giles Hayward wrote his Will, he styles himself 'gentleman'.

He bequeathed:

*To grandson, Giles Hayward, £100 at age 21, should he die before then, to grandson John Hayward at 21.*

*To granddaughter, Mary Clark, £150 at age 21.*

*To son-in-law, Thomas Clark, 1s.*

*To daughter, Margaret, wife of Thomas Clark, £100.*

*To 6 grand-children, John Hayward, Thomas Hayward, Elizabeth Hayward, Elizabeth Clark, Ann Clark and Elizabeth Turner £20 each at age 21.*

*To grandchild, Giles Hayward, 1 silver cup*

*To grandchild, John Hayward, a silver spoon*

*To grandchild, Mary Clark, a feather-bed with all appurtances and 1 copper warming-pan.*

*To grandchild, Elizabeth Clark, 1 bed with appurtances and 1 gold ring.*

*To grandchild, Ann Clark, 1 silver spoon.*

*To grandchild, Elizabeth Hayward, 1 dozen pewter plates.*

*To son-in-law, George Vincent, 1s*

*To my sister, Bazill, wife of William Andrews, 1s.*

All else he left to his son, Giles, whom he made executor.

4. *Giles Hayward 1742–1810 = 7 Sep. 1771 Elizabeth Read of Cothelstone, Somerset.*

Giles and Elizabeth had issue:

   i. *Giles b. 1772 = Sarah Bowdidge in 1798.*

   Issue: *William unmarried*
   *Elizabeth = William Budge of Crewkerne*
   *Sarah = – – – Budge of Crewkerne*
   *Edith = – – – Hole*
   *Giles m. twice*

   *Sarah Hayward d. Evershot 1807.*

*ii.* *John b. 1774 = Elizabeth Wadman in 1805.*

Issue: *Elizabeth = Edward Genge*
*Susannah = – – – William*
*(d. in London at first childbirth. Bur. Ryme, coffin arrived labelled "glass".)*
*John emigrated to Davenport, Iowa.*
*Thomas = Harriet Osmond of Trill Farm, emigrated to America.*
*Jane, through an accident when young, went insane, d. Sherborne.*
*Sarah = – – – Lomas, St. Heliers, Jersey, Wine & spirit trade, emigrated to America.*
*Anne emigrated with brother, Thomas.*

*iii.* *Elizabeth b. 1776 = Edmund Devenish in 1799. d. 1806.*

Issue: *Susanna*
*Elizabeth*
*John*

*iv.* *Thomas b. 1779 d. 1786.*

*v.* *William b. 1781 = Elizabeth Bowdidge in 1807.*
Issue: *William (3 wives) emigrated to America.*
*George = 1) Whiting of Pennard*
*= 2) Georgiana Good.*

*vi.* *George b. 1783 = – – – Bellringer*

Issue: *Susan unm.*
*Jane unm.*
*Sarah = – – – Hacker*
*George = ?*

*vii.* *Mary b. 1785 = George Silk of Beaminster in 1812.*
*Issue: Jane*
*Eliza.*

*viii.* *Jane b. 1787 (twin of Thomas, below)*
*= John Corry, wid. in 1824. When widowed, Jane returned to Ryme, d. 1884 aged 96.*

Issue: *Caroline*
     *Amelia*
     *Jane*

ix.  *Thomas b. 1787 of whom, later.*

x.  *Isaac = – – – Shepherd of Langport. Emigrated*

When, in 1771, Giles Hayward married Elizabeth Read, it was with consent of her parents, so Elizabeth was a minor. Giles styled himself 'gentleman' and the marriage was by Licence, his father, Giles and John Paltock being witnesses. The marriage took place in Ryme and not the bride's parish, which would have been more usual, so one may wonder if, perhaps, consent had been given somewhat grudgingly and that none of the Read family attended. John Paltock was buried in Ryme in 1789, he was probably the father of Robert Paltock, Surgeon and apothecary who, in the same year, was engaged to inoculate the Poor of Yetminster. Upon his marriage, Giles built a new house, presently known as the Post House, it bears a date-stone

H

G E

1772

To the east may be seen the later extension which included the small shop kept by Jane Corry when she returned to Ryme after the death of her husband. She lived to the great age of 96, until recently, her grave-stone might still be seen at the back of Ryme Church, but, leaning precariously, it now appears to have fallen completely.

Hitherto, Hayward families had been fairly small, but Elizabeth had a long child-bearing life before her and the 'newly-built' house was soon filled. Of the eleven children she bore her husband, she lost only two, the first Thomas, a boy aged seven, and an infant, Isaac, born just before the second Isaac who survived.

Giles had built up a substantial holding for himself in Ryme, but, when he came to write his Will in 1809, he had six sons to consider and two unmarried daughters as well as his wife. His Will is long and detailed and, striving for an equitable distribution of his property must have caused him many a sleepless night!

The 'Post House', Ryme Intrinseca, home of Giles and Elizabeth Hayward.
The date-stone reads:
*Giles and Elizabeth Hayward   1772*
The date of their marriage.
Their daughter, Jane Corry, in her widowhood kept a shop in the extension to
the right. She died aged 96 years

His eldest daughter, Elizabeth, had married a Mr. Devenish, she pre-deceased her father. But, his two younger daughters, Mary and Jane were still unmarried and provision had to be made for them.

To his eldest son, Giles Hayward, he left the freehold tenement and lands in Evershot which Giles already occupied. But, he was charged with paying £100 each to his sisters, Mary and Jane. The property included a malt-house. This Giles was the Churchwarden who, in 1801, signed the Agreement made between Evershot and Yetminster when Evershot arranged to send their Poor to the newly-built House of Industry erected behind Holbrook, the Yetminster Poor House.

He then considered his 2 copyhold Tenements with 80½ acres, known as 'Mundens'. He notes that his wife is entitled to these as her "Free Bench". But he leaves that part of 'Mundens' occupied by his son, John and 59 acres of named fields to Giles and John, charging them with the payment of £300 to their sisters, Mary and Jane. The other part of 'Mundens', his newly-erected dwelling-house and 21½ acres of named fields and all that part of the house called 'Cellar' at the east end of the barn adjoining the dwelling-house of John and a house called 'Flax House' he leaves to Thomas and Isaac.

He directs that his daughters, Mary and Jane, as long as unmarried, shall have the parlour and chamber over in his house with part of the garden and the use of the pump.

To his wife, Elizabeth, he leaves his copyhold Tenement in Ryme called 'Barbers Tenement', and, after her decease, to his sons William and George and William and George were to pay his executors £300. Another tenement in Ryme he leaves to Thomas and Isaac and a freehold piece of land called 'Glydes' to Isaac. After his wife's death, his household goods go to his Executors, Thomas and Isaac, except for the furniture and effects in the parlour and chamber over which are left to Mary and Jane.

Giles must have given a sigh of relief as he finally put his signature to this document. Let us hope his children were all satisfied with their portions!

In his Will, Giles Hayward describes himself as "gentleman", but the Sherborne Mercury, reporting his death in 1810 refers to "a respected farmer of that place". His signature is clear if a trifle shaky.

Elizabeth Hayward outlived her husband by twenty years. On 24 March 1828 she made her Will:

*I bequeath unto my sons Giles and John Hayward all that my leasehold land and premises situate in Rhyme Intrinseca called the Flax House and Lower Cellar with all right and title I have therein according to an agreement entered into between me and my son, Isaac as a compensation to me for yielding up my widowhood in that part of Mundens Estate which he sold by my consent.*

*I give to my sons, William, George and Isaac Hayward £5 each. Also the rest of my property, personal estate and effects, I give to my* son, *Thomas Hayward and my daughter, Jane Corry to be by them divided after payment of all my debts, funeral and other expences.*

*I nominate Thomas Hayward and Jane Corry to be Executors.*

*Four months later, on 18 July, Elizabeth added a Codicil leaving £5 each to her three grand-children, John Devenish, Jane and Eliza Silk.*

On both these documents, Elizabeth's signature is clear and bold.

Let us follow the fortunes of Giles and Elizabeth Hayward's other children, before returning to their son, Thomas Hayward and his family.

Mary and Jane both found husbands. Mary married George Silk, sail-cloth maker of Beaminster and had two daughters, Jane and Eliza. Jane married a widower, John Corry of Yarlington. When widowed, she returned to the old Hayward home, the Post House in Ryme and kept a little shop in the annexe built onto the east end of the house. She died 12 January 1884, aged 96.

A Survey of householders in Ryme, dated 1832, shows John Hayward still living there and Giles appears to have returned from Evershot. William was probably in Mudford. After the the death of Elizabeth Hayward, Thomas, as Executor, was in dispute with William over the matter of unpaid rent for lands in Ryme. An action at law had been commenced when both parties agreed to arbitration by Thomas Fooks, the Sherborne solicitor. On 25 March 1833, they met at the Angel Inn, Sherborne. The claim was for payment of £382 10s 0d rent owing for Darbies Tenement in Ryme. It was agreed that William Hayward should pay £222 2s 11d. No doubt, his mother had allowed the unpaid rent to mount up without pressing her son for payment. William Hayward's wife, Elizabeth, died in 1827 and, he himself in 1859. They had two sons, William Bowdidge and George.

George Hayward married Georgiana Good and farmed at Martock and Long Sutton, finally retiring to Yetminster to live at Rock House at the bottom of Queen Street. They had two sons and two daughters. William Good Hayward, 1854–1940, was born at Long Sutton and emigrated to New Zealand in 1874, arriving at Port Chalmers on the 'City of Vienna', an iron ship of 1,000 tons built by Connell of Glasgow in 1866. She made the passage in 89 days. By 1892, he was working as a Surveyor, and, in 1898, he was married in Palmerston North to his first

George Hayward     and his wife     Georgiana Hayward

(1812–1890)                        (1826–1906) b. Good

They retired to Rock House. Photograph taken in Weymouth, probably when their son, Harry Miles Hayward brought his bride on a visit in 1886.

cousin, Anne Mary Symes from Piddletrenthide. Her mother was Amelia Good, sister to his mother, Georgiana. It is not clear how, or where, their courting took place. Anne Mary was born in 1867 and, thus, only 7 years old when her cousin left for New Zealand. She died in 1947. There were four children but none married.

Harry Miles Hayward, 1856–1953, was born at Martock. He went into the hardware business in London, Birmingham and Sheffield. In 1877, he left for New Zealand on the sailing-ship 'Calypso', landing at Dunedin. He saw great opportunities in the colony, immigrants were arriving continuously and all needed to equip their new homes. In 1880, Harry returned to England on the 'Orient' and obtained agencies for hardware from leading Birmingham and Sheffield firms. He is said to

"Rato', Lower Hutt, home of H. M. Hayward from 1907–1953

have imported the first iron bedstead into New Zealand and to have owned the first breech-loading rifle. Later, he owned a 1907 Holsman 'High Wheels' American car, it was clutchless with a hood 8 ft. high and is now in the Car Museum in Wellington.

Harry made frequent visits to all the main Australian and New Zealand cities as well as England. In 1886, he married Jessie Luxford, and, almost immediately, took his bride on a trip to Australia and England. In Sydney, they heard of the eruption of Tarawara volcano, and, at first, it was believed that the whole of the North Island had disappeared. No doubt, on this occasion, he brought his bride to meet his parents and sisters at Rock House and his cousin, Thomas Hayward at Hill House.

In 1908, Harry and Jessie went to Lower Hutt near Wellington and lived at an imposing house called "Rato" until his death in 1953, aged 97. Harry gave a large tract of land to the town as a public park which still bears his name. He and Jessie had 2 children, Cyril George and Muriel and there are descendants. On their 60th Wedding Anniversary they gave a party for 300 guests.

78

Back in Yetminster, the two girls, Georgiana and Ada, lived on with their parents at Rock House. It must have been rather a dull life, very different from that enjoyed by brother Harry in New Zealand.

George was an active member of the Vestry. He also, apparently, took up cycling. The Sherborne Mercury records that, coming down the hill into Cerne Abbas, he had an accident, as a result of which, he was shaken but not badly hurt. George died in 1890 and his wife in 1906. Both were buried in Ryme and their Memorial also remembers William Good Hayward who died in New Zealand.

On 6 September 1899 at All Saints, Dorchester, Georgiana Hayward was married to John Henry Harris. He was a 38 year old bachelor farmer from Staffordshire, Georgiana was three years his senior. Her sister, Ada, was a witness, she returned to live at Rock House until her death in 1949. She, too, is buried in Ryme.

Thomas Hayward 1787–1862, was the second youngest of the children of Giles and Elizabeth Hayward. In 1812, he married Mary, only surviving child of William and Judith Watts of Upbury. At first, Thomas and Mary farmed at Sutton Bingham but then moved to Lower Farm in Yetminster. They had issue:

  *i.*  *Eliza Mary = Simon Goode of Yeovil. At first in the leather trade, he then opened a grocer's shop in Middle Street, near where Woolworths stands today.*

  *ii.*  *Marianne, after her sister's death, she married Simon Goode.*

  *iii.*  *William Watts, 1816–1892 = Sarah daughter of John Dunford of Lillington.*

  *iv.*  *Thomas 1826–1902 = Amelia Dampney in 1854.*

  *v.*  *Giles = Priscilla Coombs Dunford in 1859. She was sister to Sarah above.*

  *vi.*  *George Watts = 1) Lavinia Rheinhart.*
          *2) Sarah Ann Marsh 1877 in Yetminster.*
          *3) Mariam Moorhouse in U.S.A.*

William Watts appears as a competent and successful farmer, it is doubtful if the same can be said of his son-in-law, Thomas Hayward. In 1834 Hayward mortgaged 4 acres of land to one Thomas Cole of Yeovil, glover, for £100. Nine years later, he had defaulted on re-payment and Cole took possession, but, at the same Court, sold to William Watts for

£298. By 1851, he was farming at Bishops Caundle. His wife, Mary, died in 1856, and, he himself died in 1862 in Henstridge, probably staying with his eldest son, William Watts Hayward. Both Thomas and Mary are buried in Yetminster. Thomas Hayward's marriage to Mary Watts had bought another Hayward line into the family, for Mary's mother, Judith Edwards, was the daughter of William Edwards, inn-keeper and Judith Hayward. Judith was the daughter of James Hayward, inn-keeper at the Blackamoor's Head and his wife, Mary Shepherd. James was born in 1699, son of Peter Hayward and Eleanor Wright, daughter of blacksmith, William Wright.

Thomas and Mary Hayward's eldest son, William Watts Hayward, went to live at Upbury with his grand-parents. As he grew older, and, having no sons, Watts was, doubtless, glad of a young man about the farm.

In 1846, young William married Sarah, daughter of John Dunford of Lillington and they went to farm at Henstridge Bowden. The farm-house, with its large circular window facing the road may still be seen standing in a somewhat isolated position. William and Sarah had nine children of whom five died young. Of the four survivors, Sarah and Jane never married and Flora, the youngest, married J. Alan Steed of Dorchester and had two sons.

William Hayward decided to emigrate. He had seen his two distant cousins leave for New Zealand and his two uncles settle in America. First, he went to the U.S. to visit them but decided to go to New Zealand. He arrived in New Zealand about 1886 and spent some time with his cousin, Harry Miles Hayward. Later, he bought a pioneer farm near Te Horo.

On 3 January 1893, at Wellington, he married Ellen Gilbert. Ellen was born in 1857 in Barnstaple, Devon. She became a teacher, and, about 1883 came to teach in Yetminster. Her contract was signed by: Thomas Hayward, George Brake, Samuel Hallett, Abel Whittle and Charles Doddrell (clerk to the Board). Her salary was £70 per annum. In 1885, she was inspected by George H. Gordon: "Miss Gilbert has effected considerable improvement in a very backward school." Two years later, he reported: "She is painstaking and a very fairly successful teacher."

In 1887, Ellen left Yetminster to sail to New Zealand as governess to the two children of Mrs. Annie Truebridge, Alfred aged 4 and Ethel 2.

William and Ellen Hayward (b. Gilbert)
with their son, William Gilbert Hayward

Outside their farmhouse/Post Office at Hautere Cross,
Te Horo, New Zealand.
c. 1915

Mrs Truebridge was going to join her husband. She was probably related to Edwin Truebridge, assistant master at Boyles School and a nephew of the wife of J. W. Causier, master of Boyles for nearly 40 years. Mrs Truebridge and Ellen sailed from Plymouth on the S. S. Kaikoura. Ellen, as an assisted emigrant, paid £10 for her passage, the New Zealand Government paying the balance of £16.

About 1898, William and Ellen Hayward moved to a new farm at Hautere Cross, and, here, they also ran the Post Office. In 1925, William resigned after 25 years service and received a letter of appreciation from the Postmaster General and a cheque for £5.5.0.

William and Ellen had one child, William Gilbert Hayward born in 1900. By this time, Ellen was over forty years of age. At the age of 13, Gilbert left school to take over from his parents the running of the dairy farm, eventually increasing the size of the farm to 196 acres. William Hayward died in 1932 and Ellen in 1948. After Ellen's death, Gilbert sold the farm. He married Thelma Page and had two children, Joan Hayward and Kenneth Edward Hayward. Ken has two sons and a daughter, so, it may be hoped that the Hayward line, stretching back unbroken, to Thomas Hayward of Ryme Intrinseca in the 17 c, may long continue in New Zealand.

Sadly, William Watts and Sarah Hayward were never to see again their only surviving son. They retired from Henstridge Bowden to Yetminster where they lived at 'Eastover', Brister End until his death in 1892. His widow, Sarah, went to live in Dorchester with her married daughter, Flora Steeds. There she died in 1911 at the great age of 91 years. Her Obituary states that she was well known as a woman of great resource, she would have needed to be, having seen the deaths of five of her young children and having said Good-bye for ever to her only surviving son. It also states that, in her younger days, she underwent an operation which had the effect of weakening her back, so that for the last 17 or 18 years she had lain in bed. It is difficult to understand this statement. Sarah's youth was spent in the early years of the 19 c, what operation could possibly have been performed? Moreover, she had survived nine pregnancies, and, a photograph taken in 1908 in the garden of her daughter's home, shows an upright old lady, bonnet on head, sunshade in hand, standing in the doorway of a summer-house. She was buried in Yetminster beside her husband.

Thomas Hayward, 1826–1902, was something of a trial to his father, or, maybe, it was the other way round and Thomas senior was not as tolerant as he might have been! As a young man, Thomas junior joined the Methodists. His father was furious, locked him out of the house and went to bed, placing the door-key under his pillow. His mother, a kindly soul, let him in through a window. But, next morning, his father was adamant. Young Tom had to go. He went to relations in London, but, unfortunately, they turned out to be atheists, and, when they discovered that Tom had been attending a place of worship, they, too, turned him onto the street. Tom became ill with worry until the doctor suggested that a return to his native air could be his only salvation! Accordingly, he returned to Yetminster. His parents were now living in Bishops Caundle, so he went into lodgings. He returned not long before the deaths of his grandparents, William and Judith Watts, in 1852. William, after making provision for his wife and daughter, Mary Hayward, left his property o be divided amongst his six grand-children. In this way, Thomas acquired the shop and the adjacent Royal Oak Inn. Very soon, he established himself as a grocer and draper and purveyor of almost anything the village might require. In 1854, he married Amelia, daughter of William and Mary Dampney of Boys Hill. Thomas bought Hill House and lived there with his wife and only child, Theophilus, for the next 30 years. He also accommodated his shop assistants and apprentices and, for a time, his niece, Flora Hayward, was working in the shop. He also established grocery rounds, visiting outlying farms and cottages with pony and cart. A very old photograph shows the shop with a woman standing outside (could she be Flora?) and a horse and cart. On the next-door cottage hangs the Inn sign for the Royal Oak. But, most interestingly, this photograph reveals that there was an imposing porch outside the shop, going right up through the second floor to eaves level. It incorporates the present door, a window above and the date-stone.

As the years passed, Thomas's prestige as a Methodist increased, he became a Lay Preacher and entertained leading Methodists at Hill House. A staunch Temperance man, he let down the licence of the Royal Oak, thus removing one opportunity for drunkeness from the inhabitants of Yetminster. Every St. Thomas's Day, he gave an orange to every child in the village. It is said that he walked about in white kid gloves. He frequented Vestry Meetings and was a member of the School Board. There came a time when he handed the shop over to his son, Theophilus, but it was not a success. Theophilus was a spoiled young man and declared that his health would not stand up to the hard work involved, so his father took it back. However, towards the end of his life, Thomas suffered with his heart, and, finally, he relinquished both the shop and Hill House and bought the present Gable Cottage in Chapel Lane for his retirement. For centuries, this had been the farmhouse which went with the land belonging to Sherborne Almshouse and the property extended from opposite Lower Farm to the corner of High Street. John Brake was the sitting tenant, and, he too would have liked to buy. But, it appears that his offer was brushed aside by the Almshouse in favour of Hayward, who then began to complain that Brake had not quitted the property, and, furthermore, had been cutting down trees in the orchard. Having obtained possession, Hayward called the house 'Rose Cottage'.

To the north, he built a Temperance Hall and, the land to the south which had been the orchard, he sold to a fellow-Methodist, Charles Doddrell from Shepton Mallet. Doddrell built the present cottages and established a plumbing business. He evidently saw an opening for mains water had just come to the village. High up on the south wall, he placed a date-stone.

Today (1996), the original lead pipes laid along Yetminster High Street by the Yeovil Water Co. are being replaced. Doddrell, no doubt, was familiar with many of the installations.

In 1902, Thomas Hayward died. His Will, after the death of his wife, Amelia, left everything to his son, Theophilus. He had married Mary Elizabeth Ryall from another Methodist family and they had one daughter, Dulciana. Dulciana was to be given certain books from her grandfather's library and also, "my dear mother's sampler". Although it cannot now be found, this was obviously a prized possession and interesting because three other samplers made by girls at Yetminster School are known to exist. One, made by Martha Sampson, 18 Oct. 1787, may be seen in Dorchester Museum. Martha was the daughter of Robert Sampson, Rector of Thornford and his wife, the former Martha Jenkins of Chetnole and died in 1800 aged only 22 years.

Gable Cottage, Chapel Lane. The old farm-house to the land of Sherborne
Almshouse until bought by Thomas Hayward

A second sampler has recently been given to the Parish and was
made in 1813 by Elizabeth Barrett. A third, in the ownership of her
family, was made in 1808 by Sarah Shepheard.

Mary Watts, born in 1793, would also have been a young girl at about
this same period, and, possibly, attended the same school, the location
of which has not been identified.

When Thomas Hayward retired from the shop, he was presented
with a clock by the people of Yetminster. This, together with other
memorabilia, is now owned by his great-grandson. Another item is a
small spring tape-measure bearing his name, and, probably given away
as an advertisement for the shop. Amelia Hayward died in 1911, and
both are buried near the porch of Yetminster Church. Close by, are his
parents and members of the Watts family, whilst not far away, is the
grave of his brother, William Watts Hayward and his wife, Martha.

Mary Elizabeth (Polly) Hayward went to Brisbane "for her health" and died there in 1944. Theophilus lived with his grand-daughter in Kent and died at Ashford in 1950. With him, the Hayward name died out in this line.

*Giles Hayward 1829–1911*

*George Watts Hayward 1835–1917.*

Contact with Stuart Thompson, a direct descendant of Dulciana Hayward, revealed the fact that these, the two younger sons of Thomas and Mary Hayward, had, apparently, emigrated to Pine Island, Minnesota. A letter of enquiry to the local newspaper of Pine Island produced an overwhelming response. The descendants of these brothers in America are legion.

Giles left England in 1849 and went first to Wisconsin, he logged on the Menomonie River and spent the next two winters near Winona, Minnesota. In 1854, he returned to England, and, the following year went back to Minnesota taking George with him and settled on a claim. In 1859, he ws once again in England to marry Priscilla Dunford in Lillington. Priscilla was the younger sister of Sarah who, thirteen years previously, had married Giles's brother William Watts Hayward. In 1870, Giles went into the milling business, in 1877 he bought a farm, and, in 1890 was back in England, returning with 7 Dorset horned sheep. About 1900, Sarah Hayward made a prolonged visit to her Uncle and Aunt in Pine Island returning to live with her sister Flora in Fordington, where she died in 1943.

Giles and Priscilla had five children. A grandson, Al Hayward, retired to Dorchester and lived at Fordington with his fourth wife, Patricia, sadly, he suffered a stroke and has since died.

George Hayward was married in America to Lavinia Rheinhart, by whom he had two children. After her death, he returned to Yetminster to marry Sarah Marsh in 1877. Back in Pine Island, Sarah bore him four children and died in 1889 at the early age of forty years. George subsequently married Marian Moorhouse, but had no more children.

On 25 April 1905, Giles and George Hayward gave a grand party at the Opera House in Pine Island to celebrate the fifty years they had lived there.

Your presence is requested at a reception

given in honor of

the fiftieth anniversary

of the arrival in Pine Island of

Messrs. Giles and George Hayward

to be held in the Opera House

Tuesday, April twenty-fifth, nineteen hundred and five

from four to nine p. m.

Reply to Lock Box 43
before April 20th
Surprise

Invitation issued by Giles and George Hayward
to celebrate 50 years in Pine Island

———

Let us take a backward glance at the Hayward name in the vicinity of
Yetminster. We know that, in Stockwood in 1406 there was a William
Hayward, he was blind and in trouble for witholding money donated to
the Church.

In 1595, in the same place, there was a Roger Hayward. Fortunately,
his Will has survived: he had a wife, Elizabeth, and sons Thomas,

87

Edward and John and a kinsman Richard Hayward. Also, possibly, at some time, a daughter, since he mentions a son-in-law Paul Walcombe.

Roger was not greatly blessed with this world's goods.

*To Paul he left a standing bedstead & feather-bed*
*To Thomas a year old heifer*
*To Edward "one brass pot & my second-best brass pan"*
*To John "my best doublet & hose & my best jerkin"*
*To Richard one pewter platter*

The residue of his goods to his wife, Elizabeth.

The Inventory of his goods and chattels was taken by Richard Gylles, Vicar of Stockwood, John Bartlett, Edward Hayward and John Hayward.

Furniture and household items were minimal. Outside, he owned two pigs and some poultry, two cows, two three year old heifers and one one year old plus implements of husbandry. His total wealth amounted to £13 13s 4d.

It would appear that Roger's eldest son, Thomas, was absent when the Inventory was taken.

It would be interesting to speculate that he was the father of Thomas Hayward of Ryme who married Bazill Masters in 1645.

# The High Street

As late as the 19 c, we find Yetminster High Street referred to as Front Street. This was a designation found in many places, doubtless to distinguish it from Back Lane. The farm houses on the north side of the High Street have their crofts stretching out at the back. Very often, in this situation, a lane, known as Back Lane, gave access to the far ends of the crofts. However, in Yetminster, there was no such access to the rear of the farm houses in High Street, Back Lane was the road at the bottom of the crofts of the houses on the west side of Church Lane, now known as Melbury Road.

The High Street curves from the cross-roads in the west to the river at the east. Apart from the surface of the street, it is, today, probably much as it has appeared for hundreds of years.

At the cross-roads, the ways, very narrow until widened in the 19 c, went west to the Pound and Ryme Intrinseca, north to Thornford and south to Chetnole and Melbury. An early Ordnance Survey map shows a smithy on the triangle where the garage stands today and another next to Rock House. There were two or three cottages on the Garage triangle, the late Bernard Jolliffe recalled, that, in the 1920s, the occupants were Tom Jesty, haulier a Mr Slade and his son, James and Mrs L. Dyer. Whilst, at the end, facing Ryme Road, two brothers, F. and C. Roberts, ran a Cycle Shop which, later, they developed into a Garage. The other blacksmith's shop was run by Mr. Gould and, later, Mr Chant. This was demolished c 1990 and a cottage built on the very small site.

The blacksmith was vital to the economy of a settlement and it is unfortunate that so little is known of the Yetminster blacksmiths. Between 1678 and 1709, the Wright family were blacksmiths. After that date, no names are known until the Bishops appear.

In 1832, Matthew Bishop bought from Daniel Brake, part of Fairings in Church Street for £250. He died in 1843 and left the property to his widow, Sarah. In 1859, she passed it to her son, Luke Bishop. It is

High Street looking west.
Rock House on left.    Court House and Higher Farm on right.
Present garage premises at far end

described as "cottage and carpenter's shop", possibly the south end of the house plus the cottage next-door. Sarah owed £25 to Thomas Penny of Sherborne, iron-merchant. The payment and interest was secured by promissory notes of John Bishop, her eldest son, and Charles Arnold of Yetminster, cordwainer. Sarah had paid £20 for the benefit of her youngest child, Mary Ann, who, the previous year, aged only 17, had married a 21 year old Excise Officer, Alfred Rogers. It was agreed that Sarah should enjoy the premises for her life and that Luke should then sell, repay her debts and divide the remainder amongst her surviving children, but Mary Ann was to have £20 less. John Bishop was also a blacksmith.

Sarah Bishop died in 1867 aged 73. Luke Bishop sold the property to Charles Jerrard, mason, for £250.

Other blacksmiths of the early 19 c were Mark Bishop, John Padbury and James Childs. In 1840, William Ring had the smithy.

90

High Street looking east.
*On left*: "White Hart', Petty's Farm (hidden) and Manor House.
*On right*: cottages, since demolished, that on extreme right, a sweet-shop kept by Walters

To the south of the present Garage, stood two cottages on what is now actually the road. They were demolished early in the 20 c. The road must have been extremely narrow. In 1780, one of these cottages was occupied by James Arnold, shoemaker. He and his wife, Martha, brought up ten children here.

On 25 July 1798, the Sherborne Mercury carried the following advertisement:

> *Ran away from his master, James Arnold, shoemaker, William Douch, apprentice, 13, fresh colour, lost one fore tooth, strait brown hair, a well-looking and thick-grown lad, wore away an old mixed dark-colour greatcoat, brown cloth jacket and velveret breeches.*
>
> *Whoever harbours or employs said apprentice after this notice shall be prosecuted as the Law directs.*         *James Arnold.*
>
> *If the said apprentice shall return he shall be kindly treated.*

91

There is no evidence that young William every returned.

James Arnold was buried in 1838 aged 79 years. He was succeeded as shoemaker by his son, Charles, who, in 1833 had married Amy White. They had five children, including James, born in 1841. James was also a shoemaker. He was Churchwarden for 17 years and Church organist for 47 years. He is remembered for the black top hat he wore to Church on Sundays, and, his service to the Church is commemorated by a brass plaque. It is recalled that the shutter of his shop window let down to form a bench and that passing boys would thump the bench, causing nails and tacks to jump about all over the place. James Arnold died 3 January 1917 aged 75 years.

The last persons to live in this cottage before it was demolished were a Mr. Rendell, a disabled man and his sister.

On the south side of High Street, between Church Lane and the Cross, were several cottages, they appear on old photographs but all but one have been pulled down. Built right on the road and wedged into the hill, they were picturesque, but, no doubt, insanitary.

At the end of the street, next to Cross Farm, stands Priors Cleve, it is first mentioned in the Manor Court records of Upbury Prima in 1777 when it is referred to as 'Upwards'. John Upward had died and the property passed to his nephew, the Rev. William Jenkins. It is extremely doubtful that Upward would ever have lived there. Upon the death of Jenkins in 1823, his sister, Mary Jenkins, inherited. The 1840 Tithe Apportionment shows that Mary Jenkins owned a considerable amount of land in Yetminster. Robert Smith rented 102 acres including Higher Farm, Abel Whittle, the miller, rented 19 acres and Thomas Hayward 11 acres. 'Upwards', she rented to John Cake. Mary Jenkins, herself, lived in Chetnole, her brother, William, in Melbury Osmond. The small cottage stood in a large garden in the shadow of the high walls of the Tannery buildings. After its mention in the Tithe, nothing further is known of this property for another hundred years. Elizabeth Cake, possibly John's wife, was buried in 1856, aged 70 years.

After W.W.2, it was owned by a Mr. Stone. He wished to enlarge the house, and, building materials being scarce, he bought-up second-hand stone, timber etc. from wherever he could find it and the result of this somewhat piecemeal building may be seen today. However, it must be said that refurbishment carried out by the present owners has greatly improved Stone's efforts and a most delightful garden has been created.

Mr and Mrs Stone made an interesting discovery. One day, Mr. Stone rapped one of the walls in his study and decided it was hollow. He removed part of the wall and found shelves at the back on which lay a small child's shoe. The shoe was of a slip-on type with a high front and in very good condition. Originally brown in colour, Mr. Stone was advised to treat it with neat's foot oil, unfortunately this turned the leather black. The shoe is believed to date from the 17th century, and, since 1971, it has been in Sherborne Museum.

Concealing shoes in buildings was probably the most common superstitious practice of the post-medieval period. The earliest known instance of shoe-concealment dates from the 13th century and a peak was reached in the 19th century.

Shoes were hidden in inaccessible places such as chimneys, walls, under floor-boards and in roofs. Other hiding-places are bricked-up ovens and around doors, windows and stair-cases. Hiding shoes in chimneys and around doors may have been because these were openings through which evil spirits could enter the house. Chimneys were associated with the hearth which provided warmth and was the place where food was cooked, so, these also needed protection.

Shoes are often found with other objects and the shoes are usually old and worn, but this is not the case with the example found at Priors Cleve. The room where it was found lies at the north-east corner of the house and the location of the find was next to the fire-place where, originally, there was a stair-case. In old houses spiral stairs were invariably located to one side of a fire-place with the bread-oven at the other.

The large houses on the north side of High Street were farm houses, each with barns, stables and cow-sheds at the rear, and, beyond the buildings, an orchard and a close of pasture. The remainder of the fields were scattered throughout the parish. This arrangement must have made farming extremely difficult, some fields were accessible only by crossing another man's land. As late as the 1940s, an attempt was made to rationalise the land tenure, but it came to nothing because no farmer was willing to exchange a good piece of land for one that was not so good, not even if the result would be a compact farm rather than scattered fields.

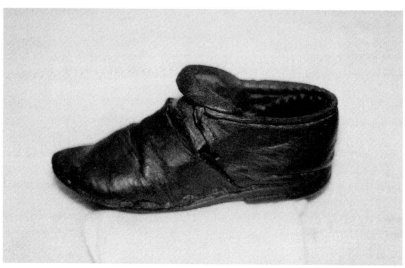

Priors Cleve and the 'hidden shoe'

In some areas, cows were milked in the fields, but, in Yetminster, it was the custom to bring them home for milking and that meant much movement of cattle. Before the coming of the Railway facilitated the movement of churns and opened-up distant markets, most milk was made into cheese or butter.

A Dorset custom was that of "Dairymen". An occupation which occurs frequently on Census returns. The farmer would rent his cows to the dairyman at so-much a head, providing pasture, winter fodder and premises. The dairyman milked the cows, generally cared for them and made what profit he could, usually by making cheese and butter. Dairymen were inclined to move around quite a lot, always in search of a better bargain!

The first house on the north side of High Street is 'Sunnyside', formerly the New Inn, when it ceased to be an Inn is not known. In the late 19 c it was occupied by Theophilus Hayward, his wife, Mary Elizabeth (Polly) and daughter, Dulciana.

Boyles School was founded in 1697 with a legacy of £700 left by Robert Boyle of Stalbridge Park to his servant, John Warr to set up a school. Yetminster is never mentioned but, it is thought, that Warr may have had some connection with the village. Warr purchased an estate upon which to erect the School and Master's house and 40 acres of land at Knighton to provide an income for the Master. Originally built to accomodate 20 poor boys, 10 from Yetminster and 5 each from Leigh and Chetnole, it was not long before the Master was permitted to take paying pupils, usually sons of farmers and tradesmen.

The first master was George Rawles, the last D. F. Gibbons, appointed in 1944.

Over the blocked-up doorway, facing the road, is a fine piece of hamstone, evidently intended for an inscription. Recently, Yetminster History Society, with the help of a generous grant from the Royal Society of which Robert Boyle was a founder member, has erected a plaque to commemorate Robert Boyle's gift.

Next to Boyles stands The Old Court House, previously known as Church Farm. Relatively nothing is known of this building believed to be part of Rectory Manor of which few Records have survived. The house is curiously L shaped and sometimes occupied as two dwellings, probably of late 17 c date, the east wing was a later addition.

Boyle's School
Yetminster
1711 ~ 1945
Endowed by

ROBERT BOYLE, F.R.S

1627 ~ 1691

for 20 poor boys
of
Chetnole, Leigh
and
Yetminster

I William Pearce being to be Licensed to teach
School in the Free School at Yetminster in
the County of Dorset and peculiar Jurisdiction
of the Dean of Sarum to which I am nominat[ed]
by the Feoffees of the said School Do freely an[d]
willingly assent to and Subscribe the Thirty —
Nine Articles of Religion made and agreed o[n]
in the Synod holden at London in the year of
our Lord 1562 and to every thing therein contain[ed]
And also to that part of the Declaration made a[nd]
established by the Canons Ecclesiastical made
in the year 1603 that is to say, I Do Declare
that I will Conform to the Liturgy of the Chu[rch]
of England as it is now by Law established

Wm Pearce

[Fif]th day of August 1762 the —
[sa]id William Pearce did Subscribe
[Decla]ration abovewritten and also
[th]e Oaths of Allegiance and —
[Supremac]y and of Abjuration before

John Tabman Sur:

School Master's Licence. 1762.
William Pearce to teach in the Free School, Yetminster

Higher Farm, Yetminster. Note thatch and gables since removed

The original dwelling of Higher Farm, next door, may have been the cottage lying north – south at the back, the part facing the road being built as the tenant prospered. Two date-stones appear on the front, A. W. 1624 and A. W. 1630. These could refer to Ambrose Willis who is known to have been in the village at that time, or, possibly, a member of the Warre family, though no Warre with a Christian name 'A' is known. An old photograph shows the house with a facade of 1½ storeys, the first-floor windows in gabled dormers and the roof thatched. The house has an open fire-place in the east room with a bread-oven and there are indications of a newel stair in the west room. The present owner found a trade-token under the floor of the barn:

*"Stephen Brassier his half peny"* and, on the reverse, *"Wilton in Wilshire 1667."*

In 1840, Higher Farm with 102 acres was leased by Robert Smith from Mary Jenkins.

Petty's Farm, Yetminster

Pettys Farm is, possibly, mid 17 c. It is thatched and built end-on to the road as if squeezed between the entrance to the rear of the White Hart and a public foot-path at the front. At one time it was divided into two tenements.

For some years, Pettys, or Coombes as it was then referred to, was held by members of the Coombes family. William Coombes, yeoman, died in 1697, and his widow, Joan, succeeded to the property. The Inventory taken of William's goods on 12 July 1697, shows that he was worth £84.

**Inventory of the goods of William Coombes of Yetminster, yeoman appraised by John Munden, John Addams and Thomas Bartlett.**

| | | | |
|---|---|---|---|
| his wearing apparrel | £2 | 0s | 0d |
| one mare & one nagg | 4 | 0s | 0d |

| | | | |
|---|---|---|---|
| 2 steers | 7 | 0s | 0d |
| 3 cowes | 7 | 10s | 0d |
| 8 young beasts | 7 | 0s | 0d |
| 65 sheep & lambs | 10 | 0s | 0d |
| wheat on ground | 8 | 10s | 0d |
| Lent corne on ground | 20 | 0s | 0d |
| wheat in barne unthreshed | 2 | 0s | 0d |
| 3 brass potts | 1 | 0s | 0d |
| 2 brass kettles | 1 | 10s | 0d |
| 1 cheese steane | | 10s | 0d |
| 1 wayne 1 dung putt 1 cart | | | |
| 3 payre of wheels & other | | | |
| plough tackling | 6 | 0s | 0d |
| 4 timber tubbs | | 10s | 0d |
| hemp & flax ready dressed | 1 | 0s | 0d |
| 1 feather bed & 1 dust bed with | | | |
| bedsteads & furniture thereunto | | | |
| belonging | 4 | 0s | 0d |
| to piggs & other small things | | | |
| omitted | 1 | 10s | 0d |
| | 64 | 0s | 0d |
| recte | 84 | 0s | 0d |

Perhaps it was a good year for corn, William's was valued at £20, that, and his 65 sheep valued at £10, accounted for nearly one-third of the total. His household goods were few. It is strange that he appears to have possessed no table, stools nor dishes. He seems to have been engaged in the usual farming activities and, also, to have grown some hemp and flax.

William left no Will and Administration was granted to his widow, Joan. She made her mark and Joseph Coombes and William Coombes signed – her sons, perhaps?

The property was passed on, to Benjamin Coombes, to Anne, his widow and Benjamin, their son.

In 1723, Benjamin Coombes mortgaged to Nathaniel Tilley of Thornford, gentleman, at the same time selling a strip of land to his neighbour, "that is to say, they did surrender about 20 ft. of ground on which Thomas Allambridge set part of his barton wall." In 1710, a Benjamin Coombes married Judith Allambridge, so there may have been a family connection here.

It is not clear exactly when the property fell to Henry Petty, but a Rent Roll dated 1776, includes,

*"Henry Petty for Gollops, formerly Coombes."*

Thomas Gollop was a wealthy resident of Lillington, grandson of Nathaniel Tilley. Gollop probably inherited the Mortgage from his grandfather.

1776 was the year that Henry Petty's daughter, Susannah, was born at Closworth. Petty, of course, was leasing the property as an investment and re-letting. Nothing further is recorded until 1815 when Henry Petty died and the 2 dwelling-houses, orchard, land called Vealhayes, formerly Coombes, passed to Susannah. She, verging on 40, lost no time in marrying William Jennings of Evershot, a gentleman of considerable wealth. So wealthy was he, that he was able to grant the Earl of Ilchester a mortgage of £2,000 on some farms. Jennings was a Land Surveyor and did a lot of work for the Ilchester estate. He also drew the plan of Yetminster Mill when Ellis Dawe was in dispute with Barrett.

At his death in 1854, Jennings left several large legacies, not only of hundreds, but some running into thousands of pounds. The unfortunate Susannah, then nearly 80 years old, was taken to the Court of Chancery by some of her late husband's kin over her alledged mal-administration of the estate. But, on William's death, Pettys Farm reverted to her and she promptly sold 2 dwelling-houses, etc., formerly Coombes, to William Andrews for £1,200. William Andrews was the sitting-tenant, but, as he was landlord of the White Hart next door, he, presumably, had been sub-letting the property.

In 1854, the property is described in the Court Book as:

*2 dwelling-houses, barn orchard, Vealhayes meadow, Vealhayes Mead 8 acres, 2 closes Eastfields Nos, 243, 215, 217, 244, 367 and 368 on the Tithe Map.*

The 1840 Tithe shows William Jennings holding Pettys which he has let to Robert Smith with 17 acres. Since Smith was also renting the much larger Higher Farm, it is unlikely that he occupied the building. It is surprising that the name Petty has survived to this day although no Petty ever lived there and Henry Petty died as long ago as 1815.

The 1832 Land Tax Return shows that Jennings had let Pettys to Ann Brake. Ann was born in 1766, daughter of William Edwards and Judith Hayward, married in 1763. Ann Edwards married Charles Brake in 1786 and he died in 1831.

The 1840 Tithe Apportionment shows that Ann had moved just down the road to Holm Farm which she was renting from John Cornick. Ann Brake died in 1845 aged 78 years.

### Devon House/Taylors

This property is, invariably, referred to as "near the Charity School". Each clerk, of course, copied details as written by his predecessors, but it seems strange to refer to it as near the Charity School, if the School was Boyles, some distance up the High Street. Could it have been the School, much nearer, known to have existed in the Church House? This seems unlikely, since this school had certainly ceased to function by the mid 17 c when Benjamin Miller took over the Church House.

This is a large house with a heated room either side of the central passage. It is possible, that at some time, it was re-fronted and newly fenestrated, previous owners found evidence of long, low windows upstairs, which might indicate that weaving was carried out, since ample light would be needed for the looms. At the back were the usual out-buildings, barns, cow-shed, stables and a malt-house with the orchard and a paddock. One small stable building with a tallot over has timber joints which indicate a 15 c origin. Down the west side of the property ran a ditch and, over this, were situated the privies.

Mains water was not brought to Yetminster until the end of the 19 c. Before that, every drop of water needed for household or dairy had to be carried in from well or pump. Privies were mostly earth-closets, small huts with one, two or three-holed wooden structures built inside over a pit which extended outside at the back. Earth would be thrown into this or ashes from the fires. One privy, familiar from the 1920s, was a three-holer with two adult seats and one low for a child, familiar and much dreaded, one may add! Once a year, this particular privy was lime-washed, a blue-bag having first been dragged through the bucket, the walls came out a tasteful shade of blue. Toilet-rolls had been invented, but the paper was harsh and coarse, the best having the texture of tracing-paper. The roll was suspended upon a holder which had two little metal hands holding the wire which was threaded through. However, this was for the women of the household, the men preferred a box with cut-up pages from the Farmer and Stockbreeder. These places were noisome in summer, freezing cold in winter and desperate after dark.

The Inventories of some more wealthy inhabitants mention chamber-pots and close-stools, but these, too, had to be emptied. Life must have been grim and even worse for those with sick or aged relatives to care for. And how much worse in pre-Jeyes Fluid days. Vinegar was much in use as a disinfectant, but we don't know if its use extended to privies.

From about 1760, there are somewhat vague references to the occupiers of this property: John Jacob, Joseph Patten, John & Mary Newman, John Taylor, Samuel Geard (Taylor's in-law), Henry Shepherd, Benjamin Coombes, and, by 1793, William Miller, and 1818, John Jeffrey, butcher. Jeffery was related to Coombes, but he soon passed the property on to John Custard of Bradford Abbas, schoolmaster, for £280. By 1838, it was in the hands of Henry Marsh Custard, his son, and then William Porter, bookseller of Yeovil. In 1842, Porter sold to Jane Bartlett, spinster, for £325. Two years later, Jane married William Notley, miller, of North Wootton, son of another William, Innkeeper. By 1848, the Notleys had moved to Joiners Mill, Martock and sold to George Read, yeoman. It remained with the Reads until the death of Mary Ann Read in 1881. In her Will, she made bequests as follows:

*to daughter, Caroline, wife of Thomas Nash, £100*
*to daughter, Elizabeth Mary, wife of George Edmunds, £200.*
*to daughter, Martha Jane, wife of Samuel Bartlett Templeman, £200.*
*to son, James Read, £200.*
*to grandson, Frank Curtis, £100.*
*Remainder to be divided between Julia, wife of Charles Holly and Mary Ann, wife of Thomas West.*
*Executors:   friend, George Andrews*
*             son-in-law Charles Holly of Quidhampton,*
*             maltster and brewer.*

By 1946, the property was owned by William and James Keech.

It is interesting to note, that when, recently (1996), the water-main in the High Street was relaid, many of the pipes serving various properties, were the original lead pipes which had lasted for a hundred years.

## Manor Farm/Bower Farm

This was a large farm occupying a corner site. It consists of a north – south block to which has been added an east–west extension. Across a small garden, the earlier block faces the east gable of the former Church House. Documentation is sparse. In 1840, Henry Redway held the property and 140 acres of land. The owner was Thomas Fooks. For many years, Fooks the solicitors, had acted as stewards for the Manors of Yetminster Prima and Yetminster Secunda, in the 19 c Fooks, himself, took over the Lordship of the two Manors. The Court Book shows that Henry Redway succeeded George Tompkins as Bailiff in 1824, and so continued until 1840, but there is no record of when he took over the farm. Not a local man, he was born in Charminster in 1783, his wife, Susannah was born in Toller Porcorum in 1788 and their son, John, likewise in Toller in 1811. So, presumably, the Redways came to Yetminster between 1811 and 1824. there is no mention of the name in the Parish Registers.

In the 1920s, Bower Farm was owned by Mr. and Mrs. Foot. Later, the Partridge family moved there from Manor House taking the name with them. In the 1980s, the farm-yard was sold for building and the house is now run as a Guest House.

### These are the field names for Bower Farm in 1840

| | |
|---|---|
| Three corner Horsehill | Pasture |
| Middle Horsehill | Arable |
| Horsehill | ,, |
| Horsehill against the lane | ,, |
| Great Down | ,, |
| Underdown | Pasture |
| Hanging Down | ,, |

| | |
|---|---|
| Five Acres | Arable |
| Quarr Ground | Pasture |
| Ryme Townsend | Arable |
| Chick Mead | Meadow |
| Great Parks | Pasture |
| Little Park | ,, |
| Green Flaxland | ,, |
| Ploughed Flaxland | ,, |
| Marle Mead | Meadow |
| Frogwell | Pasture |
| Lower Frogwell | ,, |
| Little Herbury | ,, |
| Great Herbury | ,, |
| Ploughed Herbury | Arable |

About one-third of the 140 acres was arable.

Redway leased a further 40 acres from Edward Herbert Fitzherbert, lessee of the Manor of Yetminster and Grimston named as the Glebe Lands of the Prebend.

These lands were:

| | |
|---|---|
| Townsend | Pasture |
| Lower Townsend | Arable |
| Chetenhill | Pasture |
| Long Mead | Meadow |
| Old Orchard | ,, |
| Great Thorns | Pasture |
| Little Thorns | ,, |
| Great Ham Croft | ,, |
| Little Cockeyland | ,, |

Five acres arable, the remainder pasture or meadow.

## Lease of Yetminster Farm 16 September 1757

*Anna Clapcott, spinster and Warren Lisle Esq. and Ruth his wife. (Lords of the Manor)*

*To William Tompkins of Yetminster, yeoman.*

*Yetminster Farm with houses etc. at rent of £90 per annum.*
*A further yearly rent of £5 per annum per acre to be paid for meadow or pasture or arable sown to flax or hemp.*

## Conditions

*Tompkins to live on premises*
*All hay, straw, fodder, soil and compost to remain tenant not to take more than 3 crops successively from any of the arable lands. With the third crop, to sow in grass seed and lay to pasture for 2 years.*

*In last year of tenancy, to sow in 20 acres of clover for benefit of succeeding tenant. 16 pounds of clover seed per acre.*

*In last year, Anna Clapcott and Warren Lisle to be allowed in to sow wheat crop.*

*Tenant to pay Window Tax.*

*At end of tenancy, quietly and peacably to leave.*

*Anna Clapcott and Warren Lisle to repair houses, outhouses, barns, stables, gates, stiles, hedges, ditches and, in the first year trench the Great Mayne in that part of the premises called Parks.*

*To allow Tompkins 200 wood faggots, Tompkins to fetch home with his plough.*

*The lease to run for 14 years with option to terminate at end of 7 years.*

Abstract from D.R.O. 11,249.

# Manor House/Warrs

Situated on the north side of the High Street, it would appear that much re-building of this house took place, its appearance suggests a 17 c house built using materials from an equally- good quality 16 c house.

In 1577 John Allambridge of Shepton Mallet made a gift of the property to his son, Christopher and the family occupied the property for more than two hundred years. In early documentation, it is referred to as 'Warrs'. This may be explained by the fact, that, in 1583 John transferred to Christopher an obligation signed by Richard Warre of Hestercombe, Somerset, with a Bond of £500 in case of default.

Christopher Allambridge married Mary Rocke or Rook. On 1 September 1590, he wrote his Will. He styles himself yeoman. Having left 6s 8d to the Church of Yetminster and a like sum to the Poor, he made his bequests as follows:-

*to William, my son, my table-board and my chest in the hall with my wearing apparrel therein, my silver salt and £20 to be paid him at age 21.*

*to Thomas, my son, one silver bowl and £90 to be paid at 21.*

*to John, my son, my signet of gold and £90 to be paid at 21.*

*to Margaret, my daughter, my best harness girdle and £90 to be paid at 21.*

*to Martha, my daughter, my second-best harness girdle and £90 to be paid at 21.*

*to Christian, my daughter, one harness girdle and £90 at 21.*

*to Alice Willes, my servant, ten shillings.*

*If any child should die before the age of 21 then their portion to be divided between the rest of the children.*

The tomb of William Applin, died 1610.
The oldest identified grave in Yetminster

*Remainder of goods not given, after debts and funeral expenses to
wife, Mary appointed Executrix.*
*Overseers: father-in-law, William Rocke and Barnard Jenings.*
*Witnesses: John Evered, Alexander Evered, William Rocke, Barnard
Jenings.*

Mary Allambridge re-married to William Applin, gentleman, of
Ibberton. William died in 1610 and his hamstone table tomb in
Yetminster church-yard is the oldest memorial the date of which can be
deciphered. In view of the length of time they lived in Yetminster it is
surprising that no memorial to an Allambridge has been found.

William Applin's Will is long and detailed. His property in Ibberton
he leaves to Richard Stubbs, who, in 1603 had married Margaret, eldest
daughter of Christopher and Mary Allambridge. Property in Yetminster
lately bought of Robert Dolberie he leaves to Richard Stubbs and

Thomas Allambridge with instructions to sell it and pay legacies as follows:

*to daughter-in-law Martha Allambridge £20*

*to daughter-in-law Christian Allambridge £20*

*to son-in-law John Allambridge £20*

*to Christopher & John sons of William Allambridge £5 apiece to Ezekiel, William and Robert Allambridge 5 marks apiece*

*to god-daughter Sara Masters, daughter of Humphrey Masters 50s all to be paid at age 16. The residue of money from the sale to Richard Stubbs and Thomas Allambridge.*

*Two plots of land in Yetminster, Cadwellie and Puxhodie he leaves to his wife, Mary, and then to John, son of William Allambridge.*

*John Foyle, John Minterne and William Sterr, Overseers 20s apiece. Witnesses: William Sterr, Thomas Allambrigge, Richard Stubbs, Walter Legge and Thomas Sterr.*

It would appear that William Allambridge had pre-deceased his step-father leaving five sons, nevertheless, 'Warrs' was inherited by his brother, Thomas, who, in 1611 married Agnes Clarke.

In 1611, Martha Allambridge married Thomas Grubbing and her sister, Christian, in 1616, married Joseph Greenfield, clerk.

A survey of the Digby Manor dated 1630 shows Thomas Allambridge's holding includes a dwelling-house, barn, stable and orchard, backside 1 acre, 1 close of meadow 3 acres, 1 close of pasture 10 acres and 2 closes of arable 8 acres. The rent was 6s 8d.

By 1657 Thomas had died, for his widow, Agnes, surrendered the holding to her son, John, excepting to herself "the parlour with the chamber over it and to use the kitchen and the best chamber with free egress and regresse into the forementioned premises and the little study by the best chamber."

John married and had sons, John, Thomas, Nathaniel and Christopher and a daughter, Judith. These are the boys who scratched their initials on the splay of the E ground floor window where they may be seen to this day: IA 1676, IA 1678, CA 1678 and NA 1683.

John's son, another John, was a goldsmith in Sherborne where he died in 1719. He may have been the John Allambridge apprenticed to William Bayley of Exeter, goldsmith, he was made a Freeman of the City in 1687.

In 1697 in Lillington, Nathaniel Allambridge married Judith Dunham they lived in Leigh. Nothing is known of Christopher but Judith Allambridge married George Bartlett, he died in 1701, leaving her with a son, Thomas.

In 1696, John Allambridge surrendered his customary tenement to his son, Thomas, excepting to himself "the hall, buttery, milkhouse, chamber over the hall, middle chamber, chamber over the parlour with free egress and regress into the parlour, the kitchen and the study over the buttery of the dwelling-house, also the stable, hayloft, tallot and the S end of the barn and the S garden with 2 parts of 3 of the fruit in the orchard with one ground called Holmoor and one ground called Common Mead with the use of the kitchen chamber and cock-loft".

Clearly, this except left little of the house for Thomas, it was, possibly more of an administrative arrangement whereby Thomas took over the running of the farm.

On 12 December 1700, John Allambridge of Yetminster, yeoman made his Will.

*He requested burial in the Parish Church at Yetminster.*

*to son-in-law, George Bartlett, my wearing apparel, linen and woollen and 1s.*

*to grandson, Thomas Bartlett, 5s.*

*to 3 sons, John Allambridge of Sherborne, goldsmith, £12,*

*Thomas Allambridge of Yetminster £10 and Nathaniel Allambridge of Leigh £10.*

*to daughter, Judith, "my great bible, my rack, my driping – pan, my chair of splits, my cabernett & the little box which standeth in the hall window, my amory with the frame it standeth upon, my coverlet with blanketts, sheets, boulsters & pillows, my lesser brasse pot with pot-hooks & a chimney crook, my largest brass pan, one half hogshead, two quarter barrels, the little board in the hall chamber & my chest in my son, Thomas' chamber."*

*to son, John, my friing pan, my best pewter dish*

*to son, Nathaniel Allambridge, my second-best pewter dish, a skimmer, my silver buckells, my shirt buttons and £10 which his brother, Christopher, owes him, I will pay it unto my son, Nathaniel.*

*to sonn, Christopher, one pewter dish and 20s in money to be paid within one year.*

*to sonn, Nathaniel, after decease of testator's wife, my long-legged brass pot.*

*to Judith, my daughter, my coffer in the middle chamber, my cradle.*

*Residue of goods not given, to wife for her life, both brasse, pewter and bedding and after her decease to be shared by children.*

*Funeral expenses to be disbursed by sons, John, Thomas and Nathaniel.*

*Witnesses:    Richard Brewer          Signed:*
*              Richard Brewer jun.     John Allambrig*

John died and on 20 June 1701, Gilbert Warre and Abraham Miller took an Inventory of his goods and chattels.

| | | | |
|---|---|---|---|
| his weareing apparrell | £5 | 0s | 0d |
| two feather beds & a flock bed with blanketts, coverlet, bolster & pillows thereto belonging | 6 | 0s | 0d |
| four pairs of sheets, three pair of pillowties | 1 | 10s | 0d |
| three table-cloths, a dozen & half of napkins | | 10s | 0d |
| three brass pots, two brass pans, a brass kettle, two brass skillets, a brass ladle and a skimmer | 3 | 0s | 0d |
| eleaven pewter dishes, two flaggons and a pewter chamber pot | 1 | 0s | 0d |
| a warming pan, two spits, a driping pan, a jack, fire-pan and tongs, a friing pan and two brandisses | 1 | 5s | 0d |
| three bedsteads, two chests, two quoffers, two truncks, three couberds, one settle, six chairs, two table bords, a form and fower joynt stooles, a meshing fate, three little trendles, two payles and a baccon rack | 1 | 10s | 0d |
| in money | 2 | 5s | 0d |
| in debts due from severall persons | 27 | 10s | 0s |
| | £49 | 10s | 0d |

111

It is interesting to compare the items mentioned in the Will with those in the Inventory. The Inventory, for example, makes no mention of the cradle, the silver buckles and the shirt buttons or the bible. Perhaps, these things had been given away before he died. Curiously, he never mentions his wife by name and seems more concerned with his children, particularly Judith.

John was succeeded by his son, Thomas, to whom he had excepted. The records at this point are not very clear. It would appear that Thomas had daughters Elizabeth who married Thomas Beer and Anne who married George Feaver and sons, Thomas, John and Nathaniel.

On 18 April 1745, the Digby Manor Court Book, records: Thomas Allambridge, deceased, nominated his son, John Allambridge, to be the Lord's next tenant of his tenement in the prescence of John Brake, John Hewlett and others. A heriot of £3 was paid and John Allambridge was admitted.

This entry would suggest that Thomas had died unexpectedly and intestate, and, according to the customs of the Manor, had appointed his successor in front of witnesses. John's tenure was short. He died, unmarried, in 1749. Mindful, perhaps, of how his father had died intestate, John lost little time in writing his own Will. John Allambridge of Yetminster made his Will on 10 March 1746. He styles himself "gentleman" and the provisions are as follows:

*Debts and funeral expenses to be paid.*

*Brother-in-law, George Feaver, to be Lord's next tenant to Customary Tenement called Home Tenement, Yetminster, where late father lately lived, parcel of Lord Digby's Manor, in trust, that George Feaver shall pay yearly from rents and profits, £5 to "my aunt Judith Coombes until my nephew, Thomas Allambridge, shall be 21." Then Tenement to be surrendered to Thomas Allambridge. Thomas Allambridge to enter into Bond of £100 to George Feaver to pay to Judith Coombes £5 yearly for her life.*

*Nephew, Thomas Feaver, to be Lord's next tenant to Customary Tenement in Church Lane, Yetminster called Everetts Tenement, part of Lord Brooke's Manor, chargeable with a legacy of £100 to his sister, Ann Feaver, at 21.*

112

*Nephew, John Feaver, to be Lord's next tenant of Customary Tenement called Symes Tenement and to close called Bingers, about 6 acres, in Yetminster in Manor of Mr John Haynes, clerk. Also, my close of meadow at Stakeford, Yetminster.*

*Nephew, John Beer, to be Lord's next tenant to my roofless tenement in Yetminster which my father purchased of Mr. Munden: close called the Yonder, Oat Craft, Smeth Acre, Orchard and 3 closes called Bingers. Also, Tenement called Harris's Tenement, Yetminster, in Manor of John Clapcott, chargeable with payment of £5 yearly to his sister, Ann Templemen, for life.*

*To John Beer, all principal money and interest owing to me from Thomas Beer, his father, by Mortgage and £100 for putting his life into his father's estate lying in Ryme Intrinseca.*

*To George Feaver, £100 on trust for Charles Templeman, son of niece, Ann Templeman, interest to be paid yearly towards his maintenance and education until 21, then principal of £100 shall be paid him.*

*To nephew, Thomas Allambridge, my silver tankard, cup, snuff box and whistle that were his late father's.*

*Rest of plate to nephews, John Beer, Thomas Feaver and John Feaver.*

*To servant, Gertrude Whiffen, £50 and her bed with all things belonging.*

*Remainder of goods, chattels and personal effects to nephews, John Beer, Thomas Allambridge, Thomas Feaver and John Feaver.*

*George Feaver and John Williams of Ryme Intrinseca, Executors and Trustees, to each of them, £10.*

*Witnesses: John Mose, Phillip Bearer, Thomas Chynock.*

After the death of John Allambridge in 1749, the property passed to his nephew, Thomas, son of his brother, Nathaniel. A document survives in which Thomas, a minor of about 14 years of age, elected his uncles, John Whitehead of Sherborne, carrier and John Oke of Sherborne, maltster, to be his Guardians. Until he came of age, his

The pump behind Manor House.
*"Thomas and Mary Allambridge 1788"*

property was in the hands of George Feaver. It is not known why John Allambridge should refer to it as 'Home Tenement' and not 'Warrs'. Thomas, in his Will of 1790, certainly calls it 'Warrs'.

Thomas was active in the Parish. In 1770, with Benjamin Coombs, he served as Overseer of the Poor. He married twice, firstly to Elizabeth

Jesty who died in 1770 and then to her elder sister, Mary. Both marriages were childless. A pump behind the house bears the date

A
T  M
1788

Thomas Allambridge died of inflammation of the lungs and was buried 6 December 1790, aged 55. He was buried in the Church.

On 25 November 1790, Thomas, the last of the Allambridges, made his Will. He styles himself 'Gentleman' and it reads as follows:

*To my friend, executor and trustee, George Baker of Frome St. Quinton £200.*

*To Judith Allambridge and Sarah Allambridge, both of Sherborne, spinsters, £200 each to be paid six months after the death of my wife.*

*To George Baker, £100 to invest, interest to be paid to Ann Thomas, wife of Joseph Thomas of Sherborne, for her own use without reference to her husband, and, after her death, to whomsoever she shall bequeath it.*

*To William Spooner of Sherborne, Innholder, £100.*

*To George Baker, to sell for the benefit of my wife, Mary Allambridge, my messuage and lands in Adber, Trent.*
*my customary estate of inheritance at Leigh*
*my customary tenement called "Warrs" in Yetminster*
*all other my real, customary and leashold messuages, lands and tenements in Somerset and Dorset.*

*Residue of goods, chattels and personal estate and any part of real estate not disposed of, to George Baker and wife, Mary Allambridge for the benefit of wife.*

*Witnesses: U. Shepherd*       *Mark of Thomas Allambridge*
*Wm. Read*                     *(he attempted to sign the first page,*
*Edmund Batten*                *but was, seemingly, too weak)*

Edmund Batten was a Yeovil Solicitor and great-uncle of John Batten, F.S.A. who wrote the delightful and informative, 'South Somerset Villages' first published in 1894 and recently reprinted.

115

Thomas died a wealthy man, how wise he was to appoint his friend, George Baker as Trustee, for his wife, Mary, was the "litigious widow" who so vindictively made trouble for John Warry. She survived her husband by twenty-nine years – she was buried in 1819 aged 83 years.

| Ryme Intrinseca | Protestation Return 1641/2 |
|---|---|
| Mr Richard BLANCHARD | James PIDDLE |
| Mr John STROODE | James KELWAY |
| Mr Charles BLANCHARD | Roger CHAUNDLER |
| Mr William HURCOMBE | Nicholas PIDDLE |
| Thomas HARRIS | Thomas GLYDE |
| John HULL | John BEERE sen. |
| Walter MEAD | John BEERE jun. |
| Robert WILLS | John WILLIAMS |
| William STRODS | Clement MASTERS |
| Thomas HAYWARD | James HULL |
| John MUNDEN sen. | Edward LITTLE |
| John MUNDEN jun. | William PURDUE C.W. |
| John LITTLE | John WARREN |
| Mr Nathaniel HARRIS | Benjamin WARREN |
| George HARRIS | Leonard POMEROY |
| Robert HUSDAY | Thomas WARREN |
| George HUSDAY | John PLOWMAN |
| Nicholas HUSDAY | Timothy STEVENS |
| Robert HILL | Richard DOUNTON |
| John HILL | Henry STEVENS |
| George HILL | George BRINSUME |

*Witnesses:* John ELFORD Rector. Christopher LITTLE C.W.
James KELWAY O.P. William GOFFE O.P. living in Halstock.
has taken Protestation there.

116

# The Church House

Prior to the Reformation, the Church was, for everyone, the centre of the Parish. The Chancel was God's area, and, indeed, the responsibility of the incumbent, the nave belonged to the people and was their responsibility. The two were separated by the Rood-Screen, often elaborately carved with its figures of Christ on the Cross with our Lady and St. John.

At the Reformation, many Rood-Screens were destroyed. Yetminster possessed one, the marks on the walls where it was fixed may still be seen. Benches had not yet been introduced, so the nave was a large open space able to accomodate meetings large and small, and this is where the parishioners met to conduct business of every kind. Here were held most of the social meetings and activities of the people. It was the equivalent of the modern Church hall. At festival times, people drank and danced and the religious plays of the Middle Ages were performed there. We know that these plays were performed in Yetminster because the Sherborne Churchwardens held a stock of costumes which they hired out, and, there is a record of payment by Yetminster for such hire.

However, the time came when the Bishops took a different view of the use of the nave for business or pleasure. The people were expelled, first from the Church and then from the church-yard also. What were they to do? From the 15 c onwards, in many places, they built for themselves a Church House, as near to the Church as possible. The number built is unknown and so is the number of those that have survived. It is believed that there were many in the west country, particularly in Devon.

There were Church Houses in Yeovil (demolished) it is believed to have stood on the corner of Middle Street and Silver Street, Sherborne, the long building now known as the Church House Gallery, Halstock and Evershot.

The Church House at Crowcombe in Somerset was built in 1515, and, after a period of housing the Parish Poor, it is once again used for its original purpose – it is the Village Hall.

The Meeting Room was on the first floor and the lower rooms were used for kitchen and storage.

Church Houses were mostly built between about 1450 and 1600, so they had a relatively short life. One of the uses to which they were put was the holding of Church Ales. These occasions raised money for the upkeep of the Church, much as today we might hold Coffee Mornings. The building usually incorporated a brew-house and a bake-house wherin were made the ale and bread and pastries needed for the social gatherings. The Church House was also let for private functions such as weddings. A stock of platters and utensils was held and these would be hired out, the money received all going towards the upkeep of the Church.

Although the Yeovil Church-House has disappeared, some of its accounts have survived. In 1548 the utensils owned included:

*6 dozen platters*
*1 dozen pottingers*
*2 odd pottingers*
*10 saucers (for sauce, not the items we place under cups!)*
*2 crocks and a pan*
*a pair of andirons*
*2 broches (spits)*
*a flesh hook*
*a cotterel (adjustable hook to hang pots over a fire)*
*2 dozen trenchers*
*1 brasen mortar and pestell*

In 1554 spoons were purchased for 9d a dozen. In 1569 the Churchwardens paid Walles of Melbury for new vessels and for the exchange of the old ones. Presumably, he allowed them for the worn-out vessels which he then melted down to make new. Hiring out the utensils brought in a useful sum of money. For several years, Sir John Horsey of Clifton Maybank hired 5 or 6 dozen, for estate festivities, possibly.

By the time of James I Church Ales were forbidden, but continued to be held, nevertheless. In 1607 the Yeovil Church Ale caused complaints to be made to Quarter Sessions, there was minstrelsy and dancing on the Sabbath and men carried on a cavell- staff. The Churchwardens, Thomas Marsh and Roger Traske, were themselves so carried to the Church. The "cavell" was a long pole, supported on men's shoulders with a third man astride the pole. It looks extremely uncomfortable! But all good fun, no doubt. In Montecute there is an interesting carving depicting this activity.

From the end of the 16 c to the early 17 c Church Houses fell into disuse. There was no longer the need to raise money by means of Church Ales. Church Rates and Pew Rents had come into being. Church Houses were sold off to be used for other purposes, some became Inns or private houses or shops. Some were demolished.

The location of the Church House in Yetminster remained a mystery until it was solved by a Will of 1670 and other clues. That Yetminster possessed a Church House was known from a Survey of the Digby Manor dated 1630. This recorded:

*John Minterne, gent., Thomas Hardie, gent. and Richard Coombes for a Church House or School House. Rent 1s 4d and a capon at Easter.*

These three men were the Trustees, probably the Churchwardens. Digby Manor was the successor to Yetminster Episcopi, the Bishop's Manor.

Oak House Stores and Minster Cottage, originally one building, had for long been a puzzle. It was unique in its lay-out, with false chimney-pots on the gable ends and the fire-places at the back. It was like no other building. Then, a wonderful old photograph came to light, dating from the late 19 c when Thomas Hayward owned the shop. This showed the building with an imposing porch, rising through two storeys with the door below and a window above and the date-stone in situ. Clearly, this was no ordinary dwelling-house.

The Will and Probate Inventory of Benjamin Miller, baker, for the year 1670 has survived. The Will reveals that he had a wife, Mary, and seven sons. To the eldest, John, he left £5, to William, Joseph, Thomas and Abraham £10 each and, to his two youngest sons, Giles and

Oak House Stores when owned by Roskilly. 19 c

Richard, £15 each at the age of twenty-one. The lease of the house wherein he lived, he left to his wife, and, after her death or re-marriage, to son Thomas, then Abraham, then Giles. The lease was held by Hugh Hodges and William Sansome, both of Sherborne, on the lives of these three sons. Presumably, the property was mortgaged.

The Inventory, taken by Henry Grimsted, John Miller and William Miller, values the house at £60, and, most importantly, names the rooms therein, the hall, the chamber over the hall, the buttery, the bake-house and the chamber over the bake-house.

The original building incorporated the present shop and Minster Cottage to the west which later became the Royal Oak Inn.

The exact date when they came into being is not known, but they were certainly established by 1839. The division of the original building was clumsily made with a flimsy partition actually dividing a window, a window being turned into an entrance door, an upper room of the Inn remaining part of the shop premises and the whole of the attic floor belonging to the shop, whilst part of another cottage to the west was incorporated in the Inn.

The "Royal Oak" and the shop in Thomas Hayward"s time,
showing the imposing porch which graced the Church House.
Drawn by Samantha Chaffey from an old photograph taken c. 1870

What have we today in this building?

All the windows have been changed. The shop is entered through the
doorway which was in the porch before its demolition. At the back of
the shop is a large hamstone fire-place, now obscured by shelving, to
the left, an alcove which once housed the spiral stair-case. To the west,
that part of the building which is now Minster Cottage, was the buttery
and bake-house and this has the fire-place which formerly served the
bake-house. Over the shop is a large room of the same size as the shop
itself with another handsome hamstone fire-place at the back. Next to it
is the "chamber over the bake-house" with another, smaller, hamstone
fire-place. The entire attic space over both shop and cottage belongs to
the owner of the shop.

That this building was the Church House is indisputable and accounts
for the imposing porch which was incorporated in the entrance. The

Digby Survey refers to "a Church House or School House". One might conjecture that the lower room was used for festivities with the bakehouse and buttery conveniently adjacent and that the upper room was the school-room, with the smaller heated room, perhaps, used by the master. Nothing is known of this school, but, it is curious that the Deeds of the present Devon House, a few yards to the west, recite "situated near the Charity School". It seems unlikely that the School referred to is Boyles, since that is hardly near Devon House. It poses another problem: What was the Charity?

To confirm that Benjamin Miller held the property, a Digby Manor Rental dated 24 December 1677, states: Mary Miller, assignee of Benjamin Miller, her husband, deceased, a cottage or dwelling-house called the Church House or School House with a court, backside, garden and orchard adjacent for 99 years on the lives of Thomas Miller, Abraham Miller and Giles Miller. Rent 1s 4d and a capon at Easter.

Abraham Miller appears as holding the Church House in Rentals of 1703, 1713 and 1714. It remained in the hands of the Miller family certainly until 1748 "a dwelling house called the Church House with an orchard and garden" held leasehold by Abraham Miller for the lives of Abraham Miller and Thomas Miller, his sons (a later hand has crossed this out and entered:

*Mr Thomas Gollop as tenant with James Gollop, William Bellamy and William Jesty as the "lives" named in the lease. Lord's rent 1s 4d and a capon at Easter. Yearly value £5.*

Thomas Gollop was a wealthy Lillington landowner, most probably the property had been mortgaged to him.

The next mention of the Church House is not until 1839, nearly one hundred years later. By this time it is known as 'Reads'. It was purchased, freehold, by William Watts of Upbury, doubtless as an investment, from one Peach of Crewkerne. William Watts paid £70. 14s. 9d for the Freehold. this sum included £13. 2s. 9d paid to Murley and Tidcombe, solicitors, of Crewkerne for the Conveyance. Watts's grandson, William Watts Hayward made the journey to Crewkerne to finalise the purchase. The sale included the cottage next door to the west, and this, young Hayward received as a gift from his grandfather. By this

Date-stone on Oak House Stores. A.D. 1607

time, it was already a shop, kept by John Langdon and the Royal Oak Inn, kept by John and Mary Eyears.

The name 'Reads' was taken, no doubt from the enigmatic date-stone. This refers perhaps to John and Dorothy Read A.D. 1607. Many attempts have been made to decipher the remainder of the inscription but it remains a mystery.

| AN | DO | IO | DO |
|----|----|----|----|
|  | 1607 | RE | DE |
| BE | DO | AN | SN |
| HA | ED | DE | IN |

If this does refer to John and Dorothy Read, the property could not have been owned by them in 1607 because it had not been sold at that date. Did John Read, perhaps, set up a Charity which ran the School? Did the date-stone come from another building? It was considered to be of some importance since it was replaced when the porch was removed.

## A true and perfect Inventory of all the goods and chattels of Benjamin Miller late of Yetminster, deceased, taken and appraised by us whose names are here unto subscribed the 7th day of September Anno Domini 1679.

| | | | |
|---|---|---|---|
| *In the hall* one table bord and frame, one livery table, one large carpet and one livery carpet, one forme, one joint stoole, three cushions, one paire of iron rackes, one paire of small andirons & one iron crooke. | £1 | 6s | 8d |
| Three small table bords and frames | | 13s | 4d |
| *In the bake-house,* two moulding bords, one kneading trough, two great fattes and a horse to beare them, one settle, one racke, fire-pan and tonges & other implemts. | £2 | 6s | 8d |
| *In ye buttery* three barrells, six tubs and one horse to beare the barrells, one silting trough and all the dishes and trenchers. | £1 | 0s | 0d |
| Five crockes, one furnace, three kettles, three skillets, two dozen of pewter dishes, three pewter salts, four brass candlesticks, one iron dripping pan and three tinning chamber pots | £8 | 0s | 0d |
| *In the chamber over the hall.* Two standing bedsteads, two feather beds, two rugges, two pair of blankets, two feather bolster, two paire of pillows, one cupbord and one chest. | £7 | 10s | 0d |
| *In the chamber over the bake-house* one standing bedstead, one half headed bedstead, one feather bed, two feather bolsters, one dust bed a flocke bolster, one dust bolster, two cover-leds, two paire blankets & one chest. | £3 | 13 s | 4d |
| Seaven pair of sheets, one dozen of napkins, three table cloths & all the rest of ye linning | £4 | 00s | 0d |
| Five hundred bushels of malt | £80 | 00s | 0d |
| Debts due without specialty | £60 | 00s | 0d |
| Desperate debts | £20 | 00s | 0d |
| Two cows, one bay mare & one hogge | £8 | 00s | 0d |
| all the hay and yeagrasse | £6 | 00s | 0d |
| A pile of clift wood and furzes | £10 | 00s | 0d |
| His waring apparrell & all other things forgotten and not before prized | £4 | 00s | 0d |
| His house wherein he lived, together with back-side, garden & outhouses | £60 | 00s | 0d |
| | £276 | 10s | 0d |

Henry Grimsted
John Miller
William Miller

124

Note that Benjamin Miller's wealth lay in his house, his debts and an astounding five hundred bushels of malt valued at £80!
After the decease of his wife, Mary, the property was left to his son, Thomas, then Abraham and then Giles. In 1677, Giles Miller married Bazill Hayward of Frankham, Ryme. She was sister to Giles Hayward from whom descended Thomas Hayward, who, in the latter half of the 19 c was to own the Church House, by that time a shop and Inn.

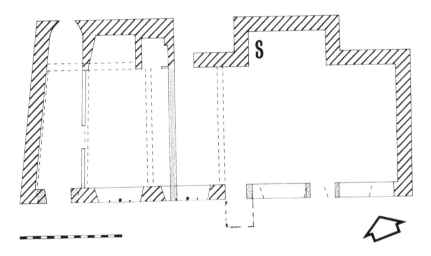

The former Church House, buttery on left with fire-place at rear. On right, presumed Meeting room, fire-place at rear and spiral stairs to left. In front, the double-storey porch which appears on the old photograph.
Taken from "The Houses of Yetminster". R. Machin

125

# Tanners

For centuries, leather was not the luxury it is today, but a commodity of vital importance to every community. Not only footwear, but breeches, jerkins, hats, belts, gloves, both fashion articles and those for work, all were made of leather. Even hides spoiled by warble-fly, that curse of the farmer and tanner, could be utilised. In many trades, such as the blacksmith or cooper, the workman needed a heavy leather apron, and a hole or two therein made no difference.

At one time buckets, bottles and jugs were fabricated from leather, and, for as long as the horse provived the principal means of transport, there was a constant demand for harness and saddlery. Carriages, too, were frequently upholstered in leather. Finer skins were used for making parchment.

We know that Yetminster had a parchment-maker, he was Robert Piddle who died in 1597. From his Probate Inventory, it would appear that he was not very prosperous! His property was valued at £12 16s 4d, and, of that amount, £8 was accounted for by the value of the lease of his house and garden which he held on the lives of Thomas and Alice Piddle. His stock of parchment, three knives and a pumice-stone were valued at only £1 2s 0d with 1s for lime. He had few household goods and Walter Legge owed him 14s.

There are Probate Inventories for three early tanners.

Robert Bailey of Leigh died in 1696 worth £167 16s 0d including the sum of £16 7s 0d owing to him. In his Will, he left his silver spoons to his daughter, Angela, 'after my wife's time' and, to his son, Robert, 'the cow-heel? crock, my little crocke, table-board and cupboard to his own use when he becomes a housekeeper'. To daughter, Angela, '£40 and one of the middle crockes when she comes to be a housekeeper'. His son, Robert, was to pay his sister Angela £5 whensoever he put her life out of the tenement. The remainder he left to his wife, Mary, and son

Robert whom he made joint executors. As Overseers, he appointed John Hardy of Batcombe and Henry Maber of Hilfield.

William Hodges and Thomas Symes took the Inventory. He was but modestly supplied with household goods but owned 6 silver spoons, 6 table napkins and 4 pairs of sheets. Outside, he had 2 cows, 2 heifers, 3 horses and some growing corn, a cart, putt and wheels. But, most of his wealth was in the tan-yard: he had 13 dicker of leather in the tan-vats, lime and water at £8 the dicker; 4 dozen of calf skins worth £4 and bark for the tanning, the lot valued at £108. Hair, horns and tails accounted for another £2.

Twenty years later, Thomas Cave of Chetnole died worth a little less, £105 15s 0d. His household goods were similar to those of Bailey. He had 8 milch cows, 1 bullock and 5 calves, one mare, 1 hog, 3 sheep and a cart and wheels. In the tan-vats he had 50 hides worth £35 and, in the lime-pits 5 raw-hides valued at £2 10s 0d. The kipps and calf skins were worth £2, the bark £2 and the mill to grind the bark £1.

In Yetminster, the first known tanner was Robert Bartlett, brother to the Vicar, William Bartlett, who suffered so much hardship, indeed, imprisonment, at the time of the Commonwealth. Robert and William were sons of John Bartlett and nephews of Alexander Bartlett. William Bartlett was born in 1583 and appointed Vicar of Yetminster in 1607. The exact location of Robert's tannery is not known, but, in his Will dated 1624, he bequeathed it to his son, Thomas, when he should reach the age of twenty-three. He refers to his house and lands at Flexlands and Flexlands was land, about 14 acres in all, on the right-hand side of the river Wriggle to the east of Upper Mill. The land had access to Mill Lane and also stretched across to Downs Lane, so, if, as it would seem, there was a house and tannery, it could have been situated either at Mill Lane or Downs Lane. The former seems more likely, since we have a reference to Joseph Hodges presented for failing to clear his ditch 'from his ground at Nether Mill to Robert Bartlett's backside'.

Robert Bartlett also mentions his wife Agnes and daughters, Christian and Agnes. He appointed his brother, William Bartlett, clerk, as Overseer.

Next, we know of two Yetminster tanners who died within a year or two of each other: Thomas Cheesman in 1729 and Thomas Rodber in 1731.

In his Will, Thomas Cheesman, the elder, left his dwelling house to his daughter, Joan, whilst she remained unmarried, and, after to his grandson, Thomas Cheesman. To his son, Thomas Cheesman, he left 1s and the rest to his daughter, Joan Cheesman and grandson, Thomas Radford. It should be noted, that, Rodber and Radford appear to have been variants of the same name. Thomas Rodber may well have been Cheesman's grandson.

When Thomas Rodber died in 1731, his possessions were valued at £52 6s 0d. His household goods were worth only £2 1s 0d. Outside, he owned a horse and harness, 1 hog, 5 beasts and some hay, the total value £10 10s 0d. His tannery held 62 hides worth £21 10s 0d, 10 dozen calves skins £10 5s 0d, bark £5, utensils of the trade 10s and horns and hair 10s.

Both Bailey and Rodber appear to have been processing a large number of calf skins, indicating, perhaps, that dairy cows were producing more bull calves than heifers. Or, possibly, calf skin leather was in demand for the finer products for which cow hide was too heavy. Bailey's Inventory includes tails, it seems surprising that these had not remained with the butcher, did ox-tail not appear in the seventeenth and eighteenth century kitchen?

The tanning process was a long one taking up to a year. For maximum efficiency it was essential to maintain a steady flow of hides going through the various processes. The requirements were fairly simple: skilled workmen, lime, bark and a plentiful supply of water. The Yetminster area abounded in lime-kilns and the quarries supplied the limestone. Tanning bark was stripped from the oak trees in the Spring as the sap was rising and crushed in a grinding-machine. The tan was extracted by soaking the bark for several days in cold water.

The tannery required a number of large, oblong baths sunk into the ground. After rough cleaning, the hides were placed in lime baths for about two weeks. They were then drawn from the baths by two men carrying poles with hooks on the ends, the weight and slippery surface making it impossible to remove them in any other way. Next, the hair was removed by scraping and the hide was then passed to the craftsman for fleshing. He placed the hide over a kind of wooden horse and, with a specially curved knife, removed the flesh. It was highly skilled work, one false move and the hide could be ruined. At this stage, where a finer leather was required, the skin might be split. The hides were then washed to remove the lime and the actual tanning process began. Suspended vertically from a strong wooden slat, thus enabling several skins to be accommodated at the same time, they were put through a succession of baths. The baths contained the tanning liquor, and, each day, the hides were moved on to a bath with a stronger solution. After several weeks, the now cured and tanned hides were hung up in an airy place to dry. Finally, the leather was oiled by hand and rolled, ready for the purchaser.

The tanners about whom we know the most are the Warrys. They came from West Coker and William and Jane Warry were in Yetminster by 1688 when their first child, Jane, was baptised, to be followed by Elizabeth, Sarah and William. They either established, or took over, a tannery at Cross Farm. Cross Farm is situated at the junction of Church Street and High Street, the Cross, the 10 c shaft of which may be seen in St. Andrew's Church, very probably stood here.

The original house was probably of two rooms and early 16 c date. In the early 17 c it is likely that alterations were made and the gable chimney-stacks added. Later in the century, a room was added to the south with a cellar beneath. Behind the house, the extensive out-buildings needed for the tanning process are still in situ though becoming more and more dilapidated. The tanning process required a copious supply of water, and, it must be supposed that there was an adequate spring or well on the property.

The Warrys prospered here as tanners for four generations and over one hundred and fifty years.

Given the inevitably revolting nature of the early stages of tanning, it seems extraordinary to our modern way of thinking, that such a business should have existed in the centre of a village. But our fore-fathers were made of sterner stuff, they did not see themselves as living in a picture-book village of thatched cottages, they lived in a working environment. Most of the dwellings along the High Street were farm-houses and behind were the farm buildings, the fields were scattered and there must have been a constant coming and going of live-stock as they were taken to and from pasture. No doubt, at times, the streets resembled a midden, but people thought little of the smells or the mess and would have accepted the stench from the tannery with all the other

129

Cross Farm. The Tannery was behind. Home of the Warry family for several generations.
Most probably, the Preaching Cross (see the shaft in the Church) stood on the triangle in front of this house

inconveniences as part of life. After all, the tanner and his family had to bear with it as well.

William Warry II married Edith Warry, a kinswoman from West Coker. Edith was born in 1710, the eldest of four daughters and four sons of Thomas and Edith Warry. Her brother, Thomas was Churchwarden of West Coker and her brother, John, an attorney at New Inn. Her maternal grandfather was a tanner. William and Edith had eight children, of whom the two youngest died in infancy. William Warry II died in 1768 and Edith in 1779.

In 1767, William made his Will. He left all to his eldest son, William, who was to pay £50 to each of his four sisters and a further £75 each after the death of his mother. He further stipulated, that, if they could not agree, William was to pay £12 per annum to his brother, John. Was there, perhaps, something odd about John Warry? No more is heard of him and no burial is recorded. To his wife, Edith, William bequeathed two beds, six pewter dishes and one dozen plates. Perhaps these items are what she had requested and she expected to continue to live in the family home with her son.

Just a month after his father's death, William Warry III went to Holwell for his bride. He married Sarah, daughter of wealthy James Cadie living at Westrow.

All the Warrys were active in the Vestry and in village affairs and, towards the close of the century, William Warry III was appointed Treasurer when the Parish embarked upon the ambitious project to build a House of Industry behind the Poor House at Holbrook. It was to house and employ 60 poor people, not only from Yetminster, but from other parishes which chose to pay to send their poor. The agreement made with Evershot has survived. According to the accounts kept by Warry, he was receiving money all the time, but nowhere are we told from whence it came, presumably money earned by the inmates, but neither do we know what tasks they were undertaking. The project lasted less than fifty years, collapsing when the New Poor Law created Unions and large Workhouses to serve each Union. Yetminster's Poor were then sent to Sherborne. No trace of the House of Industry remains, no doubt, the contents and building materials were sold.

William Warry III and Sarah had four sons, their only daughter, Mary, died. Indeed, there may have been other losses, for the five births were spread over the years 1769–1788. William died in 1801, and, within the year, his widow had followed him.

Six months previously, he wrote his Will. To his son, William, he left his estate in Stockwood lately purchased of John Axe, he to pay £400 to Axe.

To his son, John, he left a close called Whittles and appointed him Lord's next tenant of his house and several other closes. John to pay £40 per annum to his mother, Sarah. After her death, he was to pay £500 to his brother, Thomas. William Warry III had bought the house in Church Lane now known as 'Fairings', and this, with several closes, he left to his son, George, with the proviso that his mother was to live there for her life-time. George was to pay £20 per annum to his mother, and, after her decease, £500 to his brother, Thomas. All his goods, chattels and stock he gave to John whom he appointed executor.

His son, William, had inherited 'Westrow', the substantial Cadie property in Holwell, and, here he lived, ummarried, until his death, aged 56 in 1825. He was a partner in the Sturminster Bank. The previous year, he wrote his Will. He commences with some individual legacies: to Mary Wilson otherwise Lovelace, formerly of Chard, Somerset, but now of Lower Sloane Street, Chelsea, £150; to the two daughters of William Warry, formerly of West Coker who was first cousin to my father, £50 apiece; to Eunice Hammond, wife of Thomas Hammond of Holwell £40 independent of her husband; to Jonathan Cadie of Henstridge £20 and to Mary Cadie of Bishops Caundle, his sister, £15; to Elizabeth Bishop, since married, who was an old servant to my mother, £5 and to Ann Gould of Holwell, £60 over and above any wages owing to her if living with me at the time of my decease.

'To my brother, Thomas Warry of New Inn, I give two thousand pounds to be deducted out of the moneys which shall be found due to me in his hands, either individually or as a partner in the Sturminster Bank, unless he shall have settled such accounts to my satisfaction in my life-time, in which case he shall receive the £2,000 as would any other legatee.' He wishes to be buried in the family vault in West Coker Church and to have no stone or monument.

The residue of his estate he leaves to his brother George Warry whom he makes executor. There is no mention of his brother, John, and he seems not too well-disposed towards Thomas. George Warry's great grandson still lives on the estate in Holwell.

George Warry, only thirteen years old when his father died, also went to New Inn and, later, practised as a lawyer in Sherborne, his office was on the corner of Abbey Road and Cheap Street. He married Elizabeth, daughter of Thomas Cockeram of Cerne Abbas and lived in the Manor House in Newlands.

For John Warry, the last of the Yetminster tanners, life did not run smoothly. It is true, that he was in a large way of business, but, it is possible, that he was never a very robust man. He married, in 1807, Jane Cockeram, sister to Elizabeth who was later to marry his brother George, the marriage was childless, and, after only seven years, Jane Warry died.

In 1803, when High Constable of the Hundred, John had an unfortunate brush with the Law. One day, a man arrived from Hermitage, bearing a Magistrate's Warrant for the arrest of one William Bartlett, wanted as the putative father of a child born to a Hermitage woman. There was nothing unusual about this, maintenance of bastard children frequently fell upon the Parish, and Parish Overseers did their best to identify the father who could be compelled by Law to contribute to the child's upkeep. John Warry refused to serve the Warrant, because, he said, Maber, the man bringing the Warrant, was neither Constable nor Tythingman of Hermitage. He is quoted as saying: 'I bid defiance to the law, I know enough of Parish business and I am right!'

Maber went away and returned with the Tythingman. Warry then went to Bartlett's house and gave him the Warrant, saying: 'Throw the Warrant in the fire, they won't dare to meddle with thee when the Warrant is gone!' But Bartlett took it and went off voluntarily.

John Warry must have served many Warrants. Why was he so angry? Well, someone else was angry. When the news reached the Magistrate, he was anything but pleased. At the Michaelmas Quarter Sessions held at Bridport in 1803, John Warry was fined 1s and sentenced to six months in gaol for a misdemeanour by refusing to execute the Warrant of a Justice of the Peace, when, as High Constable of the Hundred, he failed to apprehend someone for bastardy.

John was locked up in Dorchester Gaol. The Gaol Delivery describes him thus:

*4 October 1803 John Warry, Yetminster, tanner, single, age 27, brown hair, florid complexion, hazel eyes, athletic build.*

*Misdemeanour: 6 months.*

When the news reached John's brother, Thomas at New Inn, he immediately made moves to obtain John's pardon. He wrote several times to Thomas Pickard, Chairman of Quarter Sessions. No reply was forthcoming. He pleaded for John, saying that he was but a young man of 27 and great injury would be done to his business if he were not released. Pickard was unmoved. But, doubtless, Thomas had access to the best advice in the legal profession as to what could be done, and, eventually, a letter reached the Secretary of State. On 21 December

133

1803 John Warry wrote a letter of apology to the Magistrates, and, on 30 December he was pardoned and released from Dorchester Gaol.

Five years later, John was again in trouble. From the end of Church Street, at its junction with Birch Lane, ran a foot-path. Known as Church Path, it ended opposite the Poor House at Holbrook. Near this path, John Warry farmed a field for his brother, George, and, adjacent to it, the widow, Mary Allambridge, held land. Warry had cut down some trees on the boundary which he believed to be his (or, rather, his brother's). But Mrs Allambridge claimed the trees were hers and accused him of damaging grass and crops, breaking six gates, twenty perches of hedge and twenty perches of fence, taking 20 cartloads of wood and 20 loads of bushes and of felling 5 oaks, 5 ashes and 5 elms!

Fooks, the Sherborne solicitor, acting for Warry, wrote: "The plaintiff is an opulent, litigious widow and the proverb of the neighbourhood for going to Law."

"The defendant is a young man, a tanner in a large way of business, but has no interest in this cause as he is merely tenant of the field in which the two miserable elms grew which are the real subject of this action, worth but £3."

In April, 1807, George Ring, carpenter, cut the trees and threw them onto petitioner's land because it was more convenient. The trees were in the bank dividing her land, Holmoor, from George Warry's close called Harris's Mead. "The fact is" wrote Fooks, "defendant being a young man, was really panic-struck at the violent ebullitions of the petitioner's temper and offered the value of the trees."

In 1768, John Warry's father, William, purchased Harris's Mead from a Mr. Beer. At purchase, William Warry had the fences made good by Joseph Child except for the fence in question. William Warry and Thomas Allambridge met to consider ownership and Allambridge gave it up to Warry. Child then laid and repaired the fence with thorns for which Warry paid. Nevertheless, in the summer, Allambridge's cattle broke it down. William Warry, also a tanner, possessed material which only a tanner could obtain, 'sloughs' (pronounced 'sloos') the inside porous substance of horns (twice as heavy as the horn itself). This substance was considered infallible for keeping off cattle as they would not go near it. Several loads were carried to the bank, which was about a mile from the tanyard. Child put it in the bank 2½ ft. high, everyone could see as Church Path was close by. The real dispute of the last twenty years, Fooks decided, was not related to right of property in the fence but to whether Warry should dig a ditch to keep out Allambridge's cattle. The reason for opposition was plain, it would have taken in and destroyed the public Church Path, throwing the path out of straight into Holmoor, causing loss of ground to Allambridge.

Witnesses were found: Thomas Swatridge, 85 years old, 60 years ago worked for Mr. Jesty who rented Harris's Mead.

Joseph Child was threatened by Mrs Allambridge, that if he did anything against her, she would trouble him for a debt of 20 years ago, witness having rented a dairy from Thomas Allambridge.

John Edmonds and William Jesty were also threatened by Mrs Allambridge.

The outcome of the case is not recorded, but the evidence gives an interesting glimpse into what was, doubtless, the subject of gossip in the ale-houses for many a day, the old men, like Thomas Swatridge, enjoying the limelight, and, perhaps an extra tankard, because, only they could recall events which had never been recorded on paper.

Five years later, John Warry was again in trouble. He held a piece of land in the Parish of Beer Hackett, and, John Munden, the Rector wrote threatening a Bill against him for four years unpaid Tithe. The land was occupied by a dairyman, John Edmonds, and Warry sent him with £10 to pay Munden, he, Munden, being at his other Living of Corscombe. But, the money was refused as being insufficient. Warry agreed to have the land measured by a Surveyor, and, it is interesting that he is speculating if the Surveyor will use Statute or Customary measurement. In the event, he used both.

Replying to queries, Warry states that the Tithe milk is not 29 gallons per annum and that the land will not find hay for three cows. He says he pays taxes to Sherborne Almshouse "whom this great Divine wants to go to Law against."

Warry was summoned to attend the Ecclesiastical Court at Sarum. Fooks wrote him a letter of instructions, but it was probably never sent. Tongue in cheek, he wrote: "You must appear in Salisbury between 9 and 12 tomorrow or stand in Yetminster Church with a sheet over you!" He suggested Warry should travel by coach rather than ride. This case lasted from 1813–1816. It is doubtful if Warry ever attended Court. The outcome is not known. By this time he was, in all probability, a sick man. He was buried, aged only 42, on 12 September 1818. Strangely, not a single Memorial stone to a Warry has survived, perhaps there were none.

It is likely that, with the death of John, tanning ceased in Yetminster. George Warry inherited the property which included 40 acres of land, and, for many years, it was let as a farm until, eventually, George sold it. The 1840 Tithe Map shows the occupier of Cross Farm as Benjamin Sampson. He came from West Milton. Ten years later, he is still there with son, Mark, daughter-in-law, Mary and three grandchildren. Ten years later again, he is still in residence, aged 82, but with another son, David.

---

## Epitaph to William Taunton
## who died 13 February 1691 aged 10 weeks

*Our life is nothing but a winter's day*

*Some only break their fast and soe away*

*Others stay dinner and depart full fed*

*The deepest age but supps and goes to bed*

*He's most in debt that lingers out the day*

*I dy'd betimes and have the lesse to pay.*

# Church Street

This short street runs from the High Street in the north to the junction with Mill Lane and Birch Lane in the south. Between these two lanes, runs a foot-path to Chetnole, at the bottom of the hill a path formerly known as Church Path, branched off to the right and came out opposite Holbrook, the Poor House. Holbrook still stands, now a private house constructed from the row of one up and one down cottages which, until Sherborne Work House was established in mid-19th century, housed the Parish Poor of Yetminster.

At the end of the 18 c, the Parish put into operation an ambitious plan. On the land behind Holbrook, they built a House of Industry to house and set to work sixty inmates. Not all came from Yetminster, other parishes were invited to send their poor. One of the parishes which did so was Evershot and two of the Parish Officers who signed the Agreement were Giles Hayward, eldest son of Giles and Elizabeth of Ryme Intrinseca who had been sent to Evershot to run the malthouse which his father owned there, and Henry Petty, wool-stapler, who gave his name to Petty's Farm in Yetminster. Although for the first couple of years accounts were kept by William Warry, the Treasurer, there is no indication of the work being carried out by the inmates. Warry died and the accounts cease abruptly. The project lasted less than fifty years because Work Houses were then established, and no trace remains of the building, which must have been substantial.

The Parish had other places where the Poor were housed: some cottages in Melbury Road, some at Brister End, and, if still short of roofs to put over heads, they would rent cottages from private individuals.

To return to Church Street. All the properties on the east side had steep gardens going down to the river.

137

Church Street, looking north.
*From right*: Cottages built by A. S. Williams for his gardener and coachman;
the Library, the former School, Hill House.
Drawing by Samantha Chaffey

## Greystones/The Crown Inn/Willis's

Arthur Cosens owned Willis's. He, and his much younger sister, Christian, were orphaned. In 1737 when he married Martha Helyar, Christian was but twelve years old. Ten years later, he surrendered Willis's to her, no doubt as a marriage portion. But, it was not until 1753 that she married John Vincent and the property passed to him. In 1785, their daughter, Anne Vincent, married Thomas Bartlett of Wareham and Willis's formed part of her marriage portion. Later, it reverted to Anne's mother, Christian Vincent, and, in 1812, she surrendered the property to her son, William. In 1816, William mortgaged to John Andrews of Leigh for £350. William must have redeemed the Mortgage, for, in 1823, following his death, it passed by Will to his nephew, Charles Oldfield Bartlett.

138

By 1840, it was the Crown Inn, rented by John Shorey together with the large field next to it and a cottage in Mill Lane. Shorey ran the Inn for the next twenty, possibly thirty, years. Following its days as an Inn, the property was next used as the Milk Factory, farmers from the area brought in their milk for processing. This enterprise was later moved to a site near the Station. The tall, brick chimney of this complex was only recently removed, painted on it were the large letters U D, United Dairies.

## The Stone House/Framptons

It seems very probable, that the site now occupied by the modern house known as "Framptons" and the "Stone House" were once one tenement known as "Framptons".

On 22 January 1900, the Rev. G. B. Southwell of Alton Pancras paid £45 for the Freehold of "all that tenement and orchard being part of a customary cottage called "Framptons", formerly in occupation of Elizabeth Partridge, widow, which the Rev. Blakeley Cooper sometime used as a Dairy House, now converted into three cottages or dwelling-houses occupied by Mary Ann Cheesman, William Brake and . . . Guppy."

From this, it would seem clear that the Rev. Southwell was paying for the Freehold of the land, orchard and out-buildings of the property then known as "Framptons" now The Stone House.

Over the years, The Stone House has been much altered. It is likely that the inglenook fire-place has survived all the alterations. It had a spiral stair-case to one side, and, most likely, a bread-oven on the other, where a way has now been made through to the present kitchen. At one time, it may have been nearly destroyed by fire, and it may have had a third storey. The north wing was added in Edwardian times and one wonders how it was permitted to extend into the road as it does, thus making the road very narrow at that point.

The Court Book of Yetminster Prima records, that, on 9 January 1752:

*Robert Frampton surrendered to Samuel Partridge "a tenement at Yetminster, house, garden and orchard, late Thomas Cheesman."*

Stone House formerly "Framptons"

*In 1757, three tenements at Yetminster passed from Robert Frampton, (deceased) gentleman, to John Shirley Esq. and his daughter, Mrs Eleanor Frampton.*

1774 Samuel Partridge of Yeovil, cordwainer, surrendered to Thomas Read, a tenement, late Framptons.

1776 Thomas Read surrendered to Samuel Partridge jun., Framptons, now in occupation of Robert Granger

These last two transactions were probably the result of a Mortgage.

In 1769, Robert Granger married Sarah Hayes, daughter of Elizabeth at the White Hart. Sarah died in 1781, but Robert lived to 1827, dying aged 84 after spending 44 years as Parish Clerk. Did he, one wonders, spend all those years at Framptons? He would have been ideally placed for carrying out his duties in the Church.

1781 Samuel Partridge Inn holder, of Bridport, deceased, by his Will surrendered Framptons to his daughter, Mary.

1793 Mary Partridge, spinster, surrendered to Edward Cooper, clerk, Framptons, now in occupation of Elizabeth Partridge.

In 1810, it came to Mary Cooper on the death of her husband and, in 1835, Mary died and it passed to her son, the Rev. Blakeley Cooper. The 1840 Tithe Apportionment shows that the Reverend Blakeley Cooper owned both the house and garden and the out-houses, yard and orchard. The former was occupied by Israel Richardson and the latter by the Reverend George Cooper who was living next door at The Vicarage.

In fact, Richardson had died in 1839.

Israel Vanderplank Richardson was born in 1785, the son of James and Anne Richardson. His mother, Anne, was the daughter of Thomas and Elizabeth Chinnock, probably the Thomas Chinnock who was landlord of The Bell Ale-house, the location of which has yet to be established. In 1819, Israel Richardson married Elizabeth Maber. Over the next ten years, six children were born to them, two dying in infancy. Until about 1823, Israel was a plasterer, he then appears in the Parish Registers as a shop-keeper, prompting the question: What kind of shop had he? He was not yet 40 years old, had he, perhaps, some illness or disability which prevented him from carrying on his trade? He was aged 54 when he died. His widow, Elizabeth, lived on until 1860 when she died at the ripe age of 77 years. On the 1851 Census, she is still living at "Framptons" with her sons, William and George. George was a shoemaker, and, two years later, he was to marry Ruth Pauley, a dressmaker. In the same year, his sister Anne married Eustace Freek, servant, of Melbury. Possibly, both had been employed at Melbury House. In 1847, sister Elizabeth married James Pitman, shoemaker.

In 1850, "Framptons" was owned by Edward Yalden Cooper and, six years later, enfranchised by the Reverend George Southwell. During the next decade, it served as a temporary school. An old photograph shows the infants' class outside with their teacher. By 1884, the property had been inherited by George Bull Southwell, curate, and he sold to Samuel Bartlett Templeman. The latter had been staying with the widowed Mary Ann Read and her daughter, Martha Jane, at Devon House. He married the daughter. Templeman was born in Weymouth.

141

He died in 1901 and his widow sold the property to Dr. William Bruorton for £450.

This would appear to be the first occasion on which Yetminster had a resident doctor. In the 18 c Henry Meech of Cerne Abbas was much called upon, he died in 1787. In 1723 we have Mr Buckland. In the 1740s, Dr. Mohun, Mr. William Saunders and Mr. Antill of Milborne Port. These were followed by Mr North, Mr. Samuel Randall of Piddletrenthide and Robert Paltock of Ryme Intrinseca.

As for School-teachers, there was a requirement that doctors and mid-wives should be licensed to practice. In 1752, George Buckland of Beer Hackett (possibly a son of Mr. Buckland mentioned in 1723), was so licensed by the Dean of Sarum.

He made this declaration:

*"I, George Buckland of the parish of Beer Hackett in the County of Dorset and Peculiar jurisdiction of the Dean of Sarum, being to be licensed to practice Physick and Chyrurgery within the peculiar jurisdiction of the Dean of Sarum, do, this present fourth day of June 1752, freely and willingly assent to and subscribe to the 39 Articles of Religion agreed to at the Synod holden in London in the year 1562 and to those articles contained in the 36th Canon and to that part of the declaration of the Act of Uniformity of public prayers now remaing in force.*

*George Buckland."*

At some time, Dr. Bruorton went to South African where he died. In 1921, Mrs Jane Burorton sold to Dr. Stanley Stephens for the sum of £850. The house was now called "Treath" and was occupied by Dr. Stephens until his death in 1939. His Surgery was a small building in the back garden, reached through a passage, now blocked, and called by the patients, "The Drain".

The present garage, which is stone-flagged and has a fire-place, housed, first the Doctor's trap, and then his car. Dr. Stevens had one of the first cars in Yetminster. The present work-shop, next to the garage, was used as stable and hen-house. In 1964, the house was sold by Dorothy Ann and Simon Stephens to Jocelyn Armstrong for £5,750. The next owner was William Edward Mackenzie Hill, then Dorothy Cullen, and, finally, in 1980, the present owners, Michael and Nora Windridge took possession.

Since its inception, the old house has seen much coming and going and many alterations, but, it is probably safe to say that the great fire-place has been there ever since the first masons heaved the stones into place and raised the rough-hewn beam across the top.


## Hill House

This somewhat imposing building, now let out in flats, has been much added to over the years. Inside the porch is a date-stone, 1698, the date of the original build, or a re-build, perhaps. The front, of three storeys and a cellar, is probably the original house. The sash windows may be later insertions.

Documentation for the Rectory Manor is sparse, but, it would appear, that the first name we can put down as an owner of Hill House is Samuel Keate. In the late 17 c/early 18 c, four Keates of Leigh were baptising children. Samuel Keate had ten children of whom six died young. His first wife, Susannah, died in child-birth in 1691 and was buried with her infant daughter. The second wife, Cecile, was buried in 1694. She was the mother of Samuel, of whom it is recorded: "he was born on 4 January 1693 at 4 o'clock in the morning, it being a Thursday."

In 1696, Samuel Keate married Mrs. Elizabeth Chapman, and, she was the mother of his remaining three surviving children, Thomas, Robert and William. One says, 'surviving' but no marriage is recorded for any of these four boys, neither is a burial, but the name of Keate dies out in the area.

Samuel appears to have moved from Leigh to Yetminster around 1700. In 1711, he surrendered the capital messuage to John Chapman, possibly a kinsman of his wife. In 1722, Mr. John Chapman, on the oaths of Mr. Arthur Cosens and Mr. Thomas Knight, surrendered the cottage and tenement, late Samuel Keate, to Charles Abington, Esq. in the 18 c, " cottage" did not have the connotation which it has today, it could refer to any dwelling. Chapman did not attend Court, but declared his intention before witnesses, a procedure sanctioned by the Customs of the Manor.

Charles Abington did not enjoy his property for long. He was a childless widower and died in 1726 nominating his niece, Ann Abington, daughter of his late brother, John, of Over Compton, as Lord's next tenant to "all that my house, cottage or customary tenement in Yetminster with the three meadows belonging thereto, called Blacklands, late in occupation of Mr Samuel Keate and Mr John Chapman and two closes of meadow lately bought of Mr John Hodges, Nether Mills and Manmead with the appurtenences thereto."

He desired to be buried at Over Compton in the vault with his wife. His Will is dated 27 July 1724 and Probate was granted 15 May 1726.

Further bequests and provisions were as follows:

*To his niece, Ann Abington, "my wife's gold watch, chain and seal with all plate, furniture, bed, bedding, woollen and linen, pewter, brass utensils and implements of household except such as shall be otherwise disposed of by this my Will."*

The pall-bearers were to have hat-bands, gloves and rings.

*"To my sister Abington, sister Young, niece Ann Abington, niece Elizabeth Lillington and niece Elizabeth Young, to each a ring value 1 guinea."*

His Executors were to give rings to other persons at their discretion.

*"To the Poor of Sutton Bingham, Over Compton and Yetminster 40 shillings each.*

*To my niece Elizabeth Lillington, daughter of Joseph Lillington, £100 at 21 or marriage. Should she die, then to nephew George Abington.*

*To my niece, Elizabeth Young, my 7 stone diamond ring that was my mother Young's, also the cornelian seal set in gold.*

*To my godson, Mr. William Prowse, my silver tankard with the Compton Coat-of-arms.*

*To my nephew, Mr. Andrew Abington, £10 a year for life and I forgive him the debt owed to me.*

*I also forgive a debt of about £40 due to me from my Uncle Charles Abington.*

*To Mr. Stephen Hodges, a mourning ring value 1 guinea.*

*To Mr. John Lane of Blandford, £20 to be paid out of such sums due to me at my death and a mourning ring value 1 guinea.*

*To my good friend William Waddon of Netherbury 2 guineas and a mourning ring value 1 guinea.*

*To each servant living with me at my death 20 shillings.*

He then refers to his other estate, the Manor of Sutton Bingham and other lands in Sutton Bingham, Barwick and Stoford late in tenure of Thomas Compton of Sutton Bingham, late in occupation of Mrs Elizabeth Young of Trent, widow, deceased or any estate inherited under the Will of the late Thomas Compton or my late wife who was his only sister.

*"I appoint my kinsman, Wyndham Harben of Newton Surmaville and my nephew George Abington of Over Compton to deal with this estate in pursuance of an Identure dated 1 July 1720 between Charles Abington of New Inn and Isabella, his wife, sister and heir of Thomas Compton of Sutton Bingham, deceased, John Clement of Hardington, gent., John Prowse of Kingston juxta Yeovil, gent., Wyndham Harben, Esq. of Newton, George Abington Esq. of Over Compton of the one part, and, Joseph Lillington of Sherborne, gent. and Elias Hosey of Sherborne, gent. of the other part.*

*"To be disposed of to the use of my nephew, George Abington and after to his heirs. Failing heirs, to my niece, Ann Abington, and, after her decease, to my cousin Charles Abington of Bristol, son of my Uncle, Andrew Abington. After his decease, to the first son of my cousin Charles Abington, and, after to my cousin, Charles Abington, son of my Uncle Charles Abington of London, gent.*

*To my good friends, Wyndham Harbin, Michael Harvey of Clifton, Arthur Cosens of Yetminster, gent. and Robert Colson of Dorchester, executors, to each a ring and to Mr. Thomas Knight of Yeovil, gent., £5 and a ring.*

*£450 to be paid to Mr Samuel Keate.*

145

A lease was to be drawn up putting his niece, Elizabeth Lillington's life into reversion, after deaths of Mr. William and Mr. Charles Tunneys, of two tenements in Sutton Bingham, Hyde and Daniells.

The Witnesses were Abraham Miller, Gilbert Warr and Thomas Melmoth.

An interesting Will and a wealth of genealogical information and how keen the Abingtons were to name their sons Charles! The giving of mourning rings was a general custom, but Abington's bequests must surely have broken the record for the number of those he wished to remember.

The Yetminster Register records that, in 1695, John Keate = Mrs Mary Young "it is not known where". Is it possible, that Mary was a kinswoman of Charles Abington's mother?

Anne Abington duly inherited Hill House. On 13 November 1734 she married Hubert Charles Floyer of Dorchester. The marriage was short-lived and childless. Floyer died 23 February 1742 aged 43 years and was buried at Over Compton. Anne Floyer lived on alone until her death in 1752. She, too, was buried at Over Compton, and, in her Will, appointed her niece, Elizabeth Lillington, Lord's next tenant to her property in Yetminster.

*The will of Ann Floyer of Yetminster.*     *15 September 1751*
*Prob.*     *22 June 1752*

*"To my niece, Barbara Abington, £500 on condition that she executes a release of all claims to my Executrix.*

*Also, to Barbara Abington, my blue sapphire seal set in gold with the Abington and Compton Arms, my green emerald ring set with diamond sparks, my silver caudle cup and cover, my silver sugar dish, silver fruit dish and silver chocolate-pot.*

*To Mrs Mary Somers of Yetminster, widow, to Mrs Sarah Clifton of Dorchester and Mrs Elizabeth Somers of Over Compton, £5 apiece.*

*To my servant, Andrew Dodge, twenty shillings.*

*To Mr Hubert Floyer, son of Rev Mr. William Floyer, deceased, £100.*

*To Mrs Mary Somers the elder, of Over Compton, £5 a year for her life, to be paid out of my leasehold estate at Sutton Bingham that now stand in the name of Mr Thomas Knight, dec.*

*To my sister, Mrs Margaret Floyer, the use of my gold watch and chain and gold seal with the Floyer and Gould Arms that was my sister Lucy Floyer's for her life and after to my niece, Margaret Cornish, daughter of said William Floyer, deceased.*

*To Mr Anthony Floyer of Dorchester, another son of the said William Floyer, my large silver soup dish with the Floyer and Gould Arms, also my diamond ring set in gold.*

*To the Rev. Mr. John Floyer, another son of William Floyer, all the rest of my plate that was my said sister Lucy Floyer's and my diamond ring having seven diamonds on the outside and a cristal on the inside.*

*£20 is to be laid out in Communion plate at the discretion of my Executrix, with the inscription "The gift of Ann Floyer for the use of the parish of Over Compton. To the aged poor of the same parish receiving no relief, £5 to be distributed by the Rector the day after my funeral.*

A bequest similar to the above was made to Yetminster Church.

*"To my sister Sarah Young and to Mrs Ann Knight of Closworth, each a mourning ring of a guinea value.*

*To my godson, Mr Samuel Barjew, my silver tankard with the Abington and Fields Arms.*

*I nominate my niece, Elizabeth Lillington, to be the Lord's next tenant to my dwelling house, out-houses, gardens, back-sides and all other my customary lands and estates in Yetminster.*

*To my upper maid living with me at my decease, one year's wages above that owing to her and such of my clothes as my Executrix shall judge fitting. To my other servants, half a year's wages above wages owing.*

*"My Will is to be buried at Over Compton in a private but handsome manner, and to the bearers and to the Rector of Over Compton and to the Vicar of Yetminster, I give hat-bands, scarves, shammy gloves, escutcheons and rings of a guinea value each.*

*To Mrs Elizabeth Feaver, daughter of the Rev. Mr. Feaver, deceased, a ring of the like value.*

*All my household goods and furniture (except my linen) all my pictures, china, plate and rings not before given and my leasehold estates at Sutton Bingham, subject to the annuity aforesaid, to my niece Elizabeth Lillington. Should she die unmarried, then, after her decease, to my niece Barbara Abington.*

*Witnesses:    Arthur Cosens*
*              Samuel Foote*

Samuel Foote was a local Attorney. Arthur Cosens lived next door to Anne Floyer at what is now Gable Court, at that time, two properties known as "Hardings" and "Grimsteads". In 1720, before Cosens took possession from John Grimstead, Abington Somers, Rector of Over Compton, had married Mary Grimstead. Mary was born in 1690, her sister, Anne, two years later. In the year 1710, Anne Grimstead's baseborn son, Thomas, was baptised. Nothing more is known of either Anne or her son, doubtless, he was named Thomas after his father.

Clearly, Anne was distributing her assets between her own relatives and those of her late husband.

Samuel Barjew was the son of the Rector of Over Compton.

The communion plate bequeathed to Yetminster Church is still in the possession of the Church and bears the inscription: "The gift of Anne Floyer."

If her wishes for her funeral were duly carried out, it must have been a quite spectacular event, no doubt the inhabitants of both villages turned out to watch, and, what a good thing she died in summer time!

She was generous to her servants, it would have been interesting had she named them all.

Elizabeth Lillington was the daughter of Joseph Lillington of Sherborne, he, too, was buried in Over Compton in 1726, aged 39 years. It is possible that Elizabeth had been living in Yetminster, for, just one year after her Aunt's death, the 19 June 1753 saw the marriage in Yetminster of Mr. Nicholas Gould of West Stafford to Miss Lillington. No doubt, the bequests of both Charles Abington and Anne Floyer had formed a substantial marriage portion for Elizabeth Lillington although it seems unlikely that the couple lived in Yetminster. No burial there is recorded for Elizabeth Gould, but, in 1756, Letters of Administration were taken out for Elizabeth Gould alias Lillington. This seems strange, since, at that time a married woman could not own property.

However, at West Stafford, on 19 September 1757, Nicholas Gould of Frome Billet was married to Husey Gould of Milborne Stileham, Bere Regis, by Licence with consent of parents. The witnesses were Thomas Gould and Ann Gould. So, Husey was under-age, and, possibly a cousin to Nicholas. This marriage, also, was short-lived. In 1760, Nicholas died and the Court Book records that his widow, Husey Gould, was admitted to the Yetminster property. In 1769, she appointed her brother, Nicholas Gould, Lord's next tenant by the oaths of Thomas Gould Esq. and Elizabeth Gould, spinster, father and sister of Husey, and Nicholas Gould was admitted. Husey married James Bullen, jun. of Devon, and, soon afterwards, died.

Nicholas Gould, evidently, did not wish to retain the property, for, two years later, he sold to John Allambridge. In 1774, John Allambridge claimed to hold the customary cottage, formerly Mrs Floyer, and paid a Fine of £15. 15s. 0d., heriot of £20 and rent of 7s 9d. Presumably, Allambridge had not paid his Fine and Heriot when he took over in 1771. The amount of both indicate that it was a property of some size, although referred to as "a cottage".

In 1783, Allambridge mortgaged to William Jennings of Puddletown, gent. and Robert Henning of Woodsforde, gent. John Allambridge died a bachelor, in 1792 and his estate passed to his kins-woman, Eleanor Shirley, and, six years later, she sold to John Barrett, sack manufacturer.

The Sherborne Mercury dated 21 May 1798 carried the following announcement:

*"To be sold by Auction at The White Hart on Tuesday 26 June an estate of inheritance, the capital mansion house, late residence of John Allambridge, Esq., deceased, containing 2 parlous and 8 bed-chambers each with a closet, 2 kitchens, pantry, larder and good undergound cellar with coach-house, stable and other convenient offices.*

*Two walled gardens, one in front of the dwelling-house, the other, of considerable extent, behind. A beautiful spot on a declivity facing a*

A. S. Williams of Hill House. c 1890

*commanding and pleasant prospect. Also, at the bottom of the garden, an orchard in its prime, meadow of 3 acres bounded by a fine trout stream. At a short distance, 3 closes of meadow, 4 acres.*

*Mr Batten Yeovil*                           *Mr Shirley Attorny Yetminster*

The "walled garden" in front of the house would be that known as "The Alcove" on the opposite side of Church Street. The property was bought by John Barrett, sack manufacturer. In 1858, Mrs Selina Barrett, wife of Thomas Barrett of West Coker, sold to Mr. James Lucas.

150

In 1863, Thomas Hayward, the grocer, purchased the estate. Probably, he took out a Mortgage with Henry Meech of Minterne Magna, since he deposited the Deeds of the property with Meech. Hayward's wife, Amelia Dampney, was connected to the Meech family and Henry may have been a relative.

Thomas and Amelia were to live at Hill House until his retirement when he moved to the Almshouse Farm-house in Chapel Lane re-naming it Rose Cottage. There, they both died.

Hill House passed to Arthur Scott Williams. He soon established himself as "squire" of the village. He took a great interest in local affairs, frequently helping out financially as he did when Boyles School was in danger of closing. His wife and daughters established a Library in a cottage in Church Street and his daughter ran a Tennis Club. The school-children could always rely upon an annual Tea-party.

In 1888, Mr. A. S. Williams was in conflict with the Vicar, the Rev. Scott McDowell. The Vicar had recently re-built the Vicarage and now wished to convert the old Rectory by the Church gate into stables. Mr. Williams wished to purchase the building to provide a home for a village nurse. In the event, neither man had his way, it remained in the hands of the Ecclesiastical Commissioners until it was, unfortunately, demolished to make way for the present Church Hall.

In the year 1890, the Church underwent a restoration, and, evidently bearing no ill-will, Mr. and Mrs. Williams gave lamps and curtains for the doors.

## Church Hatch

St. Andrew's Church, Yetminster has a clock without a face which chimes the hours, and, at 3, 6, 9 and 12 follows with a rendering of the National Anthem.

It bears the Inscription:

*"Thomas Bartholomew of Sherborne fecit. Benjamin Coome, Thomas Stone and William Bisshop Church Wardens of the Parish of Yetminster. 1682.*

It is very possible that the National Anthem was introduced for Queen Victoria's Jubilee. It is not known, what, if anything, was played prior to that. The clock required constant attention, oil, cleaning and frequent repairs. It also required daily winding, and, finding someone to take on this responsibility was a constant worry.

In 1726, the Vestry decided that the problem could be solved by building a small cottage for the sexton.

The Vestry Book, 31 August, 1726 records:

*"Buy for widow Swatridge a gown, 2 shifts and an apron and likewise erect a small, convenient house on the south side of the tower for the use of the sexton according to the discretion of the Overseers."*

*Signed: John Richardson, Thomas Allambridge, Nicholas Daggle, Abraham Miller, John Hodges.*

By the time the Vestry met on 19 December, 1726, they were able to record:

*"Order that the sexton doo ring the four o'clock bell as formerly it was done and, for so doing and for looking after the clock and chimes and keeping them in order, the said Thomas Maidment shall have his dwelling in the house at the Church built for that purpose, the whole being thirty shillings a year and we do furder order a pair of shoes for Mary Stevens."*

The Vestry, which was constantly in need of housing for the poor, thought it was solving two problems: someone to wind the clock and a dwelling for one of the parish poor.

The cottage was truly small, one tiny room up and one down and was, originally, thatched. Today, occupation by two people would be considered the maximum (and there is now a small kitchen extension) but, nearly all the sextons had several children.

Thomas Maidment continued to receive payments from the Vestry, and, in February 1745, the Overseer was ordered to buy some linsey to make Thomas Maidment a frock. Maidment was succeeded by Thomas Mose, who, in 1758 moved with his family into the Poor House at Church Hatch. He died in 1763, the Vestry paying 8s for his shroud and coffin, 3s for bell and grave and 2s to the bearers.

Peter Wheadon was a later occupant, there in 1794. By 1805, "the sextin's sallery" was £1 10s 0d.

152

The Sexton's Cottage.
Drawing by Isobel Walker from an old photograph

In 1841, William Wheadon was sexton, living with his wife and family of four children, wherever did they put them all?

William Painter moved in with his wife, Jane, to be followed by Thomas Painter who died in 1916. Thomas also worked on the Railway.

In 1901, for economy, the Offices of Sexton and Clerk were amalgamated. Henry Saunders was Sexton and Clerk and died in 1935 aged 84. After his death, Church Hatch was re-furbished and Mr Bailey became Sexton. In 1938, Mr. Jim Ellis took over and served the Church until his death in 1985.

No one could be found willing to continue with the arduous duty of daily winding of the clock. Accordingly, in March 1986, the clock mechanism was brought down and taken away to be overhauled and electrified by Geoffrey Wardle of Wylye. In October, it was back in place and, once again, 'God save the Queen' chimed out over the village (its flat note unaltered!) and Jim Ellis was recorded as the last Sexton of Yetminster. And the last of a long succession of men, who, every evening, climbed the tower to ensure that the clock continued to chime.

## Upbury

Upbury is, possibly, the oldest house in Yetminster and the Capital Messuage of the Manor of Yetminster Prima or Upbury. It is a late medieval house, reconstructed in the late 16 c/early 17 c. The front elevation has two blocked two-light windows with trefoiled heads of 15 c type. One is a tall, transomed window for an open hall, the other a smaller similar window which might have lit the solar. They are not in their original positions.

Unlike other farm-houses in Yetminster, which are sited right on the road, Upbury lies well back from Church Street with a large cobbled yard in front, barns and buildings to either side. A glance at a map will show that Upbury and the Church occupy a large island site bounded by Church Street, Birch Lane, Melbury Road and Grope Lane. There are, in addition, in Melbury Road, three cottages just perched on the edge of the site, and, it is known, that, to the north of these, there were once two or three more which fell into decay and were demolished. Until the early 19 c Melbury Road (previously known as Back Lane) was very narrow, it is possible that these cottages were erected on the waste. It is interesting to speculate that this large island site has remained virtually unchanged for hundreds of years.

As has been stated elsewhere, the Prebends let their Manors on long leases. From 1576–1729, Upbury was let to the Fitzjames family of Leweston. When the Manor passed to Lord Broke in 1729, there were 55 copyhold tenements, 203 acres of land and an annual income of £111.

10s. 6d. It should be remembered, that not all these tenements were in Yetminster, many were in Leigh or Chetnole.

The most famous tenant of Upbury Farm was Benjamin Jesty. Exactly when he took over the tenancy is not known. In 1770, he married Elizabeth Notley of Longburton and their children, Robert, Benjamin, Elizabeth, Sarah, George and Harriet, were probably born at Upbury.

Throughout the country, small-pox was a scourge which, yearly, claimed many lives, or, at best, left the victims disfigured. Jesty had noted that dairymaids, who often contracted the milder cowpox, were immune to small-pox. Two of his dairymaids, Ann Notley and Mary Reade contracted cowpox, and, later, nursed small-pox patients without any ill effects. In the year 1774, Jesty decided to vaccinate his wife and two sons with lymph taken from a sick cow. He used a stocking-needle to take infected matter from a cow's udder and insert it into the arms of his wife and two sons. All went well with the boys, Mrs Jesty became very ill but happily recovered.

It was not until 1796 that Dr. Edward Jenner, living in the remote rural village of Berkeley in Gloucestershire, carried out his first experiment. He took matter, not from a cow, but from the hand of a girl suffering from cowpox and transferred it to the arm of a boy called James Phipps.

By 1796, the Rev. Thomas Lydiat of Workton, near Kettering, had become Lord of the Manor of Yetminster Prima. In the year following, the Jesty family moved to Downshays at Worth Matravers. Here, the Rev. Dr. Bell took an interest in Jesty's experiment. Jenner had been recognised and rewarded for his discovery, but Jesty had received no recognition. Dr. Bell put forward his case. As a result he was invited to London to the Pock Institute, where the doctors were impressed by his evidence, his portrait was painted and he was presented with a pair of gold-mounted lancets.

Jesty died in 1816 and is buried at Worth Matravers. He left Upbury somewhat abruptly in 1797. It was the custom for the out-going tenant to put all in order before leaving. Jesty had not done so, but, when reminded of his obligation, he agreed to arbitration. Fooks, who was Steward of the Manor, appointed as arbitrators, Thomas Webb of Sherborne and William Warry of Yetminster, tanner. The outcome was that Jesty was ordered to repair sundry gates and fences.

Upbury. Note the 2 blocked windows with trefoiled heads of 15 c type.
Drawing by Samantha Chaffey

Regarding the two arbitrators: Warry lived at Cross Farm where the Warry family had a tannery established for many years. We know a little of Thomas Webb because he is mentioned in the Diary of James Woodforde. In 1795, Woodforde was visiting his Sister Pounsett at Cole in Somerset. Also staying in the house was a Mrs. Penny. For Sunday, 23 August, he records:

*"About 11 o'clock this morning, Mrs Penny's husband and a Mr Webb who married Penny's sister, came to Cole in a one horse chaise from Sherborne and they dined and spent the afternoon with us, and in the evening returned home to Sherborne taking Mrs Penny with them ... Mrs Penny fell downstairs this afternoon but I hope did not hurt herself much as she is breeding. Mr. Penny is a stationer at Sherborne and Mr. Webb a saddler and his wife a milliner."*

Penny was not backward if he had the chance of making a sale for he sold Woodforde "a pack of Message Cards, gilt" for 1s 2d.

We hear of Daniel Penny later in Yetminster, for he became the owner of Everards. He married Elizabeth Guppy and Thomas Webb married Penny's sister, Jane.

At about the time Jesty left Upbury, the Reverend Thomas Lydiat of Workton, near Kettering became Lord of the Manor. He corresponded frequently with Fooks, the Steward, it is unfortunate that we do not have the letters Fooks wrote in reply.

The next tenant of the farm was Samuel Eastment. Accounts have survived, in one year, for example, disbursements by Eastment amounted to £117 13s 5d, and included:

*Thomas Gill for repairing water-hatches in Longmead 24 bushels of lime @ 6d 12s.*

*Samways for glazing £2 3s 1d*

*William Goring water-hatches £1 4s 2d.½ hundred bricks 1s 6d*

*Robert Jesty & William Jesty hedging against the new barton of church-yard £1 4s 0d. 33 goads @ 6d a goad.*

Longmead was a water meadow and the channels for flooding may still be seen. The whole system depended upon flooding at the right time and in the right way, and, to this end, it was essential that the hatches which controlled the river water should be kept in good repair.

It would appear, that, Fooks sent Lydiat an annual present of game. In February 1798, Lydiat sent a letter thanking Fooks "for very kind present of brace of pheasants, which, by some unaccountable delay, did not get to Kettering till the evening of 9th inst., but, notwithstanding the delay, they were very good."

Samuel Eastment was either a very bad farmer or else a singularly unlucky one. He is constantly complaining, that, for one reason or another, he cannot pay his rent. His sheep have been attacked by disease or his crops have failed.

Lydiat complains at not receiving his rent – he cannot pay his tradesmen's bills and now has a son at University.

By 1800, Lydiat is writing about a hedge to be planted between the farm and the church-yard, he thinks a quick-set hedge would be better than a wall. He also decides to plant 50 apple trees in Home Close, half this year and half the next. He enquires frequently about the apple-trees and gives detailed instructions as to how the farmer should water and mulch them.

In August 1800, he writes that he is glad to hear the crops are good, now, perhaps the farmer will pay his rent!

At the beginning of 1803, he announces his intention of visiting the farm in the summer. In December, he writes that he did not visit Yetminster as he took the family to Margate for their health. He refers to the possibility of invasion by the French and thinks their chief attempt will be upon Ireland.

In 1805, the Prebend, Mr. Hume, died. His successor, the Reverend John White, granted a new lease to Lydiat. White, then, promptly writes a letter re/arrears of rent due to him from Lydiat, a sum of £22. The following year, Lydiat considers disposing of the Yetminster estate, there is still trouble with Eastment over non-payment of rent.

In 1807, the Rev. Thomas Lydiat died. He was succeeded by his son, also Thomas Lydiat.

For the next eighteen years, it is only the steady hand of Fooks as Steward that saves the Manor from disaster. Young Lydiat would make a splendid character for a Jane Austen novel. He was twenty-nine years old when his father died. Clearly, he considers the Manor to be a bottomless purse where money is concerned. He is living beyond his means, as well as having to support his mother and sister. He is mixed up with a set of young men, reckless and extravagant. Lydiat is constantly writing to Fooks asking for £10 and Fooks has kept the chits recording these numerous payments on account. Finally, exasperated by this young man who has not the slightest idea how to run an estate or manage money, he, evidently, writes Lydiat an avuncular letter of advice. We have only his reply to Fooks. 'Yes', he writes, 'you are quite right, I shall get away from my extravagant friends and live more soberly. I know of a place in Wales and I intend to move there.'

In 1809, The Prebend, John White, grants Lydiat a new lease for £360 per annum on the lives of:

*Thomas Lydiat aged 31*
*Anne Lydiat aged 29*
*Francis Woodford, 22, son of the Rev. Francis Woodford,*
*Rector of Ansford.*

In that same year, he mortgaged the Manor to Thomas Andrews of Bradford Abbas for £2,000. So much for his resolution to live more soberly!

In 1812, he announces that he is going to Glamorgan where he thinks he will live more cheaply away from his friends. He asks Fooks: 'How does Don turn out? I hope he makes your brother a good dog.'

In another letter, he writes that he would like to find a wife. He is waiting in Bristol for the arrival of a Mr Griffiths and his fair daughter!

When his sister writes to inform him that his mother is dying, he has to beg Fooks for yet another £10 on account as he has no money for the coach fare.

In the year following, he thinks of selling the Manor but holds on to it until 1825 then he finally sells to George Andrews of Bradford Abbas for £3,500.

By 1817, Eastment had left Upbury and the new tenant was William Watts. William was, at least, the third generation of Watts in Yetminster. He was born in 1769, son of William Watts and his wife, Hannah Gill. He had an elder brother, Samuel, a younger brother, Benjamin and two sisters, Elizabeth who married John Edmunds in 1790 and Hannah. When the elder William made his Will in 1805, he divided his customary-held property between his three sons and gave Elizabeth and Hannah £60 apiece. He died in 1809 aged 85 years.

In 1792, William Watts had married Judith Edwards, daughter of William Edwards and Judith Hayward. Like Judith's father, James Hayward who kept the "Blackamoor's Head", William Edwards was also an inn-keeper. In 1794, a daughter, Mary, was born to William and Judith Watts, and, the following year, a son, William. Sadly, only Mary survived. On 15 December 1812, she married Thomas Hayward of Ryme Intrinseca, by Licence and consent of parents, for she was under age.

Watts paid rent of £400 per annum for Upbury, he appears to have run the farm efficiently, paid his rent on time and sent in his annual statements of expenditure. He and Judith were to spend the rest of their lives at Upbury.

Some disbursements by William Watts on Upbury in the late 1830s. He made payments to:

*Matthew Bishop blacksmith*
*John Jeanes thatcher*
*John Eyears*
*Israel Richardson plastering & whitewashing*
*Matthew Hackwell for timber*
*William Andrews for thatching*
*Israel Richardson:*   *work done at the farm house riting*
                           *the tiling*
                           *man & boy 1 day 3s 6d*
                           *1 day plaistering 3s 6d*
                           *Riting the chembley & finding sement 1s 6d*
*George Frampton:*   *walling 1 day 2 men & boy*
                           *repairing of lime kiln 5s 6d 3½ days in all*
                           *Repairing the pavement around the pump self*
                           *½ day 1s 3d*
                           *putting in the flood hatches*
                           *self, man & boy 1 day 5s 0d*
                           *self & boy 1 day 3s 0d*
                           *self man & boy 1 day 5s 0d*
                           *self man & boy 1 day 5s 0d*
*Thomas Samways Yeovil*
                           *½ day self & man repairing pump 9s 9d*
                           *new leathering ascending & under flauch of do.*
                           *5s 0d*
                           *new stuffing do. 1s 6d*
*9 hogsheads lime for water-works in Long Mead @ 1s 6d 13s 6d*
*Pd. Dicker of Batcombe for sand for the same 5s 0d*
*570 ft. sawing @ 3s 0d per hundred 17s 0d*
*Paint for painting 6 new gates 8s 6d*
*5 loads stone for water-works 7s 6d*

Long Mead, by the river, was a water-meadow, extremely valuable for providing an early bite for the sheep. It depended upon a system of hatches by which the river water was let in, as required, to flood the meadow, across which ran a series of shallow ditches. The water raised the temperature, thus encouraging the grass to grow. Keeping the hatches in repair and organising the flooding was skilled work, the man responsible was known as a "drowner".

Thomas and Mary Hayward had four sons and two daughters. The eldest, William Watts Hayward, went to live and work with his grandfather.

In 1839, William Watts invested in property. He bought the freehold of the shop (the present Oak House Stores) at that time in the tenure of John Langdon, the adjacent Royal Oak Inn kept by John and Mary Eyears and the cottage next to the Inn. Mary Eyears was born Mary Edwards, sister to Watts' wife, Judith.

Information in the papers of Fooks, the solicitor, is sparse, but William Watts Hayward was sent by his grandfather to Crewkerne to finalise the purchase with Murley & Tidcombe, solicitors to the vendor, one Peach. In 1840, a builder named Peach was living in Hermitage Street, Crewkerne and, the 1841 Census names Henry Peach, carpenter, in the same street. No record has been found of how Peach came to own the property in Yetminster which was the former Church House.

On 30 June 1847, William Watts made his Will, nominating his grandsons, William Watts Hayward and Thomas Hayward to be Lord's next tenants of his Customary Tenements. To them he bequeathed his freehold property, the Royal Oak Inn and the freehold dwelling house and shop occupied by John Langdon, known as "Reads". William and Thomas were to hold the properties in trust to pay one half of the rents to "my dear wife, Judith" and the other half to his daughter, Mary Hayward, their mother.

After the decease of Judith, the Inn was to pass to his grand-daughter, Eliza, wife of Simon Goode of Yeovil, grocer and then to her children and the dwelling-house to his grand-daughter, Marianne Hayward.

After the death of his daughter, Mary, Pills Mead at Leigh was left to his grandson, Giles Hayward and an orchard called Four Acres in Yetminster to his grandson, George Watts Hayward.

Watts also owned the cottage to the west of the Royal Oak called 'Bishops', formerly 'Hawkins' in the occupation of Edward Chainey and

The old Rectory or Parsonage, mansion of the Prebend of Yetminster Ecclesia.
It was demolished early this century and the Church Hall built on the site.
A. S. Williams had wanted to buy it as a home for a District Nurse.
Drawing by Samantha Chaffey

Alfred Barnswell. This cottage was left to William Watts Hayward, charged with the payment every Saturday of 2s to "my old and faithful servant, Betty Granger". At her decease, William was to pay £7 to each of his brothers and sisters then living.

His household goods etc. were left to his wife and £50 to each grandchild except William Watts Hayward. However, in 1852, he added a Codicil revoking the sums of money which the grandchildren had already received in his life-time.

William Watts died 10 April 1853, his wife, Judith, the previous year and his daughter, Mary and her husband, Thomas Hayward, in 1856. All are buried near the Church door in Yetminster Churchyard.

Watts was succeeded at Upbury by Daniel Stone Sampson.

# Gable Court Grimsteads–Cosens– Vincent–Bartlett families

Prominent in Yetminster for three generations were members of the Cosens family. It is almost certain that the first Arthur Cosens came from Symondsbury where the family was connected with Atrium Farm. By 1710, he was in Yetminster when he acquired Leaves Tenement, later known as Hardings. In 1723, he added the next-door property, Higher Tenement or Grimsteads, which he bought from Mr. Jonas Edwards who had lately married Elizabeth Grimstead. This was the present Gable Court, which had, at an earlier date, been held by Mr. John Minterne. It was the Mansion House of Yetminster Secunda. Hardings was the property to the east, since demolished.

Arthur Cosens I was laying the foundation of an estate which would, later, result in "The seat of Arthur Cosens, Esq." being emblazoned across Yetminster on the map.

Fortunate as they may have been in their worldly possessions, their family life was affected by much tragedy.

In 1713, Arthur's wife, Mary, died. He re-married to Christian – – – – and, by her had four children of whom two survived, Arthur b. 1717 and Christian b. 1725. Arthur I was buried 20 April 1726 aged 65.

In his Will, Arthur I bequeathed Hardings Tenement to his son, Arthur II with an except to his widow, Christian, for her life, of the dwelling-house, flower garden, the court on the street side and the cellars in the garden; the closes called Chettenhill and Blacklands also three closes lying eastwards of Little Leigh Lane and a fourth on the south side of the lane. The brew-house, lower garden, orchard to remain to his son.

For his other Tenement, Grimsteads, he nominated Thomas Knight of Yeovil, gent., Lord's next tenant on the oaths of Abraham Miller senior and junior. Arthur Cosens II was admitted to Hardings, paying a fine of £23 and Thomas Knight to Grimsteads, the fine £24. These were large amounts, a widow admitted to her late husband's cottage would have paid 6d. Thomas Knight would have been admitted as Trustee of Grimsteads.

Christian, widow of Arthur I survived her husband by only nine years, she was buried 12 April 1735. In the previous February, she had made her Will. It itemizes the household possessions in great detail.

She states, that, according to her late husband's authority, his household goods, plate, linen and personal estate were to be divided between her two children, Arthur Cosens and Christian Cosens, as follows:

*To Arthur Cosens*

*the best silver tankard, the silver candle-sticks and snuffers, a pair of the largest silver porringers, a pair of large round silver salts, the least silver cup, one dozen of the second-best silver spoons.*

*All the goods and furniture in the Hall and Parlour (except the tea-table silver and silver toaster), the best bed-stead and other things thereto belonging and all the furniture in the kitchen chamber (except the chest of drawers and the linnen therein). The two largest pewter dishes, four of the smallest size, one dozen of the second-best pewter plates, the largest boyler, the largest skillet, the smallest best metall pot.*

*One fine diaper table-cloth and one dozen and five napkins of the same. Two coarse diaper table-cloths and one dozen short diaper napkins to the same belonging. Three pairs holland sheets, one pair of the best sort, one other pair marked MAC and the other pair narrow holland with a broad hem. One pair of dowlas sheets marked A.C.C. Two pairs coarse sheets which are whole, three pair of holland pillow-tyes marked A and one pair of dowlas marked C. Also all the hogsheads, half hogsheads and other barrells.*

*All the other household goods and plate, linnen and personal estate to my daughter, Christian Cosens.*

*To my son, my father's mourning-ring*

*To my daughter, my gold watch, earrings, lockets and all other rings and also my gold frame for a picture usually hung or weared with a watch and also my broad piece of gold and my wearing-apparel, to wit: silk, woollen and linnen and all other things and also my child-bed linen, quilted basket and silk mantle.*

*Also the sum of one hundred pounds to be paid her within three years.*

*All my other goods and chattels to my son, Arthur Cosens.*

*Trustees and Overseers:*

*John Channing of St. Clement Danes, Mddx., apothecary*

*William Taunton of Leigh, gent.*

*William Eynon of Yetminster, clerk*

*Thomas Knight of Yeovil, gent.*

*Witnesses: Mary Rawles, John Newman, jun., Thomas Melmoth.*

*Probate granted 25 August 1741.*

In the summer of 1737, Arthur Cosens II = Martha Helyar. She was only seventeen years old. Their first child was not born until 1745 but he was followed by a further ten. Only seven survived.

Arthur's young sister, Christian, was only twelve years old when he married, and, no doubt, she continued to live with him. In 1747, Arthur II surrendered Willis's Cottage to Christian, probably as a marriage portion. Although called a "cottage", it was, in fact, a substantial house, presently known as "Greystones" in Church Street. In the 19 c it was the Crown Inn, and, later, the Milk Factory. In 1753, Christian Cosens = John Vincent, and, as was customary, he was admitted to "Willis's" in right of his wife.

John Vincent lived at the present Ford House, at that time known as Richardsons, reputedly a fine house with delightful gardens going down to the river. Looking at Ford House today, it is difficult to imagine the fine house it once was. It was ruined by the coming of the Railway in the mid 19 c. Much of its grounds disappeared under the Railway buildings and the alteration of the road to accomodate the bridge over Railway and river, left it in a sorry, sunken situation, spoilt even further by the addition of the red-brick Railway Inn at the back.

165

But, when John Vincent returned there with his bride in the spring of 1753, such despoilation had not been dreamed of. Over the years, the couple had nine children but only three were to survive to adulthood, one died in infancy but the others in their teens. The three survivors were Thomas and William who never married and Ann who married Thomas Bartlett, solicitor of Wareham. William spent his life in Yetminster but Thomas went to Wimborne.

On 5 July 1785, Thomas Bartlett jun. = Ann Vincent by Licence. The Witnesses were Thomas Bartlett, Thomas and William Vincent, Mary Cooper, Mary Pitman and Johanna Foot.

On the previous day, the Marriage Settlement had been signed. The Trustees were George Ryves Hawker of Wareham, clerk, Edward Cooper of Yetminster, clerk and Thomas Vincent of Wimborne, gent.

Christian Vincent agreed to surrender, within six months of the marriage, her estate known as Richardsons and her tenement, formerly Thomas Read's, known as Read's Tenement, to the use of Thomas Bartlett, after his decease, to his wife Ann, and, after the decease of both, to any children of the marriage. After the children, Read's was to pass to William Vincent, brother of Ann and Richardsons to her brother, Thomas Vincent. Whilst £2,000 capital or joint stock was to be settled on Ann for life.

Thomas and Ann Bartlett had sons Thomas Oldfield Bartlett, Charles Bartlett and William Bartlett and a daughter, Alicia. Alicia was at boarding-school in Blandford. The boys went to Sherborne School. Throughout their school-days, there was much toing and froing between Wareham and Sherborne, and, en route, visits were paid to grandmother, Christian Vincent in Yetminster.

Early in the 19 c, Thomas Oldfield Bartlett kept a somewhat scrappy diary. Here are some extracts.

4 Dec 1807   *There was in our larder:*

| | |
|---|---|
| *1 cock pheasant* | *11 lobsters* |
| *3 couple wild-fowl* | *1 cod-fish* |
| *7½ couple snipe* | *2 starlings* |
| *2 couple water-rails* | *100 squins (?) or small frills* |
| *1 moor-hen* | *5 partridge* |
| *1 hare* | *2 rabits* |

166

20 Jan 1808   *A very pleasant Ball at Wareham, 15 couples began dancing at 11 p.m. Left off at 1 a.m.*

1 Feb 1808   *Charles and William went to school. My father, myself and Alicia and John Foot dined at Mr. Barker's. Met Capt. and Mrs Buchanan and Mr. and Mrs Hyde there.*

*Won a gold seal at a raffle at Symes valued at £1 16s 0d.*

3 Feb 1808   *Went to a Ball at Poole, 7 p.m.–1.30 a.m. Afterwards, two Spaniards played on the flute, beautifully.*

10 Feb 1808   *Large Tea Party*

| Ladies | Gents |
|---|---|
| *Miss Brown* | *Mr George & Tom Garland* |
| *Miss Colfox* | *Mr T. Delacourt* |
| *Miss N. & Miss S. Garland* | *Mr Wright* |
| *Miss Phippard* | *Mr I. & T. Brown* |
| *Miss Pointer* | *Mr T. Phippard* |

*(Note: The Garlands were wealthy Poole merchants trading with Newfoundland. Alicia Bartlett was later to marry a Phippard.)*

3 Mar 1808   *On Thursday morning at 4 o'clock an alarm of fire was given, when it was discovered that Mr. Panton's malt-house was on fire, which, before 7 o'clock, was entirely burned down, a great deal of malt burned but that, as well as premises, insured.*

10 Mar 1808   *Went fishing to Holme Bridge, caught in 1½ hours about 300 brace of roach.*

*Made melon and cucumber bed 1 March. Put seed in 5th Seed up 8th.*

28 Mar 1808   *Longman of Sherborne, old school-fellow called. Rode from Wareham to Corfe Castle, Worbarrow, walked on beach, Lulworth Castle, to Inn for bread & cheese and quart of beer, cost 2s. Spent part of evening with Longman at Mr. Andrews, new shopman who plays violin. Took my violin, Mr. A. gave me a mute.*
*Longman is nineteen, I am twenty. Sent a letter by him with 7s to Charles and William at school.*

167

3 Apr 1808   *Three corpses carried to be buried at the same time such a thing never seen before in memory of oldest men in Wareham Mr. Tuck, Mr. H. Bestland, Mrs Smith who was insane.*

19 Apr 1808   *Caught a thirty pound salmon.*

23 Apr 1808   *Went to Blandford for Alicia. Bought a Siberian crab-apple to put in walled garden and half a hundred sea-kale plants.*

25 Apr 1808   *My father, myself and sister went to Yetminster. Father and sister by chaise. I went on horseback. We all went to Sherborne Sessions and then back to Yetminster with Charles and William. Returned home Fri. 29 April. Dapper, the little dog went with me and ran by my horse all the way there and back.*

30 Apr 1808   *Planted 32 filberts which I brought from Yetminster.*

9 May 1808   *Went to Blandford with Alicia. I bought a multiplying reel and a fishing-rod. The reel cost 10s 6d, the rod 7s 6d. Also bought new pair of brown top boots.*

5 Jun 1808   *Pony 'Snip' killed, aged 16.*

24 Aug 1808   *Went to Dorchester to see sham fight between 1st and 2nd German Dragoons. Saw chalk figure of George III on horseback.*

17 Oct 1808   *Went to Yetminster and stayed two weeks. Old John Besant and myself shot at woodcock which we killed.*

10 Mar 1809   *Made a sparagrass bed, plants given by Mr Stains from his own seed.*

23 Jul 1810   *My Danish mare had a mare foal.*

His mother, Ann, is never mentioned, it is presumed she was an invalid. She died in 1817. His father, Thomas, died in 1836, aged 81. Thomas Oldfield Bartlett was later to become Vicar of Swanage, he was inducted on 20 March 1817 when he was 29 and died there in 1841.

His grandmother, Christian Vincent, nee Cosens, was buried in Yetminster, 19 June 1810, aged 86 years.

On 4 November 1805 she made her Will.

To her younger son, William, she left her estate in Symondsbury centred on Atrium Farm and 'Willis's' in Yetminster together with

Whittles Orchard (under the Will of one John Reynolds, whoever held this land was charged with the payment of 20s per annum to the Poor). The remainder of her estate in Yetminster, she left to her son-in-law, Thomas Bartlett. Her servant, Joney Hooper, was left £10 per year for life.

Some mystery surrounds her elder son, Thomas. He appears to have become a black sheep. Her son, William, is charged with paying his brother 12s per week (just about twice the weekly wage of a labourer at that time). But Christian, obviously, does not trust Thomas, for she states categorically, that should he in any way mortgage or promise the money before he receives it, then payment will cease forthwith. Payment will also cease should Thomas make any threats against William.

Two years later, she added a Codicil reducing the payment to 9s weekly and re-iterating the consequences to him should he in any way threaten or obstruct William in the enjoyment of his inheritance.

It would be interesting to know just what kind of life he was leading. A spendthrift? A gambler? A drunkard? And what had caused his downfall. William Vincent lived on in Yetminster, at 'Slades', the present Rock House. On 20 December 1820, he wrote his Will. He bequeathed Atrium Farm to his niece, Alicia Oldfield Phippard, subject to the payment of £50 per year to his brother, Thomas. He then revokes the £50 and reduces the payment to £40.

To his nephew, William Oldfield Bartlett, he left "the tenement where I now live" and land called Downs.

To nephew, Charles Oldfield Bartlett, Trendle Mead, 4 acres, subject to the payment of 20s per year to the Poor under the Will of John Reynolds.

To his servant, Daniel White, annuity of £10.

To his servant, Julia Cooper, annuity of £5.

William Vincent died, aged 57, on 8 October 1822.

To return to Arthur Cosens II, who, in 1737 had married Martha Helyar. Between 1745 and 1767 she bore her husband eleven children, of whom four died in infancy. A record only slightly better than that of Arthur's sister, Christian Vincent, six of whose nine children died though only one in infancy. Amongst rich and poor alike, infant mortality was high, due, no doubt, to inadequate nurture and the incidence of infectious diseases against which there was no immunity. The death of a child was accepted, everyone knew, that, in a couple of years it would be replaced by another. As one woman remarked: I was 'baby' three times.

In 1764, when he had six children and a baby, Arthur turned his attention to the seating arrangements in St. Andrew's Church. He claimed the right for himself and family to occupy pews in the Chancel and for deceased members to be buried under the Chancel. He based his claim on his occupancy of Hardings and Grimsteads. The Vicar opposed him but he put his case before the Dean who ordered that his claims be published in Church. The Dean's Consistorial Court sat to hear the objections of the Churchwardens, John Hewlett, Thomas Bellamy and John Wiltshire and any other inhabitants, but none came to object, so the Dean confirmed the Cosens family in their possession of the pews. Cosens was an influential man in the parish, so maybe the objectors thought better of their protest. But one can see their point, the pews occupied the greater part of the small Chancel, leaving room for persons to pass in single file only.

The Dean also granted Cosen's claim to a vault beneath the Chancel, provided the Vicar was paid his dues each time the vault was opened up for a burial.

On 17 September 1768, Arthur II made his Will, not a moment too soon, just over a month later, he was in his grave in the Chancel and the fee of 6s 8d was duly paid to the Vicar. His eldest child, Arthur III was 23 years old and the three youngest but eleven, nine and four. His wife, Martha, was insane.

It must have been a worried man, already sick, who, nevertheless, was able to formulate the provisions he wished to make for his wife and children. Martha's mental illness may have commenced with the birth of her last child, Elizabeth, born and buried in April of the previous year.

That the welfare of his wife and minor children might be ensured, Arthur appointed as Trustees John Chafie of Sherborne, gent., Thomas Melmoth of Yetminster, shopkeeper, and his two eldest children, Arthur Cosens and Mary Cosens. His estate was extensive, embracing Minsons in Symondsbury in the possession of Richard Knight, lands and tenements in Cattistock, Chilfrome and Longburton and the manor

170

of Hilfield as well as his holding in Yetminster. His estates were to be shared between his four sons, Arthur III receiving one of the Yetminster properties. His three daughters were left £500 apiece at age 21 or marriage.

He left 10 gns. to his late servant, Thomas Melmoth and certain items to his children:

*To Arthur: silver decanter with cypher and little silver tankard. All the furniture belonging to the Grey Room which I lately built.*

*To John: largest silver tankard which was mine before marriage and my silver watch.*

*To Mary: my two large fluted candle-sticks with the snuffers and stand. The mourning diamond ring which I had for Mr Helyar.*

*To Martha: my 2 silver porringers and the mourning diamond ring I had for my mother and all other my mourning rings whatsoever.*

*The rest of plate, mine before marriage or purchased since, to Arthur together with all my other rings and gold watch and all my old pieces of coin, my books, my bureau in the study and bureau and book-case in the hall.*

*Remainder of goods, chattels and personal estate to aforementioned Trustees for benefit of wife, Martha Cosens. Should his wife recover her senses and be capable of managing her own affairs, then Trustees to hand over to her.*

Arthur Cosens III inherited heavy responsibilities: a mother insane, two sisters approaching marriageable age and four younger siblings to be educated.

Martha Cosens lived for another 30 years, she died in Dorchester and was buried in Yetminster 9 October 1798 aged 78. The Chancel floor was opened for her burial at a fee of £5 5s 0d. It is not known if she was living permanently in Dorchester or visiting her son. Charles Cosens was certainly living in High West Street in 1830 and may have been there earlier.

In 1777, Martha, sister to Arthur III married Edward Iliff of Littleham, and, presumably returned with him to Devon.

171

John Cosens went to London, in 1783 he was a Surgeon Apothecary in Bloomsbury.

Robert Cosens matriculated at Wadham College and received his B.A. in 1779. On 14 January 1784, he was installed as Vicar of Longburton, a position he held until he died, unmarried, in 1826.

Charles Cosens married and had a son Robert, b. 1820. In 1836, Robert matriculated at Pembroke College, Oxford and was awarded his B.A. in 1840. On 28 March 1842, he was installed as Vicar of Longburton. He married Penelope, daughter of Col. Henry King of West Hall, Folke and had a son and a daughter. He died in 1867 aged 48.

Throughout the years, Arthur III, like his Cosens and Vincent forebears, was active in the Parish. He was also hospitable, the Sherborne Mercury reported:

*25 Dec 1809. Arthur Cosens of Yetminster gave an excellent dinner to 140 inhabitants of Yetminster. The day was spent "with great hilarity and good humour". The health of the donor and God save the King with many other toasts were drunk for three times three.*

Somewhat late in life, on 3 June 1802, Arthur III married Elizabeth Jeffrey.

On 24 June 1810, the Mercury published the following:

*Arthur Cosens of Yetminster, aged 65. In the morning he attended the service in Wells Cathedral where he was on a visit to a near relative and, whilst at dinner, awful to relate, fell from his chair and instantly expired. In the year 1807, he was called to fill the high and important office of Sherriff of Dorset, the duties of which he ably and honourably discharged. In private life he was honest and sincere and much respected as an honest man.*

His body was brought back to Yetminster and buried on 2 July 1810. There is an elaborate memorial on the Chancel wall to an honest man who was "High Sherriff during the contested Election of 1807 and discharged the duties thereof with honour to himself and satisfaction to the County."

His widow survived him for 22 years. She was buried 16 October 1832, aged 74 years.

Upon the death of Arthur Cosens, the Yetminster estate passed to his brother Robert, and, after his decease, to his brother, Charles. Arthur's widow, Elizabeth, having the right to remain in occupation for her life. At the White Hart, on 3 August 1864, the mansion house and lands in Yetminster and Leigh were auctioned. By this time, Hardings was derelict and had been pulled down.

At the time of the 1840 Tithe Apportionment, Robert Cosens had let the land, variously, to Ann Brake, Peter Brake, Elizabeth Edmonds, Simon Cox, William Loveless and John Stephens. The house he let to Ann and Eliza Brake.

So ended the Cosens connection with Yetminster.

———

At the time of the 1840 Tithe Apportionment, the Rev. Thomas Oldfield Bartlett held 90 acres of land in Yetminster, Ford House and Bridge House, all let to John Shorey and Henry Meech. His brother, Charles, held another 10 acres and the Crown Inn, let to John Shorey. One hundred acres out of the total acreage of 1,460 acres.

### Field names of the holding

| | |
|---|---|
| *Thorney Coppice* | *Little Common* |
| *In Common* | *Northfield* |
| *Villhays* | *Old Orchard* |
| *Thorns* | *Hamcroft* |
| *Little Hamcroft* | *Red Gate* |
| *Broad Moor* | *Little Moor* |
| *Little Trendle Mead* | *Great Trendle Mead* |
| *Lower Staple Cross* | *Copse Ground* |
| *Earthpit* | *Dry Close* |
| *Little Copse Ground* | *Staple Cross* |
| *Peasehill* | *Spring Mead* |
| *Lower Spring Mead* | *Easterfield* |
| *Reads Orchard* | *Kennell Orchard* |
| *Sycamore Ground* | *Whittles Orchard* |

Robert Cosens held 80 acres.

### Field names of the holding

| | |
|---|---|
| *Beckerswell* | *Hardings Common* |
| *Coles* | *Gallytrams* |
| *Chetenhill* | *Bowbridge Mead* |
| *Blacklands* | *Lower Stoneylands* |
| *Higher Stoneylands* | *Stakeford Mead* |
| *Furzy Close Mead* | *Furzy Close* |
| *Higher Horsehouse* | *Lower Horsehouse* |
| *Horsehouse Mead* | *Willis's Field* |
| *Old's Mead* | *Home Orchard* |
| *Staple Cross* | *Higher Staple Cross* |
| *Three Acres* | *Higher Orchard* |

## Population of Yetminster and surrounding villages

| | *1801* | *1851* | *1901* |
|---|---|---|---|
| Melbury Osmond | 335 | 364 | 249 |
| Melbury Bubb with Woolcombe | 107 | 157 | 86 |
| Chetnole | 168 | 227 | 215 |
| Leigh | 300 | 440 | 313 |
| Batcombe with Newland | 155 | 227 | 98 |
| Yetminster | 479 | 666 | 551 |
| Ryme Intrinseca | 123 | 216 | 165 |

# Queen Street/Church Lane

This is a short lane, running from the foot-path known as Grope Lane, in a northerly direction to join the High Street nearly opposite the "White Hart". At the lower end, to the east, stood a public well, and, it is believed, the stocks.

The houses on the west side are the older, all had crofts running down to Back Lane/Melbury Road.

The first is "Everards", one of the few properties which retained, over the centuries, the name of an earlier occupier. It is unfortunate, that, only quite recently, the name was changed, first to Rose Cottage, then to The Muntings.

This cottage has a cross-passage, an unheated central room and two rooms to the north and south respectively. An R.C.H.M. Survey of 1939 states: ". . . the north room has cross-chamfered ceiling beams and an open fire-place with a chamfered bressemer and a fragment of wall-painting in the N.E. corner."

No trace of this wall-painting remains today.

To the west of the fire-place, in an unusual position, on the west wall, rose a newel stair-case, the wall has been pushed out to accomodate it.

A crucial feature, clearly visible from the street, is a relict wall-plate beneath the present eaves on the east. This is broken on the south side of the cross-passage so that it runs on a lower level over the cross-passage and north room and indicates that the house was of two builds. It may even have been single-storey with an attic.

We may suppose that it was the home of the Everard family who left three excepts. On the other hand, when Thomas Allambridge bought the property in 1738, it is referred to in the Manor Court Record as Church Lane Living.

The Muntins formerly Everards

The three excepts were:

1573 Robert Everard to son, Alexander
he excepted, the hall, the chamber over the hall, the chamber within the hall, two milk-houses and kitchen.

1604 Alexander Everard to son William
he excepted the hall, the chamber over the hall, the buttery, the milk-house within the buttery, the cock-loft, kitchen.

1625 Agnes Bartlett to son John Everard
the hall, the loft over the hall, the buttery within the hall, the milk-house, the cock-loft, kitchen

The 1635 "Ship Money" lists Ambrose Evered and John Evered. The Protestation Return of 1641 names John Evered. The Register of Ryme Intrinseca records in 1654 William Payne of Whettle, Somerset, age 30

176

= Edyth Everard, daughter of John Everard of Yetminster, age 19. They were married before Walter Foy, Esq. J.P. This was during the Commonwealth when marriage in Church was not accepted.

An Inventory, dated 5 October 1592, relating to John Evered, blacksmih, has survived. We may, perhaps, assume that this John and Alexander were contemporaries, brothers, possibly. So John may have been living elsewhere.

The Willl of John Evered, yeoman, dated 26 April 1680, names his wife, Mary and daughters, Edith Paine, Anne Chaffie, Mary Furber, Jane Oldis and Joan Chisman. He left them 5s each with 1s each to his grand-children.

John was buried on 14 May 1680. note that his eldest daughter was the Edith who married William Payne in 1654. It is probable, that the Everard name died out with John.

The next known occupier was Ralph Gillingham, in 1720, the property passed from him to Edward Harris jun. In 1738 it passed to Thomas Allambridge, and, upon his death in 1745 to his son, John. Soon after, John himself died, unmarried, and it was inherited by the Feaver family. John's sister, Ann, had married George Feaver. The property remained in the hands of the Feaver family, though they never lived there, until 1803 when Catherine Feaver of Woolland sold to William Edwards. In 1763, he had married Judith, daughter of James and Mary Hayward of the Blackamoor's Head. William was also an innkeeper, and, presumably, retired to Everards. He died there in 1817 and Judith the following year. Both were in their seventies. Judith left the property to her son, William in London. In 1839, William Edwards, now styling himself "gentleman", of 5, Globe Terrace, Mile End, sold to Daniel Penny, banker, of Sherborne for £200. This was the very year in which he had refused to help his brother, Peter, to get to Tasmania!

The Penny family were to own and let Everards until 1959 when it was sold to Bertram Jesty, builder, of Ryme for £1,300. The croft reached west to Back Lane/Melbury Road. Jesty cut this off, made an entrance to the north of the house and built three bungalows. It was awkwardly contrived.

The next owner was a Mrs. Haddock, followed, in 1962, by Mr. & Mrs Scutt, a Mrs Stileman in 1970, L. J. Sutton in 1978 and Mr and Mrs J. Carter in 1983.

During the Penny ownership, the house was rented, for three generations, to the Foot family. The south room was the 'parlour' and the north room the kitchen/living room, from here, the spiral stair-case still gave access to the upper floor, it was not until after 1959 that the present stairs in the south room were installed.

In 1573, when Robert Everard was making his except to his son, Alexander, Elizabeth I had been on the throne of England for fifteen years. The old cottage has seen over four hundred years of history, what stories it could tell of those who have passed through its doors!

## Spring Cottage

The history of the three cottages next to Everards is very much mixed up with that of "Fairings". But the first, Spring Cottage, in the 1870s, was owned by Henry John Spencer, a retired grocer. He lived alone and appears to have suffered greatly with an injured leg. At one time, he allowed John Read to live rent-free in the cottage and to take in lodgers, on condition that Read's wife attended upon him. The cottage is very small, it is difficult to imagine just where the lodgers went!

When Spencer died, in 1878, his Will left everything to his niece Mary Ann Spencer. A letter dated 1877, states that Miss Spencer has been admited to a Lunatic Asylum. The Vicar, George Southwell, had been appointed Executor. Accordingly, he wrote to Fisherton House, the Asylum in Salisbury, to have this fact confirmed. Southwell knew his parishioners (and human nature)! He sent the letter to Fooks, the solicitor in Sherborne, to have it posted there, because, he said: ". . . our Post Office here, and it would be just the same at Leigh, would probably be spreading abroad all kinds of reports for village gossip."

Poor Miss Spencer! On 29 December 1878 she wrote a letter to Miss Louise Loveless of Ivy Cottage. She paints a graphic picture of life at Fisherton House, as she sees it. The doctors are rogues and cheats, the nurses big, over-fed hussies. She is afraid to eat anything for she is convinced she is being drugged, her hair is white, her teeth falling out, and, after two years, her clothes are falling apart. She has no money, though she knows her house and furniture have been sold. To get away from the prying eyes of the nurses she is writing the letter in the summer-house, where, understandably, since it is December, she is

178

half-frozen. She writes: "I cannot feel sorry to hear the poor old man has gone, I have no doubt now, that he was for years dosed and made irritable just as I have been, which accounted for his strange and unnatural behaviour for years to myself and those about him, it was not in his nature to be like that."

H. J. Spencer's goods were sold at auction in 78 lots and realised £23 16s 3d. All lots were sold except for 48 bottles of the sauce which he had, apparently, invented when he had his grocer's shop.

John Ring was paid £6 7s 6d for Spencer's funeral, not a great increase on costs in the 18c.

The Account included:

| | | | |
|---|---|---|---|
| *Elm coffin and shroud* | £3 | 0s | 0 |
| *Pall* | | 5s | 0d |
| *Bearers 5s each* | 1 | 10s | 0d |
| *Bell & grave at Chetnole* | 1 | 10s | 0d |
| *Clerk's fees at Yetminster* | | 2s | 6d |

## Fairings

This property probably dates from the early 17 c. It is thatched with mullioned windows, and, over the years, has been altered. Behind, on the south side of the plot, were the outbuildings and the croft ran down to Back Lane, the present Melbury Road. Last century, a small tin chapel was erected in Melbury Road, a bungalow has now been built on the site, plus another bungalow to the north. Thus, the ends of all the crofts on the west side of Queen Street have been developed.

The first mention of this property is probably to be found in the Will of John Allambridge, dated 1746. He appoints his nephew, John Beere, to be Lord's next tenant to his roofless tenement in Yetminster which "my father purchased of Mr. Munden." John Beere was not admitted until 1750 when he paid the Fine of £16 which was due to the Manor Court.

This ties in with an entry in the Court Book of Yetminster Secunda dated 1768. William Clarke, gent. by direction of Charles Francis and Elizabeth his wife (late Elizabeth Beer, widow) passed "all that roofless tenement in Yetminster" to the use of William Warry, tanner.

179

Fairings, Yetminster

The tanner, William Warry III died in 1801. In his Will, he left the property to his son, George Warry, with the proviso that his mother was to live there for her life. William had left Cross Farm and the tannery to his son, John, so presumably, he was providing a home for his widow. She, too died within the year and it is not mentioned again until sold in 1822 by George Warry to Richard Dodge for £250. It is referred to in documentation as "part Beers, now, or late, in occupation of ?Thorne". If this name is indeed Thorne, the only mention of the name in Yetminster is in 1788 when Timothy Thorne of Dorchester married Susanna Besant of Yetminster.

George Warry himself never lived there. He was a solicitor, firstly, in London at New Inn and, subsequently in Sherborne where he was in partnership with Peter Batson. Their Office was in Abbey Road, and, George lived at the Manor House in Newland, the present Council Offices.

Richard Dodge died in 1850 and left the property by Will to his nephew, John Minchinton of Bradford Abbas. Two years later, he sold to William Groves, the younger, miller for £400. Groves remained there for only seven years before he sold to James Read. The latter died, intestate, in 1865 and Mary Ann Read inherited. In 1878, she sold to Albert Ryall, baker, for £425, and, in 1897, his widow, Mary Ann Ryall, sold to William John Pardy Foot for £650. In 1903, another baker, Arthur George Baron, bought for £600 and, three years later, sold to yet another baker, Samuel Rowland of Sturminster Newton.

The bakers continue: Eli Turner, Fred Cobb, Herbert Clement Vowles. By this time, the price had risen to £900.

Albert Ryall was granted enfranchisement. The southern end of Fairings, now part of the house, was originally a separate cottage made from a former carpenter's shop. When Mary Ann Ryall sold in 1897, she kept this cottage for herself, but no garden, so stipulated that she should have access for coal, the use of the pump and the right to bury her night-soil in the orchard.

The bakery was in the building which is presently a garage and continued there for 60 years. Vowles sold in 1939 fo £1,100. In just over one hundred years, the property had quadrupled in value.


## Rock House/Slades

This is a substantial house with a cellar and a large garden on the corner of Church Lane/High Street.

From the early part of the 18 c, John Haines of Cattistock, clerk, was Lord of the Rectory Manor, or Parsonage, which he purchased of the widow of John Richardson. He also purchased Slades of Lewis Norman, Slades was part of Yetminster Prima. There is no record of the death of Norman, we know that he was Overseer of the Poor in 1723 when the Vestry agreed "out of the Poor Stock to pay Mr. Buckland £3 of the £5 he demands for curing of William Moor who was much hurted and

*By direction of the Executors of the late Mr. William Jerrard.*

# Freehold Country Properties,

IN THE PICTURESQUE, HEALTHY VILLAGE OF YETMINSTER,
OVERLOOKING THE BLACKMORE VALE,

## DORSET.

### Lot 1.

# ROCK HOUSE, YETMINSTER,

**A Commodious Residence** of mellowed stone, standing well above the road, and only a short walk from Station, Post Office or Church. **It is built** on the **solid rock,** in which is cut dry cellarage, on the ground floor are **Entrance Hall, Dining-Room,** 17-ft. by 12-ft. 6-in., including the semi-circular bow window, **Drawing-Room,** 15-ft. by 12-ft. 9-in., **Capital Kitchen,** 16-ft. 6-in. by 13-ft. 6-in., fitted with a Scotch Grate in a tile setting which has the appearance of a good register-grate, with convenience for cooking, Second Kitchen, Large Pantry, Lavatory.

**Oak Principal Staircase,** Servants' Staircase, **Four Bedrooms** (two being 16-ft. 6-in. by 14-ft. and 17-ft. by 15-ft. 3-in., including the bow window), and a Room which is admirably adapted for bathroom and lavatory. 3 Large Attics. Detached Coal Store to hold truck, cool larder and E.C. **The Yeovil Corporation's water supply** can be laid to house, in addition there is a large galvanised rain-water cistern and good well with pump.

**A stone and tiled Building,** 20-ft. by 11-ft., with good approach from road, would make a **capital Garage** there are also a **two-stall Stable** with loft, Cow-shed and other useful outbuildings.

**A large Garden** of **rich deep soil** planted with several fruit trees and having a glass-house, also a **well-stocked Apple Orchard.**

*Rock House with its Outbuildings and a large amount of Ground, forms a pleasant Freehold Home for a family, or it would make an excellent small Hunting-Box, most conveniently situate for either the Blackmore Vale or Cattistock countries.*

Having been in the late owner's occupation, **Vacant Possession can be given on completion.**

### Lot 2.

# A BLACKSMITH'S SHOP,

With **Plot of Ground,** let to Mr. Gould on a yearly Christmas tenancy at a rent of £8 per annum, Landlord paying rates amounting to about £1 per annum.

**Lot 3.**

# A neat stone and slated
# Dwelling-House,

In excellent order, situate in **Church Lane, Yetminster,** containing Entrance Passage, 2 Sitting-Rooms, Kitchen with range, **3 Bedrooms,** Garden at back and front. Let to Mr. Causier on a quarterly tenancy at £12 per annum, tenant paying rates in addition.

*This Lot is sold subject to the right of the occupier of Lot 4 as well as of the cottage now occupied by Mrs. Jerrard to take water from the well on this lot, the cost of keeping the pump in order to be shared by the respective parties.*

**Lot 4.**

# A Picturesque old Stone Cottage,

With partly-thatched and partly-galvanised roof, adjoining Lot 3 in Church Lane, Yetminster, and containing Sitting-Room, Kitchen, **3 Bedrooms,** boxroom, washhouse with copper, and fuel store. Garden at front and back. Let to Mrs. Park at a rental amounting to £8 9s. 0d. per annum (paid by instalments of 13/- every four weeks), tenant paying rates in addition.

## HY. DUKE & SON

ARE FAVOURED WITH INSTRUCTIONS TO OFFER THE ABOVE

### FREEHOLD PROPERTIES

FOR SALE BY AUCTION AT

# THE "WHITE HART" INN,
# YETMINSTER,

On *TUESDAY, OCTOBER 21st,* at 3 p.m.,

Subject to the Common Form Conditions of the Dorset Law Society and such special conditions as shall be then and there produced or in the meantime may be seen at the Offices of—

*MESSRS. ANDREWS, SON & HUXTABLE,*

*SOLICITORS,*

*DORCHESTER and WEYMOUTH,*

or of the AUCTIONEERS, DORCHESTER.

LING, PRINTER, DORCHESTER.

Sale of Rock House in 1913

D.R.O. PE/YET: SC 1/7/5

183

wounded by Mr Norman's plow and dung-put." In Dorset, the 'plow' is the team of horses, not the implement which is known as a 'zull'.

In 1756, John Haines wrote his Will. He had two young sons at Oxford, both intending to be clergymen. He left his books and manuscripts to be divided between them, £500 to John and £2,000 to Nathan at age 21. The Rectory Manor and Slades he left to John and lands in Oxfordshire and Warwickshire to Nathan.

In 1822, John Haines jun. died and left Slades to his daughter, Harriet Haines, six years later, she sold to Edward Herbert Fitzherbert for £420. During this seventy odd years, several persons were involved with Slades, some as mortgagees. In 1794, Thomas Webb of Sherborne passed it to Edward Hayes jun., currier. He mortgaged in 1803 to James Baker of Cattistock for £200, two years later, there is a new mortgagee, Vaughan Jones. In 1811 Edward Hayes died intestate and Vaughan Jones, Daniel Basant, gent., Mary Hayes, widow and Richard Andrews and his wife, Mary pass it to William Vincent.

Richard Andrews is described as 'plasterer' but he was, in fact, landlord of the White Hart and had married the sister of Edward Hayes.

William Vincent was unmarried and the son of John Vincent and Christian Cosens of Ford House. He died in 1823 and left Slades to his nephew, William Oldfield Bartlett, son of his sister, Ann and Thomas Bartlett of Wareham. In 1831, William Oldfieeld Bartlett, clerk, of Canford, sold to William Culliford for £450. In 1840, Culliford sold for the same amount, to Richard Dodge, baker, who already held Fairings, next door.

The next, known, owner, is George Hayward and his wife, Georgiana. George died in 1890 and his wife in 1906, their two sons emigrated to New Zealand, one daughter lived on there until her death, the other married and left Yetminster.

Until c 1880, there were probably just two properties on the east side of Church Lane, The Blackamoor's Head and the house on the corner of High Street, presently known as The Laurels. c 1880, two cottages were built, end-on to the lane, just behind The Laurels, possibly on part of the ground of this property. Thomas Ryall occupied the inner cottage and called it "Briar House." This and The Blackamoor's Head have been dealt with elsewhere.

In 18 c Court records, The Laurels is referred to as Balls and Daggles, references to either name are sparse. A Mr. G. Ball died in 1713 and a Mrs Ball in 1739. Nicholas Daggle died in 1729, his wife, Gertrude having pre-deceased him in 1717. In 1742, Thomas Daggle died and the property passed to his daughter, Mary. Six years later, it went to Mr. George Brown in right of his wife, possibly, Brown had married Mary Daggle. In 1765, George Brown of Sutton Waldron, weaver, sold the property to Jeremiah Cole, clothier, of Fontmell Magna. There is a note in the Court Book, that permission was given for Cole to devise his Tenement for any number of years. He had bought it as an investment, normally, the rule was that holders should live on their properties. In 1785, Jeremiah Cole died and his son, also Jeremiah, succeeded, he passed it on to Isaac Cole, and, in 1797, Charles Bull Hart, mortgagee, and Isaac Cole pass it back to Jeremiah Cole of Fontmell Magna. At that time it is described as 'late in occupation of George Brake, now Charles Brake.

# The Ryall Family

Thomas and Amelia Hayward's only child, Theophilus, married Mary Elizabeth Ryall, known as "Polly". This Ryall family originated in Lillington and Thornford. By the latter part of the 18 c, they were staunch Methodists.

Of all the documents studied in the course of research, Wills often prove to be the most revealing and indicative of the character of the testator, particularly, perhaps, in the case of women.

Here is the Will of Alice Ryall of Lillington, daughter of Nicholas and Alice Ryall, made in 1734.

*In the Name of God, Amen. I, Alice Ryal of the parish of Lillington in the County of Dorset, being of great age, but of disposing mind and memory, thanks to Almighty God for the same, do make and ordain this my last Will and Testament in manner and form following, revoking all other Wills by me formerly made.*

*In the first place, I commend my soul into the hands of Almighty God hoping for eternal bliss through the merits of my Blessed Saviour and Redeemer, Jesus Christ and I desire that my body may be decently buried in the churchyard of Lillington aforesaid, under my father's tomb-stone.*

*As to my worldly goods which God hath bestowed upon me, I give and bequeath them as followeth: I give to Katharine, the wife of John Wiltshire of Stalbridge in the County of Dorset, yeoman, the sum of twenty pounds and my bed which I usually lye on and the bedstead and bed-clothes thereunto belonging, excepting sheets and pillow-biers. Also, I give to the said Katharine Wiltshire my warming-pan and great crock and my gold ring whose posey is 'God have Peace, my Love encrease', together with the third part of my wearing linnen, such as shifts and caps to be equally divided betwixt her and two others to be under-named at the discretion of my neighbour, Jane Shirring of Lillington, widow.*

Item *I give to my kinswoman, Rose Ryal, who now lives with me, the sum of twenty pounds and my best suit of wearing apparel and one of the two remaining gold rings, of which she shall have the choice, together with one other third of my wearing linnen to be equally divided at the discretion of my neighbour, Jane Shirring, abovesaid.*

Item *I give to my nephew, William Mitchel of Whitfield in the parish of Lillington, yeoman, the sum of twenty pounds. and I give to his daughter my third remaining gold ring.*

Item *I give to my brother's son, William Ryal of Whitchurch in Dorset, one shilling.*

Item *I give to Grace, the wife of Hugh Orchard of Chediock in Dorset, yeoman, five pounds.*

Item *I give to William Shirring, now labourer in the service of my nephew, Thomas Mitchel of Lillington, twenty shillings.*

Item *I give to Mary Ryal of Lillington, aforesaid, my best flannel whittle and the remaining third part of my wearing apparel to be equally divided at the discretion of the said Jane Shirring.*

Lastly *All the rest of my moneys, goods of all kinds, bonds, bills and other debts which remain after my own debts, funeral expenses and Legacyes are paid, I give and bequeath to my nephew, Thomas Mitchel of Lillington, yeoman, whom I constitute the sole executor of this my last Will and Testament desiring him to cause my body to be decently buried according to the directions given above and to entertain and present my neighbours who shall attend my funeral in an handsome manner. And I likewise desire him to be kind and helpful to Mary Ryal above-mentioned and it is my Will that he give my chest to Katharine Wiltshire, above mentioned. I publish and declare this to be my last Will and Testament, and, in witness thereof I have hereunto set my hand and seal the third day of August in the year of Our Lord one thousand seven hundred and thirty-four.*

| | |
|---|---|
| *In the prescence of*<br>*John Shuttleworth, clerk* | *The mark of Alice Ryal* |
| *The mark of Joan Jefferey*<br>*The mark of Mary Whiffen* | *Probate: 19 Jan. 1736/7.* |

Nicholas Ryall, father to Alice, died in the summer of 1693 leaving a wife, Alice, a son William and daughters Elizabeth, Alice, Elinor and Grace Michell, widow. He also left grandchildren, unnamed.

John and William Ryall took the Inventory of his goods and the value came to the considerable sum of £360. The livestock accounted for £204. As well as six owen, presumably used for ploughing, he owned four horses. He was certainly one of the wealthier yeomen of the district. Alice, with her sister Elinor, was appointed executrix of their father's Will. She must have been a mature woman at that time and outlived all her siblings. Despite her "great age" Alice had clearly given much thought to the disposal of her belongings and must have been a kind and delightful person. She had probably spent the whole of her long life in this tiny village.

Many people of quite modest means owned gold rings and Alice had three. Rings with "poseys" seem to have been popular, too . . . Jane Sherring must have had her ingenuity tested to the full when it came to dividing Alice's wearing apparel into three equal parts. How thoughtful of Alice to request her nephew to be "kind and helpful" to Mary Ryal. Mary, perhaps, had not been blessed with great intelligence, or was she simply aged, frail and forgetful? Finally, Alice wishes the neighbours to *enjoy* her funeral, being regaled with refreshments and presents – the usual white gloves and hat-bands, no doubt.

Once the Ryalls embraced Methodism, they tended not to have their children baptised in the Parish Church, and tracing them becomes a little difficult. Thomas Ryall, 1773–1849, may have been descended from Alice's nephew, William. On 19 February 1805, Thomas Ryall=Mary Chapman, daughter of Richard and Ann Chapman of Lillington. Until about 1812, they farmed at Higher Farm, Gussage St. Michael. There may have been a good reason for their choice of Gussage, it was nearer to Blandford where there was a Methodist place of worship.

Thomas and Mary had issue:

*Rebecca 1806–1876.*
*Thomas 1808–1890*
*Susanna 1813–1904.*
*John 1814–1856 = Emily dau. of Esau Critchell of Batcombe.*
*Samuel 1820–1882 = Elizabeth Martin.*

By 1830 the Ryalls had moved to Sherborne, where Thomas established himself as a maltster in Long Street. In 1837, he moved to Bowden. On 22 May 1837, he inserted a notice in the local paper:

*"Thomas Ryall, snr., maltster, respectfully informs his friends and the public generally, that, though he has removed from Sherborne, he resides within a short distance of it and that they can still be supplied with malt and hops of the best quality on application to his daughters, Rebecca and Susanna Ryall, straw-bonnet makers, Cheap Street, Sherborne. Thomas Ryall returns his sincere thanks to his friends for their past favours and assures them that it shall be his constant endeavour to give them satisfaction both in article and price."*

The straw-bonnet shop was situated at the upper end of Cheap Street, possibly one of the small properties opposite the Dentists. Later that year, 1837, Ryall's land in Sherborne was sold by Auction at The King's Arms. In 1843, authorisation was granted to distrain on the goods of Thomas Ryall for the recovery of £30. This sum was due to William Fooks as Receiver, as rent for the estate of James Barrett, deceased. Thomas died in 1849. He, his wife and all his children except John, were buried at the Methodist Church in Sherborne.

In 1833, a mare owned by Thomas Ryall, jun. met with an accident. She became jammed between a wall and a gate-post at Mead Gate. She was found the next morning by a dairyman arriving to milk his cows. Although in a deplorable state, Ryall insisted on putting her on a hurdle and dragging her home. Needless to say, the unfortunate animal did not survive the night.

In 1851, Thomas was in Batcombe working as a farm bailiff. His brother, John, was also in Batcombe, having married Emily, daughter of Esau Critchell of that place. On the Census, John described himself as "local preacher". Very soon, he emigrated with his wife and young family to Wisconsin, continuing to work for the Methodists as a circuit-rider and doing carpentry as a side-line to keep his family. There, in 1856, he died aged 43, leaving Emily to bring up the children, Esau, Mary, Emily and Thomas. This, she did by working as a seamstress. She died in 1894, and, in 1983, her great, great grandchildren, Mary and Lois, paid a visit to Yetminster.

Samuel and Elizabeth Ryall kept a grocer's shop in Charmouth. Only two of their children survived. Mary Elizabeth (Polly) born in 1864 married Theophilus Hayward. Samuel Thomas, born in 1868, in 1897 married Rebecca Collis at Ryme Intrinseca.

About the year 1880, a pair of houses had been erected in Church Lane, Yetminster, on the east side, end-on to the road. An entry in the Vestry Book for 1881 refers to these houses, in the context of rating for the Poor Rate:

*"that the new houses in Church Lane be rated as follows: Thomas Ryall at £3 occupied by himself*

*William Jefford at £2. 10s now in the occupation of Frank Chapple"*

Ryall occupied the inner property and called it 'Briar House'. He was now over 70 years old, and, living with him, was his sister, Susanna, neither had married. Rebecca had died, unmarried, in 1876 and Samuel died in 1882, so they were the last of the family. Thomas was to spend 10 years in Yetminster and Susanna twenty-four. He bought all the property on the east side of Church Lane, the former Blackamoor's Head and cottage adjoining which had belonged to Abraham Donne, he bought from Donne's grandson, John Donne Brake, grocer, son of Peter Brake and his wife, Mary, who was the only child of Abraham Donne. A portion of land, 80 ft.×50 ft., Thomas Ryall gave for the building of a Methodist Manse, the present Red House.

On 4 March 1888, Thomas and Susanna each made a Will.

*Will of Thomas Ryall of Briar House, Yetminster.*

*To Susanna Ryall, premises in Cheap Street, Sherborne in Occupation of William Salter Gillard, tenant.*

*Should Susanna pre-decease him, then house in Cheap Street to "my niece, Mary Elizabeth Hayward" after her death, to children of said niece.*

*After decease of sister, all interest in estate in Yetminster to nephew, Thomas Samuel Ryall.*

*To Thomas Samuel Ryall, after decease of sister, all furniture, plate, linen, china, books, prints, pictures and all personal estate in Yetminster now in occupation of himself and sister.*

Also, "my 26 shares in Sherborne Gas & Coke Co. and shares in London and South West Railway Co., value £295."

Property in Yetminster held jointly with sister to be sold and divided equally between surviving nephews and nieces.

To sister-in-law, widow of late brother Samuel Ryall, annuity of £10 per annum.

Should sister pre-decease him, whole of residuary real, leasehold and personal estate to Edward Broadlake Dingley of Sherborne, gent., nephew Thomas Samuel Ryall and Benjamin Baverstock of Thornford, yeoman, to invest for benefit of nephews and nieces.

Executors: Susanna Ryall, Edward Broadlake Dingley, Thomas Samuel Ryall and Benjamin Baverstock. To each (except sister) £10.

Codicil: dated 17 October 1889.

Re. additional purchase in Yetminster of property adjoining present property, bought of Abraham John Donne Brake, grocer, portion 80 ft. long×50 ft. wide given for Methodist Minister's house.

Interest in said property for life to Susanna Ryall then to nephew, Thomas Samuel Ryall.


## Will of Susanna Ryall

To Mary Elizabeth Hayward £100.

To niece, Emily Ryall, daughter of deceased brother, John Ryall, £50 in consideration of her great care and attention in nursing her mother, Emily Ryall, widow of John Ryall.

To Mary Elizabeth Hayward, property in Cheap Street, Sherborne.

£400 to Trustees, Alfred Dingley of Sherborne, draper, Caleb Ryall of Thornford, yeoman and James Russel of Yetminster, gent. Income to niece, Emily Ryall.

Codicil: dated 8 February 1896.

191

*Dwelling-house, gardens and premises in Yetminster in occupation of Messrs. Stone, Jesty and Guppy to nephew Thomas Samuel Ryall.*

*£50 to new Wesleyan Chapel in Yetminster.*

*To Susan Sarah Brake, if living with me at the time of my death, £40.*

*Furniture and effects to Thomas Samuel Ryall.*

The Dingleys were prominent members of the Methodist Church in Sherborne, as was Benjamin Baverstock who had married a Ryall.

In December 1891, all was not sweetness and light between Haywards and Ryalls. Thomas Ryall had died the previous year, the aged Susanna was still at Briar House. Theophilus and Polly Hayward were living at Sunnyside, Thomas and Amelia Hayward were at Rose Cottage in Chapel Lane. He had developed a heart condition and was far from well but still struggling to keep the shop going. Samuel Thomas Ryall was staying with his Aunt Susanna. He had recently returned from visiting his Cousin Emily in America and now sat down to write to her.

*Yetminster*

*Dec. 21 1891.*

*Dear Cousin Emily,*

*I received your letter just a week ago today, but as Mr. Russell was here at the time, I thought I would hear all I could from him then I could tell you all he wished to be remembered to you. He said that Mrs Russell used to very often speak about the walks that you two used to take. He looks rather worn out, of course, he naturally would after losing his wife.*

*He came on the Friday and stayed until Wednesday following. The Haywards and him are at swordspoint. I do not wonder at it after they found out that he was persuading Uncle against them. They would have had the biggest share if he had not put his head to work. He told me that in the first Will that was made, all this property here was to go to Polly. I was to have had the house in Cheap Street and*

192

*the houses in Bristol Road, Sherborne were to be sold for the rest of the relations. Now the Will is a new one, I am to have all the property here and everything in the house that is specified in the Will and an Inventory. Mr Russell took off everything here so that no one can take a thing out of the house.*

*Polly is to have the house in Cheap Street then it is to go to Dulcie. I am glad that Haywards won't get very much benefit from it. I am to have part of the Gas Shares and R. R. shares. The rest of the property to be sold and divided between the rest of you. Everybody here says it was a good thing Mr Russell was here or else Hayward would have had the biggest share. Mr Hayward is very gracious to me with his shaking hands.*

*Last Monday, Mr. Russell and I drove into Sherborne to see Mr. Bartlett and I had a talk with him, he said that Haywards had not got much money as he had considerable business of his pass through his hands, getting money from him for other people. While in Sherborne, I saw A. Dingley and also a Mr. Cox and I asked them if they knew where I could get work. They told me that Hayward had offered his business for sale and advised me to go and talk with him and ask him his terms and they would tell me whether it was worth it. They said that the goodwill of the business was out of the question altogether nowadays.*

*So, on Friday last, I went to see the Lord of the Manor as they call him here, he said that now he thought he should try and keep it on himself, he had given up part of the journeys into the country and he thought he could manage it. He went on to say that he wished his son could take it on again but his health would not stand it. When his son took it on before and his health failed, he took it back and paid him what he gave for it. He said he thought Uncle would have done more for him. He was very much disappointed because Uncle (Thomas Ryall) had altered his Will and that he should alter his now.*

*Then I fired in. I asked him if that was any part of the business I had asked for. Did he not expect to do more for a son than Uncle a niece and if there were not five more relations that had as much claim on Uncle and Aunt as Polly had. I felt equal for the occasion and I told him I did not care how much he did for his son, that was*

193

*not my business, but that I should look out for my ends as well as I could, and for the other relations abroad. He did get rattled! He hummed, he rubbed his hands and I said Good morning.*

*I think the reason he told me all this was I told him I thought of setting up a business here if he did not want to sell his. He advised me not to, that the competition was very close, there were enough shops here and a lot more objections. I told him they said such things everywhere, I knew I had lots of friends and thought I could have a very nice little business. I really believe I could, if I had a shop set up next to him, you cannot hear one single person that has a good word for him or his son, even his own nieces and nephews talk about them.*

*The Sunday before last, Mr. Thomas, the minister, was here to dinner and we were talking about the Chapel. I thought it was just comfortable and he thought it was hot, so we all passed our opinions.*

*Monday morning, I went down to Polly's. She was out in the kitchen so he called her she came in and just said, Good morning. Then she went into the parlour, I could see there was something the matter, so I walked in. She asked me how I liked Mr. Thomas and I told her, Very well. Then she spoke about its being warm, I told her I had a talk with Mr. Thomas yesterday about it and that we were two against two up at Aunt's. So she says that if I had been used to fresh air I would have thought it was warm and close. The slur way it was said was enough to cross my skin, so I told her I had been used to as much fresh air as she had. She told me she did not want any argument and for me to go out of the door. As I went, she said they did not want me there very soon again, and you bet, I don't go again.*

*I can't see for the life of me what I said that should cause that. I think that Hayward has told them what I said, I do not care as I am right. The next time I saw her, she said, Good morning and so did I. I saw her one evening and she passed the time of day and that was all. I won't speak to her unless she speaks to me. I should like to have a talk with you for an hour, to tell you all I have heard, as I cannot express myself on paper so well.*

*Aunt seems to keep up very well indeed at her age in life, she seems to make a mountain out of nothing that is of any consequence. Mr. Thomas Chapman invited me to spend Christmas Day with him, but I am going to stay home with Aunt.*

194

*Last Thursday, there was an Excursion to Plymouth from Yeovil for five shillings and sixpence return, so Charlie Tribley and myself went. It is a very pretty place, a person could spend a week there and then not see all the sights of interest. We went to the top of the old Eddystone Lighthouse and out on the Pier and through the Royal Naval Yard, saw two second-class war ships being built. I also called on Libbie's uncle, he seemed to be pleased to hear about them. His wife took us up and gave us wine and biscuits and asked me all questions concerning them and treated us royally. I enjoyed the day very much.*

*My skates are either in with my tools or else down in the box in the cellar with the plane, I forget which. I hope that Tom is better by this time, I only wish he could take a trip over here where he would only have to eat and sleep, the same as I am doing. Today and yesterday are cold and frosty days like winter but there is no snow yet.*

*Now this is a supposition which none of us can tell anything about: suppose Aunt should die while I am here and the Will is not altered between this and that, which it cannot be legally as it is a joint Will, I should come in for this house and its contents. Do you think any of you could come over if I paid half your fare, that is paid it one way and you paid it the other. I should not know what to do with all the things there are here and, perhaps, you would like to have something for a remembrance. Of course, it is not for the value of any one thing.*

*I would like you to see that either of us did not get any more than is allotted to us, it would be satisfaction to me. Of course, any one of us may be gone before Aunt, we cannot tell and I suppose it is not right for me to say such a thing, but, it happened to cross my mind when I heard how things were left.*

*I am very glad to hear that you are having such a good time visiting your friends. You see, it was a good job for you when I came away, now you have not get to got up and get a breakfast for anyone but yourself.*

*Aunt has just come downstairs, I asked if she had got anything to say. Tell her that I am neither dead nor alive, I am cold. She is knelt down by the fire calling for her dear, oh dear, another dear and laugh! She wanted to go out on the cistern and wash out some*

195

*handkerchiefs this morning, but we would not let her. She says I am a naughty chap. She wishes you one and all to have a Happy New Year and says you know I am a rascal.*

*If the sea freezes up, Aunt and I are going to skate over and see you all. Aunt just tells you that I am a regular thief for sugar!*

*I now must close. Oh dear, says Aunt, with her mouth open yawning!*

*Hoping to hear from you soon. I remain,*

*Your affectionate cousin,*

*S. T. Ryall*

*P.S. Aunt says she will write when it is warmer as she has not got much circulation of blood to keep her hands warm.*

*I just told Aunt she was good-looking and she said I was telling a story!*

For this letter, the author is indebted to Lois Greenwood, her grandfather, John Greenwood married Mary Ryall, sister to Emily to whom the letter is addressed.

The Ryalls in England certainly kept in touch with those in America and, at some time, Emily paid a visit to Yetminster. It is sad that there should have been such friction between Ryalls and Haywards.

And all over money.

Susanna Ryall died on 8 March 1904 aged 90 years. With the rest of her family (except John, who died in America) she lies buried at the Methodist Church in Sherborne.

# Chapel Lane

This short lane cannot have been so named until after the building of the Methodist Chapel. It runs from the lower High Street, round in a horse-shoe bend and back to the High Street again next to Ford House. On the west, ran the high wall of Bower Farm yard. At the bottom of the lane is Lower Farm. To the side of Lower Farm is a foot-path leading to Beer Hackett and this probably contributed to the lane's importance. In the past, foot-paths were vital links between one settlement and another. In an age when only the better-off owned horses, most people walked. Foot-paths provided short-cuts and were, probably, more pleasant to walk on than the rough and pot-holed roads, they had not been churned up by the wheels of carts and the feet of horses or other livestock on the move.

It was not uncommon for a man to walk seven miles, or so, do a day's work and walk home again, in all weathers. Gloving was a popular home occupation for women, and, they, too, would walk several miles to the factory to deliver their work and obtain a fresh supply. Both Yeovil and Milborne Port were local centres for glove-making. So any means of shortening the journey was welcomed.

Part of Beer Hackett is known as Knighton and some of the field names contain the element "spital". Centuries ago, the Knights Hospitallers held land here, this would make an interesting area for research.

Lower Farm, previously known as Ring's Tenement, is thatched of 2½ storeys, and probably of early 17 c date. It has several of the small circular windows which appear to have been popular in Yetminster around that time. The front-door is interesting as it is hinged at the centre as well as at one side. In the 1980s the house changed hands and was found to be in such a deplorable condition that it was pulled down to first floor level and re-built. At that time, the out-buildings were still intact, even the chains in the cow-shed were just as they had been when the last animals had been restrained for the last milking.

Lower Farm, Yetminster.
The date-stone reads:
*Thomas and Sarah Ring 1707*

A date-stone over the door reads T $\overset{R}{S}$ 1707. Thomas Ring and his wife, Sarah. No marriage has been traced for the couple, but, Sarah, wife of Thomas Ring was buried in 1711.

A Thomas Ring buried sons named Thomas in 1690, 1692 and 1693 and Richard, son of Thomas and Sarah Ring was buried in 1704.

Between 1705 and 1709, the Yetminster Secunda Court Book records Thomas Ring exchanging small pieces of land with various individuals: William Harding, William Hodges, John Caffe and Lewis Norman are all mentioned. In 1724, he mortgaged for two years to Thomas Knight of Yeovil. In 1731, the property passed to his son, also Thomas, of Odcombe. This transfer was made on the oaths of Thomas Knight, gent. and William Watts, which would imply that Ring was too old or infirm to attend the Court.

No Will has survived for this Thomas Ring, but, in 1696, Thomas Ring of Yetminster, yeoman made a Will naming his brothers, George, Richard, John, Anthony, sister Elizabeth Ryall of Thornford and numerous nephews and nieces. The bequests are monetary in the main. The document is mutilated. Unfortunately, this mutilation includes the portion where he refers to "my house in Yetminster". At this point, he is concerned with Mary Chubb, widow, of Yetminster. He left her 10 shillings and instructed Thomas Ring of Leigh to pay her 10 shillings yearly during her widowhood. A beneficiary made responsible for paying an annuity was usually the person who had inherited the property. Possibly, this Thomas Ring inherited the farm and took up residence there with his wife, Sarah, perhaps carrying out some refurbishment and proudly erecting the date-stone in 1707.

Susanna Chubb was also left £5. A Mary Chubb died in 1708 and Susanna in 1744. As Executors, Thomas Ring appointed Richard Ring and his sister, Mary, son and daughter of his brother, Tristram Ring. They were to receive 2s 6d each for their pains and Richard also received "my lesser Bible".

The Thomas of the 1696 Will died the following year as did his brother, George, who also left a Will naming the same brothers. The 1697 Inventory of Thomas Ring, yeoman of Yetminster, shows that his possessions were valued at £102, of this amount his seven milking cows were worth £28 and he was owed £40. George Ring of Leigh, husbandman, was worth only £23. 17s. 0d and £10 of this amount was a debt due from a Mr Ryall. But he owned a Bible and some other books.

Thomas Ring's interest in Mary and Susanna Chubb should not be ignored. In 1681, Dame Dorothy Gorge's Charity paid William Chubb £1. 15s. 0d towards his expenses in carrying his daughter to London for the cure of the King's Evil. He was accompanied by Thomas Miller, also taking his daughter and paid £1. 10s 0d.

The King's Evil was scrofula, tuberculosis of the lymph glands, it was believed that it could be cured by the touch of the Monarch.

In 1709, the same Charity apprenticed William Chubb to a barber and George Chubb to a "founder of clockwork", both in London. Is it too fanciful to suppose that George was a diligent apprentice, and that either he, or a descendant was concerned with the manufacture of the Chubb lock and safe?

In 1740, Lower Farm passed from Thomas Ring to Philip Smitheram. He was born in 1710, the son of Andrew and Elizabeth Smitheram. In 1733, Philip married Susanna Hewlett, two years later, she was dead, and, in 1740 he married Elizabeth Hewlett, probably a cousin of Susanna. The Hewlett family were well-off and lived at Caine's Living and Barick's Living at Hamlet. Philip and Elizabeth had three children baptised in Yetminster, Elizabeth in 1741, Sarah in 1744 and Thomas in 1745. The Register records that Thomas, son of Philip and Elizabeth Smitheram was buried in woollen 10 May 1745.

On 3 January 1745, Philip wrote his Will. Probably, he was already feeling ill, since most men left Will making until advancing years advised them it would be prudent so to do.

He was anxious that his debts should be paid and that provision should be made for his young wife and daughters. He appointed his brother-in-law, John Hewlett, Lord's next tenant of his property in trust for his children, except that his wife was to have Woodlands and the two Easterfields, 16 acres in all. His sister, Elizabeth Smitheram, was made co-partner in trust with Hewlett. He instructed that his stock and implements should be sold to pay his debts, and, if insufficient, part of the tenement, also, should be sold, any surplus going to the maintenance of his children.

When his youngest child was aged 21, his sister, Elizabeth, was to sell the tenement and divide the proceeds between the two.

*To his wife, Elizabeth, he left his household goods.*

*To daughter, Elizabeth, one large holland sheet at age 21.*

*To daughter, Sarah, a diamond ring at age 21.*

*To his two sisters and brother-in-law, John Hewlett,1 guinea each to buy a mourning ring.*

*Executors: John Hewlett.          Elizabeth Smitheram.*

Was the holland sheet the "child-bed linen" which seemed to be of importance to some testators, and, usually left to the eldest daughter?

Philip Smitheram was buried the 4 February 1746. It could be that he lived for a year after making his Will or for only a month. The Registers at this time were badly kept. Days and months were given but rarely years. Frequently, the only way of calculating the year is by noting the date of the Visitation and working from that.

In Chetnole, the Hewletts, the Jenkins, the Smitherams, were all connected. There must have been great concern, when, so soon after the burial of her only son, Elizabeth Smitheram was left a widow with two small daughters. No sooner was Philip Smitheram in his grave than Mr Henry Jenkins stepped forward, and, on 30 April 1747 married Mrs Smitheram. A month earlier, Mr. John Jenkins had married Martha Hewlett. John may, or may not, have been brother to Henry. Martha was the daughter of Edward and Mary Hewlett wheras Elizabeth Smitheram was the daughter of John and Elizabeth Hewlett. Tragedy struck again, on 13 June 1748, Mr. Henry Jenkins was buried.

Nothing more is known of the family for thirty or forty years. In 1778, John Hewlett left £20 each to his nieces, Sarah and Elizabeth Smitheram. It would appear that they went to live in Sherborne. On 12 August 1783, Elizabeth Jenkins from Sherborne was buried in Yetminster. The previous year, her daughter, Betty Smitheram was also buried.

1785, and the Court Book records that Ring's Tenement passed from George Young of Alton and Sarah Smitheram of Sherborne, spinster, to Robert Sampson, clerk. The involvement of George Young is not clear, possibly the property was mortgaged to him.

Sampson sold Common Close, 5 acres to John Martin of Yetminster, linen draper and Northfield, 4 acres to William Jenkins of Melbury Osmond. Two years later, Sampson was dead and Ring's Tenement passed to William Jenkins, clerk.

It will be recalled that, in 1747, John Jenkins had married Martha Hewlett. In 1752, a daughter, also Martha, was born to them. On 28 May 1772, Martha Jenkins married Robert Sampson, Rector of Thornford.

Following the Rector's death, his widow returned to Chetnole. Their daughter, Martha Sampson, attended Yetminster School, an establishment so far unidentified. On 18 October 1787, she completed a Sampler. It bears the quotation:

*"The noblest employment of the mind is in the study of the works of the Creator."*

Her Sampler may be seen in Dorchester Museum. Martha died in 1800, aged 22 years.

On 8 October 1805, her sister, Mary Sampson, married John Perkins, jun. of Henley, Crewkerne. The witnesses were Susan Perkins and William Jenkins.

The mother of the girls, Martha Sampson, died in 1790, just five years after her husband, the Rector of Thornford.

With the death of Robert Sampson, Ring's Tenement passed to the Rev. William Jenkins of Melbury Osmond, he died in 1823 and Mary Jenkins, spinster, of Chetnole, inherited. William Jenkins was aged 76 when he died, he had been Rector of Melbury Osmond for 40 years.

Mary Jenkins died in 1850, leaving a considerable estate in Yetminster. Some she left to the Rev. John Jenkins Matthews of Melbury Osmond and some to Mary Perkins of Chetnole, widow. Mary, born Sampson, was the widow of John Perkins, he died in 1827, aged 53 years and was buried in Melbury Osmond. Ring's Tenement came into the hands of Mary Perkins. The 1840 Tithe shows her as the owner and Thomas Hayward as the occupier. Mary Perkins also died in 1850 and she left Ring's to Charles Perkins, her son. Thomas Hayward had been the tenant for upwards of thirty years, but now he left for a farm in Bishops Caundle. Possibly, Charles Perkins wished to sell and Hayward was unable to buy.

For one hundred years Ring's had been involved with the Hewlett and Jenkins families and those with whom they had inter-married. It is likely, that, throughout this period, it was let.

### Gable Cottage/Rose Cottage/Almshouse Farm

The Almshouse of St. John in Sherborne owned much land, gifted by various donors at different times. In the year 1410, one Elizabeth Latymer made a grant of land in Yetminster. There may have been others. From later Leases and Surveys, we know that the Freehold in Yetminster of the Master and Brethren of Sherborne Almshouse consisted of a messuage, dwelling-house, barn, garden, orchard and backside.

Common Close 12 acres          Peasehill
Chettenwells 2½ acres          Park 3 acres

Scotland Cross 8 acres        Plott with barn 1 acre
Subtree in Beer Hackett 9 acres.

A Survey of Digby Manor dated 1630 shows Henry Palmer as the Freeholder, but his name is crossed out and John Minterne substituted.

In 1633 the "herbage" was let to James Fisher and the "herbage" of Common Close and Peashill to Hugh Beard.

Later tenants were:

| | | | |
|---|---|---|---|
| 1641 | Thomas Bound | Rent: | £33. 4s. 0d |
| 1715 | Edward Harris | | £16. 10s. 0d |
| 1715 | Thomas Read | | £23. 0s. 0d |
| 1726 | Edward Harris | | £18. 0s. 0d |
| 1760 | Mary Read widow | | £44. 0s. 0d |
| 1771 | Thomas Allambridge | | £44. 0s. 0d |
| 1779 | Benjamin Jesty | | |
| 1785 | William Warry & Benjamin Jesty | | |
| 1801 | John Warry | Rent: | £80 |
| 1810 | John Warry | | |
| 1840 | George Brake Farm-house, garden, orchard+land 57 acres. | | |

It is interesting to note, that, in 1840, the field names have not changed but there seems to be an increase in acreage. Leases were usually given for 7 years.

The farm-house, now known as Gable Cottage, dates from the 15 c. Originally, it may have been an open hall house, subsequently improved by the addition of a few extra courses of stone to accommodate the dormer windows and allow for an upper storey. The orchard extended to the South as far as High Street, but some of this land was lost in the latter part of the 19 c when the road was altered to accommodate the bridge over the Railway.

In 1879, Thomas Hayward, the grocer, with retirement in mind, was considering selling Hill House and buying something smaller. His health was not good, he had a heart condition. He was born at Lower Farm in 1825 when his father held the tenancy, so the Almshouse farm was not far from his birth-place.

Sherborne Almshouse agreed to sell "the two cottages, garden and small orchard now in the occupation of John Brake" for the sum of £180. It would appear, that, at some time, the house had been divided.

John Brake, the sitting tenant, was, not unnaturally, concerned. He wrote a neat and careful letter to the solicitor offering to buy the property himself. Not knowing how much to offer, he left the space blank and Fooks suggested "a pound or two more than Hayward's offer". To no avail, the Almshouse appears to have had no concern for its sitting tenant who was about to be made homeless as well as losing his livelihood. Possibly, Brake might have had difficulty in raising the purchase money, whereas Hayward owned, not only Hill House but the Shop as well. Brake's offer was refused, on 29 April 1879 he was given notice to quit. By 19 June of the following year, he was still in possession. Hayward complained. He also complained that Brake was cutting down trees in the orchard.

With the farm-house sold to Thomas Hayward, the Almshouse was left with the land. In 1883, an agreement was reached with William Dicker to let the barn, barton, outbuildings and 43 acres of land late in the occupation of John Brake, for £45 per annum. This did not include Chettenwells 2 acres or the Almshouse Common 8 acres, these were leased to Charles Read, Inn-keeper, for £16 per annum.

Hayward named his newly acquired property "Rose Cottage". He lived there until his death in 1901, aged 76. Amelia stayed on until she, too, died in 1911 aged 82 years.

As a Methodist, Hayward was much concerned with intemperance. To the north of his property, he built a Temperance Hall. The orchard, to the south, he sold to a fellow-Methodist, Charles Doddrell from Shepton Mallet. Doddrell built two cottages and incorporated a shop on the corner from whence he ran a plumbing business, no doubt a lucrative undertaking in a village which was only just beginning to experience the delights of mains water. High up on the South facing wall, Doddrell set his date-stone

C D

1897

The arrival of mains water must have caused a minor revolution. For the very first time there would be no more going out in all weathers to well or pump for every drop of water needed for household use, dairy or watering of animals. As people watched the laying of the pipes along the High Street, they must all have wanted, at the very least, a sink with

Date stone on corner shop.
*Hill View*
*Charles Doddrell*
*1897*

a cold tap over it. When, recently (1996), the pipes in the High Street were re-newed, some were found to be the original old lead pipes. As time went on, demand would grow for more ambitious amenities, for hot water on tap, for baths and flushing closets. Life was to be transformed . . . by water running through a pipe!

Charles Doddrell died 3 June 1927 in the Yeatman Hospital. He was 70 years old. His wife, Abigail, had died the previous year. They had three daughters who remained unmarried and a son, William Ewart Doddrell who died 12 July 1966. He married but had no children.

## Watts' Tenement

From the 1840 Tithe Map, it would appear that there were but two properties on the triangular piece of land opposite Lower Farm, one was the almshouse Farm-house, the other known as Watts' Tenement.

In the year 1690 it was held of the Manor of Yetminster Secunda by William Barber. He died and the property passed to Thomas Uvedale with an except to William's widow, Grace, for life, of "the north end of the dwelling-house from the entry, the orchard, barn, one stable or out-

# YETMINSTER, DORSET.

# To be Sold

## BY AUCTION,

# By Percy and Son,

AT THE WHITE HART INN, YETMINSTER,

## On Monday the 24th of February next,

AT THREE O'CLOCK IN THE AFTERNOON PUNCTUALLY,

*Subject to such Conditions as will then be produced,*

## A CUSTOMARY COPYHOLD

# TENEMENT,

## Called WATTS'S,

Now in the possession of Mr. SAMUEL WATTS, in the following lots:—

Lot 1. A DWELLING-HOUSE, OUTHOUSES, GARDEN, and ORCHARD, containing, by estimation, one Acre; and a COTTAGE adjoining.

Lot 2. An ORCHARD, called *Four Acres,* by estimation four Acres.

Lot 3. A CLOSE of ARABLE, called *East Field,* by estimation four and a half Acres.

☞ To view the Premises apply to the said SAMUEL WATTS; and for further particulars, either to Messrs. RUSSELL, Solicitors, Beaminster; or FOOKS and GOODDEN, Solicitors, Sherborne.

*January 28th,* 1834.

*J. Penny, Journal Office, Sherborne.*

Sale of Watts's Tenement in 1834. It was bought by Samuel's brother, William Watts of Upbury.

D.R.O. D148 30/35

206

house, two gardens, one meadow called Headlands, and two closes called "Bingers 5 acres." Thomas Uvedale was given special licence to let his tenancy which was to be kept in repair.

Grace Barber lived for only four more years. In 1693, she made her Will. She made bequests, mostly monetary, to a number of people:

> *Joan Wickham, the 4 children of Robert Symons, William Wickham, Anne Wickham, Mary Wickham, Elizabeth Wickham, Elizabeth Symonds, Joan Barrett, Joan, wife of James Fluellin, Giles Little, Thomas Taylor, Anne Barber, William Edwards jun., Mary, wife of Thomas Glyde, John Barber, Bridport, the wife of Thomas Udall.*

> *Executors: William Wickham, Jane Wickham and Matthew Hutchins.*

> *The Witnesses:  Elianor Minterne*
> *Elianor Minterne the younger*
> *Joseph Slade.*
>
> *Mark of Grace Barber.*

Comparison of Joseph Slade's signature with that of the hand of the writer of the Will confirms that he was the writer.

Joseph Slade was the School master, and, as such, frequently called upon for such tasks as the writing of Wills. In the year 1679, Joseph Slade was licensed to teach a Grammar School. Like surgeons and midwives, school masters had to be licensed by the Church. Yetminster came under the peculiar jurisdiction of the Dean of Sarum, so, it was he who granted the licence. The Licensee made a declaration that he subscribed to the Thirty-nine Articles of Religion and would conform to the Liturgy of the Church of England.

Later, Slade seems to have fallen upon hard times, he is recorded in the Vestry Book as receiving Parish Relief, payments were made regularly from 1698 until his burial 21 January 1712.

The Inventory of Grace Barber's goods names the hall, kitchen, inner and outer buttery and the chamber over the kitchen and the room within the hall. Her goods were few. Most of her wealth lay in money out on loan to several men. Rather than keeping it under the mattress, she was making her money work for her, possibly her only source of income.

Her possessions were few but sufficient for the time in which she lived. However, although she owned two tables, there is no mention of a stool or form. Perhaps the house had fixed window-seats and benches within the inglenook, even so, one might expect some kind of movable seating. (See Inventory)

No Memorial stone for Grace has survived, but one of the fine hamstone table-tombs in Yetminster Church-yard commemorates Ann, wife of Joseph Barber of Ryme and daughter of John Dawes of Cattistock. The date is illegible, probably early 18 c which would fit in with the Ann Barber a beneficiary in Grace's Will.

In 1698, Thomas Uvedale sold to William Watts the "customary Tenement in Yetminster, formerly William Barber." No doubt, Uvedale had been holding the property as "caretaker" during Grace's widowhood. In her Will, Grace left 1s to Bridget, wife of Thomas Udall, probably the same man with a variant spelling of his name, by no means unusual.

In 1735, William Watts made his Will. He was buried 8 December 1735. To his son, William, he gave his apple-mill and cider-press and nominated him Lord's next tenant to his property in Yetminster and, also, to another in Leigh.

To his son, Henry, he left his wearing-apparel, and his wagon and dung-pot and ploughing-tackle to be divided between his sons Henry and Joseph.

His son, Henry, was to receive the money due to him in the hands of John Everett of Holnest, to be laid out to add some of his children's lives to his cottage at Leigh, and,

*" if my son, Henry, shall live to the age of 60 years and be in want, I desire that my son, William, shall pay him 1s a week for as long as he lives."*

*"To son, Joseph, my long trendle and the great chest & £40.*

*To daughter-in-law, Elizabeth Watts in London £20.*

*"To grandsons, William and Edmund, £20 apiece.*

*"To grand daughters, Sarah and Katharine £10 at age 21.*

*"To grandson, William Watts in London, my two silver spoons marked W.W.*

*"To son-in-law Thomas Whiffen 1s.*
*"To son-in-law Andrew Lumbard 1s.*

The residue of his estate, he left to his son, William.

Edmund Watts "of London" was buried in Yetminster in 1731. It would be interesting to know what took a farmer's son from Dorset to London. What trade did he follow? Did he prosper? What became of his four children?

The next William Watts died intestate in 1766 and administration was granted to his widow, Elizabeth, Edward Hayes, Inn-keeper and George Sherring of Lillington, yeoman.

Following, came another William. He died in 1806 appointing his son, Samuel, to be Lord's next tenant of his property in Yetminster, his sons, William and Benjamin, receiving pieces of ground and his daughters, Elizabeth and Hannah, £60 apiece. The residue of his estate he left to Samuel whom he appointed Executor. At this time, Samuel Watts was 40 years old.

By the year 1831, Samuel Watts was in difficulties. He took out a Mortgage for £200 with Samuel Scott of Sherborne, gent. The following year, it was renewed. In 1834, Samuel sold a piece of land, Eastfield 4 acres, to William Loveless, cooper, of Leigh. Charles Cosens of Dorchester appears to have become a co-mortgagee with Scott. Samuel Watts took out a new mortgage for £100 with Thomas Cole of Yeovil, glover. Next, the property was about to be auctioned when Samuel's brother, William bought it in for the sum of £200. Samuel Watts was buried 4 September 1844 aged 79.

William Watts was farming at Upbury, successfully, it would appear, since not only was he able to buy his brother's property, he also bought the Shop and the Royal Oak Inn. William died in 1853, in his Will, he left the Chapel Lane property, "formerly Samuel Watts" to his grandsons, William Watts Hayward and Thomas Hayward, except for a piece of land at the NW corner, N to S 70 ft., breadth at S extremity 30 ft, bounded on W by Parish road, which was surrendered by William Watts in his life-time to Edward Broadlake Dingley and, on which, a Chapel has since been erected. It was built in 1849. E. B. Dingley was a leading Methodist in Sherborne.

At their grandfather's death, William Watts Hayward was farming at Henstridge Bowden, and Thomas was able to take over the Shop and the Royal Oak.

The 1840 Tithe Map shows that William Watts had let his property in Chapel Lane to William Bartlett. But, there is no sign of Samuel, perhaps, he had been taken in by one of his relatives. The map shows Watts' Tenement right on the lane, immediately below the Almshouse Farm. If it is the same building, today it is a row of cottages.

---

**The Inventory of the goods & chattels of Grace Barber, widow of Yetminster in the County of Dorsett late deceased, taken and appraised the 23rd day of February in the year of our Lord God 1693 by Thomas Ring, Thomas Read & John Brewer all of the Parish of Yetminster, aforesaid.**

**In the chamber over the kitchin**

| | | | |
|---|---|---|---|
| *Impr.* One feather bed, bedsteade with all the furniture thereunto belonging | £4. | 0s. | 0d |
| In the same chamber a dust bed and bedsteade & furniture | £1. | 0s. | 0d |
| One chest | | 10s. | 0d |
| One trunke & coffer | | 4s. | 0d |
| One warming pan, a firepan & toasting iron tongs | | 6s. | 0d |
| one pannell | | 3s. | 0d |
| one spade | | 1s. | 0d |

**In the inner buttery**

| | | | |
|---|---|---|---|
| 1 trendle 3 cheese vates | | 2s. | 0d |

**In the outermost buttery**

| | | | |
|---|---|---|---|
| five barrells for beer | | 10s. | 0d |

**In the Roome within ye hall**

| | | | |
|---|---|---|---|
| 1 barrell, 1 little tubb, 1 trendle, 1 peck measure, 1 half peck 1 Turne & reel for wool | | 6s. | 0d |

---

**In the hall**

| | | | |
|---|---:|---:|---:|
| one table with a frame belonging to it | £1. | 00s. | 0d |
| five sacks and bags | | 8s. | 0d |

**In the kitchin**

| | | | |
|---|---:|---:|---:|
| One brass pan & 3 kettles. Two skillets | £1. | 15s. | 0d |
| Two brass pots | | 12s. | 0d |
| Thirteen pewter platters little & great | | 16s. | 0d |
| One table with a frame | | 10s. | 0d |
| one pair of iron doggs, one spit, three back crooks, three pair of pot-hooks, one frying-pan. | | 6s. | 6d |
| Three candlesticks | | 1s. | 0d |
| three tubs two pails | | 8s. | 0d |
| A pair of bellows | | 10s. | 6d |
| In money on severall Bonds from severall men due to the Testator | £75. | 0s. | 0d |
| In desperate debts | £5. | 8s. | 0d |
| Money in house | £5. | 0s. | 0d |
| in wearing apparel | £5 | 0s. | 0d |
| in lumber stuff | | 5s. | 0d |
| | £99 | 12s. | 0d |

Witness our hands
    Thomas Ring
    Thomas Reade
    The sign of John Brewer

# The Brake family

As early as 1524, the Brake name occurs in the Yetminster area, in that year, in Chetnole, Michael Brake was assessed on the Tudor Subsidy at £1 on wages. In 1543, Michael Breke, alien, was assessed at £2 on goods. Richard Brake appears on the 1635 list of those contributing to "Ship Money" and his Will of 1642 has survived.

His wife, Elizabeth, was buried in 1636 but he left daughters Joan, Katharine and Anne and sons Dennis, Ralph and George. The Parish Registers record the burial of a Ralph in 1678 and the baptism of Radolphus, son of Ralph in 1681. In the late 17c/early 18c a Ralph, a Richard, a Dennis, a Thomas and a John were baptising and burying children. The records are incomplete but the Brakes increased and multiplied. It would be impossible to follow them all: here are just a few.

David Brake, baptised in 1711, became Parish Clerk, through the years, he witnessed numerous marriages and was buried 18 June 1783.

In 1727, John Brake=Margaret Douglas.

Margaret and Elizabeth were the daughters of William Douglas and his wife, Elizabeth Hayward. Douglas was a Scotch pedlar, as such, he travelled the country with his pack of small items which might tempt the country housewives, pins, needles, ribbons and laces and other trifles. On an isolated farmstead, the arrival of the pedlar was a welcome diversion for the mistress, her family and maid-servants. He was often offered food and drink and given permission to bed down for the night in a barn if he so wished. Country dwellers could not indulge in the modern pastime of "shopping", a visit to the weekly market, perhaps, or an annual one to the Fair.

Scotch pedlars usually stayed at home during the winter months and set out on their travels again in the Spring.

About 1706, William Douglas=Elizabeth Hayward, the elder "we know not where nor when". The Parish wished to get a Removal Order for Douglas, so he was not recognised as belonging to the Parish, but, seemingly, nothing was done. Two daughters were born: in 1707 and 1709, and, in 1710, William Douglas died, presumably, away from home, since no burial has been recorded for him locally, or, indeed, anywhere in Dorset. Elizabeth applied for relief, and, a tussle ensued between the Overseers, who had a right to take her late husband's goods, and her husband's creditors who had a right to the Pack goods.

In 1723, in one of their periodic swoops on unemployed young people who were prone to make a nuisance of themselves in the village, Elizabeth and Margaret were ordered by the Overseers to find themselves masters. We don't know if they did so. Elizabeth was in trouble again, when, in 1731, she bore a child to John Old of Minterne Magna, but, fortunately for her, he married her and took her off to Minterne. She had been on the verge of being taken before the Ecclesiastical Court in Salisbury.

Margaret Douglas, in 1727, had married John Brake. They had several children, and, after his death, Margaret appears to have kept an Alehouse, a not unusual occupation for a widow. In 1748, she married the widowed Henry Fox and they continued to run the Inn, known as the "Fleur de Lys". Henry had children by his late wife, Constance, and he and Margaret had two daughters, Margaret and Lettice. Henry Fox died in 1761 and Margaret continued at the Inn until her own death, she was buried 29 December 1772. There is evidence that Margaret also acted as midwife and boarded paupers for the Parish.

The antecedents of Ralph Brake are uncertain. He could have been the son of Ralph, who, in 1704, armed with a Settlement Certificate from Yetminster Parish, took himself off to Thornford with his wife, Elizabeth, perhaps returning to Yetminster with his son after the death of his wife.

On 5 January 1753, Ralph Brake=Sarah Shave, daughter of James and Mary Shave. This appears to have been his third marriage. Ralph was, most likely, a thatcher. The couple had three sons: Robert, James and Ralph. By 1761, Ralph was sick and unable to provide for his family, accordingly, he had recourse to the Parish. But, Ralph must have been seriously ill. On 5 October 1761, the Vestry Book records:

*"We authorise the Overseers to put Ralph Brake under the care of Dr Bragg and to provide the said Ralph Brake with lodgings and all*

*necessary accommodation as long as he is under Dr Bragg's care and it is necessary for him to be in Sherborne."*

*Signed: John Topham, Thomas Allambridge, Timothy Hewlett, William Warry.*

Who were these men? Topham was the Vicar. Allambridge the last of the Allambridges of the present Manor House, then known as "Warrs", Hewlett lived at Yetminster Hamlet, a member of a well-off family, Warry was the tanner of Cross Farm.

There is no indication of the nature of Brake's illness, but, it was almost unprecedented for a sick person to be sent out of the Parish for treatment at Parish expense. Hutchins notes that Dr Bragg was an eminent surgeon known for his cure for cancer. Is this a clue?

However eminent, Bragg was unable to cure Ralph Brake. After spending six weeks in Sherborne at a cost of 25s 9d for lodging and £5 5s 0d for Dr Bragg's attendance, Brake was brought back to Yetminster. Denis Cockram was paid 1s 6d for the journey. Two months later, on 31 December, Brake was buried. The Parish paid 13s 6d for the expenses of his funeral.

Over the years, much money was expended on Sarah Brake and her sons. Sarah even made the situation worse! Mrs Fox was paid 2s 6d for attending Sal Brake in labour, on 3 November 1765, Sarah, bastard of Sarah Brake was baptised. Payments were made to various women for looking after Sarah's children and there was much expenditure on clothing. The 8d paid for 'leaders' for Sal Brake's bastard gives a picture of this toddler being guided through the rough and miry streets of Yetminster wearing, perhaps, the cap and stockings which cost 1s 3d and the "coats", i.e. petticoats which depleted the Poor Accounts by 2s 4½d.

The three boys were fast growing up and ready to be apprenticed so that they might no longer be a charge upon the Parish. In 1772, it was decided to send Robert, the eldest, to the Newfoundland trade. In a maritime county such as Dorset, this was a popular option, no fewer than twenty-four parishes taking advantage of it. From the view-point of the Vestry, it was ideal, for it ensured that such boys would never again be able to claim a right of Settlement in the Parish.

Boys and girls maintained by the parish sent out as apprentices were kitted out by the Overseers, and, the clothing provided was invariably of better quality than the garments normally provided.

The Overseers expended a total of £2 17s 2d on Robert Brake when they purchased his clothing for Newfoundland.

| | |
|---|---|
| 5 yds. & 3 qrs. of blanketing @ 1s 6d | 8s 7½d |
| 1 yd. & 3 qrs. of canvas & 2 & ½ thread | 1s 8½d |
| buttons & tape | 8d |
| 7 yds. check @ 14d yd. | 8s 2d |
| Buckels | 3d |
| a Hatt | 1s 6d |
| pd. for making the cloathes | 4s 0d |
| pd. more for Robert Brake's clothing | 19s 11d |
| to carry him to Poole & other exps. | 6s 0d |

Young Robert was, doubtless, very pleased with himself as he bade farewell to his mother and brothers and set off for Poole and the unknown.

The Vestry, also well-pleased, decided to send James & Ralph for sea services as well. At the same time, Joseph Cheesman's two sons were also kitted out but it is not known if they, too, were sent to Newfoundland. Talyor Bishop was paid 12s for making the clothes, 4 pairs of stockings were purchased for 6s 8d and a pair of shoes for each boy cost 12s.

Sarah Brake never saw her sons again. She was buried on 8 April 1808 aged 84 years. There is no record of the fate of her daughter.

## The Brakes in Newfoundland

We do not know the exact arrangements made for the Brake boys, usually, a boy was apprenticed to the Master of a vessel "to learn the art and mystery of catching fish." There was a constant demand for crews to man vessels sailing from south coast ports to the fishing grounds. Poole had a long history of trading with Newfoundland stretching back over hundreds of years. By the 18c many of the wealthy Poole merchants, such as the Lesters and Garlands, had established trading-posts in Newfoundland. In 1790, Benjamin Lester supported 3,000 people and there was a permanent population of 10,000.

The ships owned by the merchants went to the fishing-grounds for the season, their catch of cod was then salted and dried and brought back to Europe, much being sold in Portugal. Those working for one of the merchants traded "per contra" receiving wages and payment for sealskins, oil and the skins of small mammals they had caught and buying their food, items of clothing and other necessities. Vessels set out from Poole laden with these trading goods. They also gave passage to men who had been recruited to work in Newfoundland – carpenters, bricklayers and other craftsmen who had responded to advertisements placed in local papers such as the Sherborne Mercury. There is also evidence that deserters from the Militia found the colony a useful haven.

The Wills of persons dying in Newfoundland were entrusted to returning Masters to be proved in England, thus, probate might take several years. Masters might also bring back small items, such as watches, for repair.

We don't know if the Brake boys served their seven years apprenticeship at sea and then settled, or whether they made just one voyage and then remained on land. Robert Brake, the first to arrive, settled at Twillingate. From 1783, he worked for Slade & Co., his wages were £20 a year. His name appears on their ledgers until 1815.

The Slade ledgers show purchases made by Robert Brake which were settled "per contra" against his wages. To begin with, he bought mostly brandy, tobacco, molasses and beer. A couple of years later, he had probably married, for his purchases change to flour, oatmeal, butter, pork, etc. and he bought a pair of boy's hose and two pairs of women's hose.

By 1788, Robert was selling sealskins and seal-oil to Slades and 37 gallons of berries. Gradually, he began to prosper. His income increased, and, by 1795, he bought rum only once (on Dec. 24th!) and tobacco twice in the year. He now spent his money on food, clothing, materials and household articles. For several years, Mrs Brake did laundry for single men: Ben Toravil, Sam Shappick, Richard Murton, Thomas Clarke and James Gale among them, for which, in just one year, Slades paid £9 10s 2d.

In 1815, Robert was still buying from Slades: 4 pairs boys' shoes, 6 cotton shirts, 1 woman's gown, 1 pair light shoes, 1 fancy waistcoat, 1 pair cloth trousers, 1 plush jacket.

He was still selling to Slades: sealskins and seal-oil, fish and berries. He was buying no fewer than 7 pairs of men's shoes, 3 boys' shoes and a pair of women's shoes. This would indicate that he had a number of grown sons.

Did Robert, perhaps, recall the shoes with buckles which the Yetminster Overseers had bought for him all those years ago and which he had worn so proudly as he set off for Poole and the unknown? No doubt, the long winter evenings were much given to story-telling and the passing on of family history to the younger generation who could not have imagined what life was like in far-off Dorsetshire. When the "Yetties" visited Newfoundland, they found that the Dorset accent had survived, and Dorset songs which had been remembered and passed down.

Robert was fortunate in the number of sons he had fathered, from the age of about 15, boys did a man's work, but, by custom, the money they earned went to the father. This was an equitable arrangement, they were still living at home, families were large and there were often younger children to be provided for.

Commencing in 1814, James Brake, son of Robert, had an account with Slades, and, it would appear, that he was married. His purchases included: 1 leather cap, 1 cloth jacket, 1 cotton gown, 1 girl's frock, 1 pair women's hose. He was also selling cod-fish and oil to Slades.

Ralph Brake settled in Bay of Islands and remained there until his death in 1842. He married Jane . . . who died in 1819, aged 46. Ralph, it is believed, had eight or ten sons, of whom only one, Edward, was educated, he was sent to England for that purpose, probably so that he might learn the 'ins and outs' of trading.

In 1818, Ralph built a substantial boat, 49 ft. × 14 ft. of 43 tons. He named the vessel "Hope". Colonial Office Records of 1830 state:

*Mr R. Brake to be paid for hire of his vessel last autumn by Quebec merchants. The vessel was afterwards lost.*

J. B. Jukes, a geologist, met Ralph Brake during a brief stay in Bay of Islands in 1839. He wrote:

*"We anchored at the head of the Humber Sound in not more than 8 ft of water. We found here an old man, residing with his family in a*

217

*small wooden house with a garden attached. He had lived in this spot
for sixty years and had several sons. One of these, a cripple, was with
him, the other six, he said, were away in the woods hunting, either for
deer, beavers, otters, martens or other fur-bearing animals."*

The sons were: Edward, Robert, James, Thomas, William, John, Joseph and Ralph probably the cripple.

Edward Brake traded first with Joseph Bird of Poole and Sturminster Newton, and, later, with his son, Thomas Street Bird. This raises an interesting question: did Edward spend his period of "education" in Poole or Sturminster?

Joseph Bird owned just one ship, the "Joseph".

In Sturminster, his shop was the Market House.

A local Census of Sturminster inhabitants taken in 1801, shows Joseph Bird sen.

*Joseph Bird jun. clothier, married with 2 children*

*Thomas Bird gent. married with 2 children*

*Edward Bird, maltster, married with 1 child.*

Each of these families had a living-in servant, so all were prosperous.

On 14 May 1801, Joseph Bird put an announcement in the Sherborne Mercury:

*Joseph Bird of Sturminster Newton, after trading for thirty years is
now selling up. 10%–15% off prime cost will be given.*

*Superfine and second cloths*
*Forest and Yorkshire*
*beavers, kerseymeres, swansdowns, etc.*
*also, Irish dowlas, sheetings, prints, muslins, lawns*
*Manchester goods – all sorts*
*velverets, corduroys, mancoes, camblets*
*Men's and boys' hats*
*all sorts of stockings, gloves & ribbands*
*black lace & white thread ditto*
*Great variety of haberdashery*

*All those indebted to Mr Joseph Bird are asked to discharge same
within 3 months.*

The Market House, Sturminster Newton where Joseph Bird had his shop

He was succeeded by his son, Joseph. Thomas Street Bird lived in Poole.

On 20 August 1842, Edward Brake wrote to Thomas Street Bird from Bay of Islands.

*Sir,*

*With sorrow I must inform you of the death of my father which happened on the 4th of May. He was taken ill and speechless three weeks before his death.*

*I have sent you one tuin of fur, containing*
*30 beaver skins*
*4 otter*
*18 martens*
*10 yellow fox*
*You will please to send me the following articles:*
*½ pieces of swanskin*

1 piece blue serge
12 pairs swanskin breeches
6 men's swanskin pea-jackets
12 cotton sheets
12 white flannel shirts
18 pairs men's yarn hose
12 pairs men's shoes
6 small boys' shoes
6 men's fine blue cloth jackets with black buttons
½ piece blue cloth
12 clasp knives
12 hatchets
12 covered hats
50 salmon twine
2 dozen cotton handkerchiefs
½ yd. lining
12 St Peter fishing lines
½ (?) job leather
Gun (description unclear)
4 black waistcoats
6 pairs blue cloth trousers
1 sizeable woman's black gown
1 sein for caplan & lance 20 fathoms long 3 deep

I should wish for to have a good Headstone for my father and mother as their bodies is remaining alongside of each other, similar to this form with a gilded angel on each side.

| | |
|---|---|
| Jane Brake | Ralph Brake |
| Sacred to the memory of | Sacred to the memory of |
| Jane Brake who departed | Ralph Brake who departed |
| this life Aug 23 1819 | this life May 4 1842 |
| aged 46 years. | aged 82 years. |

"Behold and see as you pass by
As you are now so once was I
As I am now so you must be
Prepare for death, to follow me."

*You will, if you please Sir, to deliver the legacies to whom it may be due and leave the rest remaining as usual together in partnership, which is to say, Edward Brake, Robert Brake, James Brake and Thomas Brake.*

*I must inform you that we have had a very bad fishing this year with salmon and cod.*

*Wishing you a pleasant winter, I remain your humble servant, Edward Brake and brothers.*

So, Edward was in partnership with three of his brothers. One may note, that, with the exception of the black dress, he is buying only men's clothing. No doubt, the women were in the habit of buying material and making their own gowns, etc., by so doing they were more likely to get a garment which fitted! No sizes are specified for the men's wear, it must have been hit or miss whether a garment of the right dimensions was found.

Most probably, an order was sent by one of the last boats to leave for England before the winter set in, delivery of the goods could not be expected until the following Spring.

Will of Ralph Brake *of Bay of Islands, Newfoundland planter.* *dated 5 August 1838.*

*Just debts to be paid*

*To son, John Matthews Brake* £40.
*To son, Joseph Matthews Brake* £100.
*To daughter, Elizabeth Matthews wife of Thomas Park of Bay of Islands* £20.
*To daughter, Jane Matthews, wife of William Whocier? of Bay of Islands* £20.
*To son, Robert Matthews Brake* £100.

*These legacies to be paid out of property in England.*

*Residue to sons:* *Robert Matthews Brake*
*Ralph ,, ,,*
*William ,, ,,*
*Thomas ,, ,,*
*James ,, ,,*
*Edward ,, ,,*

*so long as they continue together in co-partnership. "If any of my sons part from the said company prior to my decease, at my decease he shall be paid £100 as his share.*

*"If any son die during my life-time his share shall go to the survivors.*

*William Blanchard of Bay of Islands, Executor in Bay of Islands. Joseph Bird of East Orchard, merchant, Executor of property and effects in England.*

*Mark of Ralph Brake.*

*Witnesses: William Wolfe. Mark of William Gaulton.*

This Will is interesting because it reveals that each of Ralph's children had been given the name 'Matthews'. Was this their mother's name? And, another speculation, had Ralph actually married her? Had he not done so, this would not have been unusual in the Newfoundland of the time.

That Ralph should have property in England is another point of interest. Where was it? Since Joseph Bird of East Orchard was involved, one might guess, somewhere in the Sturminster Newton area. What was the nature of the property and why had Ralph invested therein?

Ralph Brake died 4 May 1842. On 27 January 1844, William Wolfe, one of the witnesses, was in Poole swearing an affidavit as to the authenticity of the Will before James Farr, Minister of St. Peter's Church, Parkstone. It would appear, that, after that, nothing was done until 1866, by which time, Edward Brake his brothers, Robert, Thomas and James also Joseph Bird, were all dead. Administration was granted to Edward's brother, William, as next of kin. This information has been extracted from comments on the Will at the P.R.O., but there are added notes which cannot be deciphered which may throw more light upon what happened. If only Ralph had described the location of his property in England and its nature.

A year later, Edward wrote again to Thomas Street Bird. His order was much the same as the previous one. It also included 12 pewter plates, 2 good cheese, 2 pair blankets and 12 small fox traps. Also ordered:

*1 woman's handsome silk gown and 1 gold ring, put together and marked J.I.*

He concluded:

*I should thank you to acquaint the shoemaker concerning the shoes sent me last year. People could not wear them by means of coming down behind. I should like, therefore, to have them banned.*

*Concerning of my father's Will, I should thank you to act as you think proper for our benefit at the less expense. This, I hope, will find you quite well as it leaves me and my brothers at present.*

*Wishing you a pleasant and prosperous winter,*

*I remain, dear Sir, your obedient servant,*

*Edward Brake & Co.*

*I have sent you two watches to be repaired.*

Who, one wonders, was J.I. who was to get (or give) a silk gown and a gold ring?

A wedding in the offing, perhaps. One can only hope that both gown and ring fitted the recipient.

It would seem that some shoe-maker had been tempted to off-load sub-standard footwear on the settlers.

It must have been a frustrating life, a wait of up to a year for an item upon which one had set one's heart or which was desperately needed for the everyday routine of fishing, trapping or hunting.

What a large part the harsh winter must have played in everyone's life when an ordinary business letter could end with a wish for a good one!

By 1849, Edward was living at Meadows Point, Bay of Islands, married with four children. There are Brakes there to this day who know nothing of their forbears. It was not unusual for Newfoundlanders to marry Indian women. One of Edward's brothers, James, married a Micmac Indian. A sister married Edward Crocker from Dorset, first settler at Trout Cove. They had nine children.

In 1849, Bishop Field undertook a Visitation of Newfoundland on the Church ship "Hawk". Arriving at Bay of Islands, he writes in his Diary:

*"We found Edward Brake at home and placed in one of the loveliest and most fertile spots of nature's own work. One feature of this locality and of the whole Bay of Islands, is the predominance and*

*luxuriance of deciduous timber, birch, beech, poplar and ash. The hills are clothed from their bases at the water's edge to the very summits of 400 feet in height.*

*Edward Brake has a house and well-stocked garden at the base of one of the mountains. His father came from Dorsetshire, (Yetminster, I think) many years ago and lived in this locality some sixty years. He died in the year 1840 and left ten sons, of whom, this Edward alone received any education, being sent to England for that purpose. He has a wife and four children, and, one of his brothers who appears weak, lives with them, unmarried."*

Later, he visited Tucker's Cove, the residence of another Brake, Edward's brother, and writes:

*"We landed on the beach, close to what might be called a natural garden – a thick border of beautiful rose trees covered with flowers of two colours and very fragrant, the bees were very busy among them, French willow was interspersed also in full flower, and, within the borders, gooseberries, currants and raspberries in abundance. The gooseberries were equal to garden fruit, smooth, thin-skinned and with a beautiful bloom. Enough were soon gathered for a substantial pudding.*

*J. Brake showed us the skins of three wolves he had killed close to his own house last winter – they were large, 6 ft. from tail to snout. They are caught in traps and then shot. "They were shocking fierce and dangerous entirely!"*

The Bishop travelled on to meet another of Edward's brothers, married to a Mic-mac Indian, and then to Deep Cove, another settlement of Brakes, with them an old man named Crocker from Trout River, also from Dorset and married to a sister of the Brakes and has nine children.

Bishop Field's visit, of course, took place in July and August, before the dreaded winter had the country in its grip. He was an observant man, and, wherever he went, held services and baptised the children.

The fate of the third brother, James Brake, is uncertain. He has not been researched and there is a suggestion that, either he never left

224

Yetminster or that he returned. In 1781, in Yetminster, a James Brake=Ann Painter or Ryme. They had four children, Betsy, Jane, James and Ann. James Brake died in 1799 aged 42 years. This would correlate with the birth-date of 1758 of James, son of Ralph and Sarah Brake who should have departed for Newfoundland. No other birth for a James Brake has been found in the records.

The Sherborne Mercury frequently carried advertisements relating to Newfoundland, for example:

*18 March 1799. Placentia, to be sold a good settlement.*

| | |
|---|---|
| *1 wharf 300 ft.* | *2 hacks* |
| *1 store 60 ft.* | *3 gardens* |
| *1 store 40 ft.* | *1 large stage* |
| *1 store 24 ft.* | *7 large shallops* |
| *1 large cook room* | *or boats* |
| *1 house annual rent £25* | *1 boat or skiff* |
| *3 punts* | *1 large lumber boat* |
| *some goods in store* | *1 yawl* |

*Property of de la Taste, Chevallier & Co. Jersey.*

*24 February 1813. Wanted for Newfoundland*

*1 carpenter, 1 wheelwright, 1 mason & 30–40 men*
*Apply to Mr Colbourne, Sturminster Newton.*

In Sturminster, in 1830, there was a John Colbourne, swanskin manufacturer.

*11 February 1807. Wanted a clerk in a store in Newfoundland. A steady man, well acquainted with accounts who may have been accustomed to serve in a grocer's or draper's shop. Apply: Mr James Langdon, Asburton.*

## More Emigration

Over the years, many members of local families either migrated or emigrated. What has become of them is not always apparent, they simply disappear from the records. The Brakes were no exception. Often, the only clue to the whereabouts of a missing family member is a chance mention in a Will, a reference in a Manor Court Book of a property transaction, a gaol record, or, perhaps, an item in the local press. Occasionally, welcome information comes from descendants who have traced their families back to Yetminster from some distant place. Such information is of tremendous value to the local historian and warmly welcomed.

In the year 1825, a "lease for lives" for a property in Mill Lane granted by the Digby Manor to Ellis Dawe, the miller, names the "lives" as Bernard Brake of Yetminster, flax dresser aged 30 and William Brake of Yetminster, mason, aged 28.

In 1851, Mrs Ann Dawe, widow of Ellis, was granted a mortgage on the property by Mr John Chapman of Lillington, the "lives" being, Bernard Brake, now U.S.A., aged 56 and William Brake, now Newfoundland, aged 54.

This property has been identified as one of the cottages on the right-hand side going down Mill Lane. The two are presently known as "The Pottery" and "St. Francis", of the two, the latter seems the more likely. The cottage was let by Ellis Dawe to George Brake, thatcher. His wife, Grace, died in 1824, aged 56 and George in 1827, aged 58 years. The couple had four children:

*1789 Charles baptised by the Parish*
*1792 Bernard*
*1794 William*
*1797 Nelly*

*Charles Brake=Mary Hunt in 1811*
*William Brake=Ann Edmonds in 1818*
*Nelly/Eleanor=James Hyde of Castleton in 1817*
*Bernard Brake moved to Sherborne where he m. Sarah Burrows.*

c. 1832, Bernard Brake left his wife and family and went to America, never to return. No Brakes appear on the 1834 Terrier and Map of Sherborne as either owners or occupiers of property, so, presumably, Sarah and her family are in lodgings, with a member of her family, perhaps, for William, Joseph and Sarah Burroughs appear.

One of the Brake children, Hezekiah Brake, also went to America, and, at the end of his life (he died in 1903) he wrote a book: "On two continents – a Long Life's Experiences".

What follows is taken from this book. Although he is writing about his own family, some of his information is known to be incorrect. For example, he writes that his grandfather, George Brake, was a very poor man with twenty-two children! And that George lived with his, Hezikiah's family, until his death in 1827. George certainly died in 1827, but he is buried in Yetminster and had four children only. He is, perhaps, confusing George with his Burrows grandfather. He also states that his father, Bernard Brake, was a weaver of sail-cloth and linen, he may have been in Sherborne, in Yetminster, he was a flax-dresser.

After his father left, Hezekiah went to work in Milborne Port in a glove factory and became engaged to one Harriet Hobbs, but Harriet's father, on his death-bed, begged her not to marry but to care for her mother. Hezekiah was devastated, and, in 1836, walked to London where he found his uncle, James Hyde. He refers to his aunt as "Mary", but Hyde had married his father's sister, Eleanor Brake. Uncle James had a livery stable and Hezekiah went to work for him. Two years later, having learned the business, he set out on his own, working in various places. Uncle James succomed to drink, as did his two sons, Nelly also died.

At one of his many positions in London, Hezekiah met and married Charlotte Cranham. He says, that, although of humble birth, Lottie's sister was the wife of Lord Crump! Well, it would not be the first time a member of the aristocracy had picked up a parlour-maid, but who was he?

On 1 May 1847, they sailed for Quebec aboard the "Royal Albert". The following year, they went on to America, to Albany. Hezekiah wanted to find his father. At the time of his last letter to his wife, Sarah, Bernard was in a boardinghouse at 23 Steuben Street and planning to send for his family. After considerable searching, Hezekiah learned that his father had been seen alive one morning in Steuben Street and that evening found dead from cholera on the wharf.

Over the next few years, Hezekiah and Lottie went to New York, Richmond, Virginia, Baltimore and New Jersey. They tried hotel-keeping and worked in New York for a wealthy paralytic.

Next, they tried Minnesota, they built houses for sale, hauled freight, fished and farmed. They also adopted a seven year old girl called Lizzie, all their own children had died in infancy. They went to Minnesota in 1852 with $3,000 and left in 1858 with $99.

Next, they went to New Mexico and started farming, growing grain, cabbages and cauliflowers and making butter and cheese, most of which was sold to the Army at Fort Union. In 1861, they moved on to Council Grove, Kansas, here they farmed, dairied, grew peaches and hauled timber. Lizzie had married Newton E. Fisher, but was soon a widow with two children. Hezekiah was active in local affairs and, eventually, owned 240 acres of land. In 1884, aged 70, he sold his farm and built houses for rent to provide an income in retirement.

Lottie died in 1893 and was buried in Greenwood Cemetery, Morris County, Kansas. Hezekiah survived her by ten years.

# Basket makers

For many years, in the Batcombe area, the Dicker family had been sieve makers. John Dicker, then his son, Elias, who married Elizabeth Crabb at Batcombe in 1795. Elias was also "chapel clerk" and ran the Sunday School at Batcombe, for which he received payment from the Parish.

In early days, Sunday School was not simply a religious meeting. Many labourers' children had to work from a very early age to augment the family income, even if they earned only a few pence, every penny helped. Sunday was the only day on which they were free and the Sunday School was the place where they might learn to read, and, possibly, to write as well.

Information on emigrants arriving in Australia included their ability in reading and writing: some could do both, many were totally illiterate, but a surprising number could read but not write. Had these people, perhaps, attended Sunday School in their places of origin?

In 1799, Elias and Elizabeth had a son, David, who later migrated to Melbury Bubb, where, on 2 October 1821 he married Maria Mitchell. In the following year, their first child, Elias, was born. There followed George, William, Sophia and Cordelia. The baptisms of William and Cordelia are recorded in Yetminster, so David may have been working there. It would seem that Maria did not enjoy the best of health. On several occasions, the Overseers of Melbury Bubb paid doctors' bills for attendance on Maria Mitchell. There were charges of 5s for ointment and lint and 3s for "dressing the breast". This was nearly three years before her marriage, but, doubtless, this condition and the bearing of five children in eleven years contributed to the early death of a young woman in poor health, living in poverty on a woefully inadequate diet.

Early in 1832, David must have found himself unable to support his wife and young family and he applied to Yetminster Parish for relief.

Vestries were ever mindful of the ratepayers who provided the money which they distributed and any applicant whose entitlement was in doubt was referred to the Magistrate. Although no record survives, David must have been examined concerning his place of Settlement, for, on 16 February 1832, the magistrate made an Order removing the family from Yetminster to Melbury Bubb, the latter place having been decided upon as the Parish to which he belonged.

Maria Dicker was ill. The removal of a sick person was not permitted, and, on account of Maria's condition, the Order was suspended.

Maria died and was buried in Yetminster on 3 March 1832. Two days later, the Removal Order was re-imposed and Yetminster Overseers were ordered to convey David and the children to Melbury Bubb. Melbury was obliged to find housing for the family and to pay them maintenance. It was also ordered to pay Yetminster the sum of £2 6s 0d, the amount expended by the Parish on the Dickers since the suspension of the Order.

It is unclear just why David Dicker had been reduced to asking for Parish Relief. Like his father and grandfather, he was a sieve-maker by trade. Possibly, with his wife's illness and the care of his young family, his work had gone by the board.

Happily, things were to improve. On 21 October 1832, he took to wife Elizabeth Andrews of Woolcombe. She was 41 years old and born in Beer Hackett the daughter of John and Betty (b. Downton) Andrews. Just a year after their marriage, a daughter, Maria, was born to Elizabeth. She was to be her only child, and, sadly, died in 1849. The family was still in poverty for the Vestry accounts record that Elizabeth was paid 1s 6d a week for 4 weeks "for her child". With the help of a mature woman, life for David and the children must have improved considerably. Indeed, it seems incredible, that, only nine months later, he was able to buy a property for himself, albeit with the help of a mortgage.

About a mile outside Yetminster on the road to Leigh will be found Stakeford Cross. It is no longer a cross-roads, since the fourth road, which joined up with Knighton Lane, has disappeared. About 1820, Charles Brake had enclosed a long, narrow piece of waste and built thereon. On 23 July 1833, this property was auctioned at the White Hart and purchased by David Dicker. He was to live there for the remainder

# FREEHOLD PROPERTY,

## AT YETMINSTER DORSET, FOR SALE.

## TO BE SOLD BY

# AUCTION,

## BY PERCY AND SON,

## On Tuesday, 23d July, 1833,

### At the WHITE HART INN, YETMINSTER,

At Six o'Clock in the Afternoon precisely, subject to such Conditions as will be then produced,

### THE UNDERMENTIONED

# FREEHOLD PROPERTY,

### Situate at YETMINSTER aforesaid.

#### LOT 1:

A Stone-Built DWELLING HOUSE, CIDER HOUSE, with STABLE, SHOP, GARDEN and ORCHARD behind the same, containing 1 Acre (more or less), now in the Occupation of Mr. John Ring.

#### LOT 2:

A DWELLING HOUSE, now divided into Two Dwellings, with a large GARDEN, now occupied by Joseph Whittle and Robert Buglar.

☞ The above Premises are well supplied with good Water.

For viewing the same apply to the respective Tenants ; and for further Particulars to Messrs. FOOKS and GOODDEN, Solicitors, or Messrs. PERCY and SON, Surveyors, &c., Sherborne, if by letter post paid.

W. W. PERRY, MERCURY OFFICE, SHERBORNE.

Sale of property at Stakeford Cross bought by David Dicker 1833

231

of his life. The property had an ample supply of water, this may have been from a well or from the stream which still flows on the other side of the road. A plentiful supply of water would have been essential for soaking the willows.

David Dicker was buried in Yetminster on 8 July 1869. By this time, the children had grown up and left home. George Dicker was a policeman in Abbotsbury, Elias had died, but his son, George, was a grocer in Blandford. In 1856, Cordelia had married John Bird, a shoemaker. They emigrated to South Africa where John became a policeman in Stellenbosch. Sophia married Luke Bishop, blacksmith at Henstridge.

Elizabeth Dicker stayed on at Stakeford, but she was becoming more and more frail and ill. At a cost of 10s, a horse and van were hired and she was taken to Henstridge to her stepdaughter, Sophia Bishop. There she died, aged 80 years, and was buried in Yetminster on 30 September 1871. A woman to be admired, she had devoted nearly half her life to someone else's family.

William Dicker was the only one of the children to remain in Yetminster where he set up as a basket, sieve and rake-maker. In 1855 he married, probably Matilda Paulley. To begin with, they lived in Church Street. Later, he bought the property at Brister End now known as Willow Farm, it was then a small cottage, but he built another dwelling adjacent to it with buildings at the back for his business. William himself was a sieve-maker, he employed others for the basket and rake making. George Henry Chedzoy looked after the basket making, and, later, his son, Arthur Chedzoy. During the first World War, Arthur's wife kept the business going with the help of Mr Hallett of Ryme, nearly blind from birth, he was exempt from military service. After the War, Arthur Chedzoy returned safely and carried on until about 1924 when he left Yetminster. Arthur Chedzoy was also Secretary for the area of the Wiltshire Working Men's Club and was organiser of the annual Fête at Yetminster. At the annual gathering of Club members, they marched with their band for Church Service (one year in Yetminster, the next in Ryme), then back to lunch in a tent in a field loaned by a farmer, usually by Mr Willis of Upbury.

William Dicker bought more land at Brister End and started a farm. From 1858–1901, he was Parish Clerk and his long service in that capacity is commemorated by a plaque in Yetminster Church.

Basket making at Willow Farm. c. 1917
Mrs. Arthur Chedzoy with Roland and George
Nora Jolliffe
Mrs. Rendell's family
Joe Hallet          Bernard Jolliffe

Baskets were in demand for all manner of purposes: eggs, fish, vegetables, fruit, butcher's and baker's baskets, laundry baskets, almost any commodity that needed transporting required a basket. Dicker made butter baskets and baskets for use in the gloving industry. He received orders from many places in the area, some, sent on postcards, have survived.

Addressed to William Dicker, Basket-maker, Yetminster, all appear to have arrived safely without benefit of postcode!

The postcards measure 4 in. × 3 in. and are ready stamped ½d. They are post-marked in the 1870s.

In 1876, John Samways from Evershot Station wrote:

*"Please forward to Evershot Station 6 (weighing out) coal baskets and 6 (carrying out) baskets at once and oblige."*

Brister End
The Lashbrook brothers with the waggon made for Vowles the miller.
They came from Beaworthy, Devon. Richard John m. Laura Rendell.
Benjamin James m. Flora Shorey of the Sussex Inn

Also in 1876, W. Hodge of Glastonbury asked:

*"When may I expect some baskets? I am quite sold out."*

P. Southcombe in Stoke sub Hamdon, enquired:

*"Sir, can you make me a few small glove hampers?
If so, I will send you the sizes."*

From Holwell, G. Hann sent some information:

*"Dear Sir, the weatheys are not Sold, going to sell them by the bolt as
they are, he asked me 1s 4d for a bolt, you better see them, but it is no
use for you to see him as he haven't forgot you."*

J. Head of Somerton was getting impatient:

*"I shall be glad to have the baskets on order without delay."*

The Jolliffe family c 1910
George and Maria Jolliffe (b. Rendell).
*From left:* Bill, Jim, Bernard (baby), Tom and Charles
*At back:* Maria's daughter, Laura


In 1872, a lady in Maiden Newton:

*"Please send as soon as possible*
*1 doz. half bushel baskets*
*½ doz. drop-handle do."*

And, finally, a postcard more or less ignoring the printed instruction: 'The address only to be written on this side'. The other side was blank. It was posted in Blandford on 11 January 1871 by an unnamed correspondent, who wrote:

*"Mr. James Dicker at the Royal Oak Inn, Church Street, Wimmycombe did you recived my letter are you coming to Yovel for i have not recived your letter."*

On the same day, 11 January, it was stamped Henstridge, and, on the following day, 12 January, Yeovil. Arrived there, the sorter, no doubt, decided that 'Dicker' must mean William Dicker of Yetminster.

Matilda Dicker died in 1889, aged 64. There were no children. William then married Ellen Rendell, daughter of Charles and Edith Rendell of Preston. Edith had been born in Yetminster. In 1893, Ellen's daughter, Maria Rendell, married George Jolliffe. They had a family of sons. Maria's daughter, Laura, married one of the Lashbrooke brothers. They had arrived in Yetminster, probably from Devon, and set up in business as waggon-makers at Brister End, next to the Sussex Inn. One of their waggons, made for Vowles the miller, may be seen in Dorchester Museum. During the first World War, they worked for Westlands making aeroplanes.

William Dicker, Parish Clerk of Yetminster for 43 years, died 31 December 1901 aged 75 years. Ellen Dicker died in the same year aged 54 years.

––––

To see the basket making process carried out just as it was by the Dickers and Chedzoys, it is recommended that a visit be made to Coates Willow and Wetlands Visitor's Centre at Stoke St Gregory, Somerset. They have been making baskets since 1819. There is also a small Museum, exhibiting many of the articles made of willow – chairs, baby-carriages and even a coffin!

# The Anne and Mary Charity

In St Andrew's Church, Leigh may be seen a brass tablet bearing the following inscription:

*"A Christmas Gift to the Poor of Leigh in the name and memory of Anne and Mary*

*ANNE*
*Daughter of Richard Hare of Leigh*
*Died April 5th 1853*

*MARY*
*Daughter of Thomas Samson*
*of Kingston Russell, Dorset*
*Died October 22nd 1855*

*Buried in the same grave in Holy Trinity Churchyard, Brompton in the Parish of Kensington, Middlesex."*

The Charity provided money to buy, annually, a blue coat for a boy and a red cloak for a girl, a condition being that the two recipients should be pupils attending Leigh Parish School. They were chosen by their fellow-pupils.

At first sight one might think that here were two little girls, friends in life and united in death. Read on . . .

The Hare family first appears in Leigh in 1774, when, following the death of Agnes Yeates, Richard Hare took possession of Black Barn, part of the Manor of Yetminster Secunda. Richard was the son of Richard Hare who married Ann Ridout at Holnest in 1734. Richard, the son, married Jane Granger. They had a daughter, Anne, and a son,

Black Barn, Leigh. Home of the Hare family

Richard. In 1795, Richard Hare m. Jane King. The witnesses were Thomas King and William Barrett jun.

Hare was a butcher. On 29 November 1799, the Sherborne Mercury records: "Hare, butcher of Leigh was stopped by three foot-pads at Holmbushes and robbed of £14. He was unharmed."

Thomas King is believed to have been an elder brother of Jane King. A liaison developed between himself and Anne Hare, and, on 28 March 1806, a son, Thomas Hare, was born to her. It was not until 18 August that he was baptised and entered in the Register as "base".

The couple never married.

On 16 September 1818, Thomas King married Ann Bewsey by Licence. She was born in 1793, the daughter of John and Elizabeth Bewsey of Leigh, and so considerably younger than King who was born in 1767. Children, David and Jane, were born to them. Thomas King died 1 November 1857 aged 89 years and 11 months. His wife, Ann,

The 'Anne and Mary' Charity Plaque in Leigh Church

died 10 April 1875 aged 83 years. Their son, David died in 1881 aged 61 years and is interred in Tottenham Cemetery. Also commemorated on Thomas King's tombstone is one David Ferguson who died in 1884 aged 63 years.

Thomas Hare 1806–1891.
Son of Ann Hare of Leigh
He founded the 'Ann and Mary' Charity
Photo courtesy of John Andrews, his great, great grandson

On 3 July 1820, just two years after the marriage of Thomas King, Ann Hare married William Barrett. There were no children.

The Barrett family held "Whitehall" at Leigh, and, after William's death in 1841 at the age of 83, Anne went to reside with her son.

Nothing is known of Thomas Hare's early life, he must have received an education, for, in 1828 he was admitted a student at Inner Temple and called to the Bar in 1833.

By the summer of 1837, Thomas was determined to marry Mary Samson of Kingston Russell. Her brothers opposed the marriage but Mary was equally determined. Her elder sister, Catherine, had married Thomas Hare's cousin, Thomas King Hare, son of his mother's brother, Richard Hare and Jane (b. King).

In July 1837, Thomas Hare wrote a long letter to Thomas Samson, Mary's brother, setting out his assets, which were few, but included "a small estate in Leigh" settled on his mother for her life and worth, he says, perhaps £1,000, and his prospects, which were, at that point, unknown and dependent upon his abilities and his connections amongst solicitors who might introduce him to business. In short, Thomas was poor. What funds he had, had largely been expended upon his professional education, costs of admission to the Inns of Court and calling to the Bar.

Thomas begged, that for their sister's sake, the brothers might overcome their animosity and be present at the marriage. Her brother, Charles, had refused to allow Mary to be married from his house in Manchester. So, they were married in Liverpool where they had friends. On the Marriage Certificate, Thomas Hare gave his father's name as Thomas King. They honeymooned in the Lake District before returning to London to part of a house at 19 Tollington Park, Hornsey Road, which Thomas had rented as their first home.

Thomas Hare prospered. As a lawyer, he was untiring. He wrote a number of pamphlets and was particularly interested in putting forward a new system of proportional representation. At one time, he was a member of the Charity Commission, which, possibly, gave him the idea for a Charity in memory of his mother, Anne Hare and his wife, Mary Samson.

He might have mentioned himself, but did not. By this time, fifty years had passed since the village was agog with the news that Anne

Hare had been delivered of a son out of wedlock. Probably, there were few who remembered.

On 4 April 1843, the Manor Court Book of Yetminster Secunda records that "Black Barn" passed from Thomas Stone to Thomas Hare of Osmington and Thomas Hare of the Inner Temple. Hare of Osmington was Thomas's cousin who had married Catherine Samson, his wife's sister.

It is not clear how Thomas Stone came to be associated with "Black Barn", a mortgage, perhaps. When Richard Hare took possession in 1774, the property passed first from Agnes Yeats to Thomas Stone and then to Hare.

Thomas Hare's portrait hangs in the National Portrait Gallery, it shows a benevolent, white-haired old gentleman who bears a striking resemblance to his descendant, John Andrews.

Thomas Hare died of pneumonia on 6 May 1891 and was buried in Hook, Surrey.

# Tailors and Tape

Thomas Wright, tailor, of Yetminster died in 1672. The Inventory taken of his goods must be one of the most detailed ever recorded. The document measures 34 in.×7 in.

On 18 November 1672, four men, Thomas Ring, gent., John Allambridge, John Miller and John Wright, set about this lengthy task.

The house was not large: just four rooms, hall, parlour, parlour chamber and chamber over the hall plus the shop. No kitchen or buttery is mentioned, so, possibly, shop and kitchen were one and the same. He owned the usual furniture and household goods and

*"an earthern pot with the King's Arms on it*
*"a Bible and another book*
*"7 silver spoons belonging to the children*
*"3 gold rings, 5 silver spoons & a bodkin.*

Wright appeared to be comfortably off though his own wearing apparrel was valued at only £2 10s 0d.

But his widow had a good wardrobe:

*"a cloth pettycote & wastcote*
*"a stuffe pettycote & Xtning whittle*
*"a cloth wastcote*
*"a green serdge cote*
*"a tammy pettycote*
*"a red serdge wastcote*
*"3 whittles*
*"a wastcote & a child's hood*

The whole valued at £4 5s 0d.

No doubt, she pulled it all out of the chest and complained that she hadn't got a thing to wear.

Wright also owned 5 pairs of shears and 5 pressing-irons.

The appraisers moved to the shop.

Here, they recorded no fewer than 69 items. Every piece of material, braid and trimming was measured to the last quarter of a yard, buttons were counted by gross and dozens. In all, about one hundred yards of material of various kinds were measured:

*cloth of varying shades of grey, cinnamon & stone*
*serdge —— brown & cinnamon*
*fustian – striped & bird's-eye*
*canvas, dowlas & lining*
*calico buckram and cloth buckram*
*striped linen*
*striped inkle & braid inkle*
*green silk lace & green worsted lace*
*black & brown thread*
*23 doz. cote thread buttons*
*17½ doz. cote gimp & 3 gross 1 doz. breast gimp*
*17 doz. wastcote thread buttons*
*3 doz. cote leather buttons*
*3 gross 7 doz. brest silk buttons*
*3 gross 3 doz. cote silk buttons*
*silver braid & looping & filleting*
*2½ doz. strawberry tipt buttons*
*a piece of Melbury tape*
*14 yds. of ribbon*
*9 lbs. of whalebone*
*Remnants of galloon & other cloth*
*Man's cloth stockings @ 3s 6d, Youth's @ 2s 9d*
*Women's stockings 4s*
*fustian drawers @ 3s 6d, canvas drawers 1s 6d*

| | | | |
|---|---|---|---|
| *In all* | *£38* | *7s* | *8d* |
| *Household stuff* | *27* | *19* | *2* |
| *Good debts re'cd & money due* | *40* | *00* | *00* |
| *Total* | *£106* | *6* | *10* |

How long did it take the four men to measure all the material and trimming and to count the dozens of buttons?

Here we have a good idea of what the well-dressed Yetminster man was wearing in 1672 – a beaver grey coat, perhaps, with a cinammon waistcoat, trimmed with braid and sporting silk buttons and brown serge breeches plus a pair of drawers, fustian or canvas to choice. Some of the linen, no doubt, was intended for shirts.

It is unfortunate that the Will has not survived, it might have revealed some interesting family relationships.

One item mentioned in the Inventory is "a piece of Melbury tape". This takes us to Melbury Osmond where there was a thriving business in the manufacture of inkle tape. It was a narrow tape much in demand by tailors and corset and bodice makers, for it was very strong and used to form the channels into which the whalebone was inserted.

Inkle-weaving is slightly different from normal cloth weaving. The warp is put on the small inkle-loom and the weft passed to and fro, but, on the finished tape, the weft is seen only at the edges where the turn is made, in the tape itself, the weft is completely hidden by the warp. This gives much greater strength than in normal cloth weaving where warp and weft appear equally, criss-crossing each other.

Flax was grown in many local areas, including Yetminster. Inkle-loom weaving was ideal as a cottage industry as the loom took up so little space.

Melbury Osmond was renowned for its tape, and, it is interesting that the industry was flourishing as early as 1670.

A Parish Survey of 1800 shows that a large number of the inhabitants were still, at that date, engaged in spinning and weaving flax.

Flax spinning differs somewhat from wool spinning. The combed flax, which resembles a tress of long hair, is fixed to the distaff and bound, criss-cross fashion, with ribbon or tape. It is essential that, throughout the spinning process, the flax is kept damp, so the spinner has a small bowl of water in which she constantly wets her fingers.

The Survey shows 65 households and 335 individuals, many, of course, were children.

Henry Farr appears as Tape Manufacturer and Thomas Cave and his son, John, as linen manufacturers.

Fifty women were engaged in spinning and six women and eleven men were weavers. There was one flax comber, three women spoolers and one warper.

The remainder of the adult population was made up as follows:

*The Rector, the Rev. William Jenkins*
*Schoolmaster Abraham Fiander*
*Miller Richard Daw*
*4 farmers employing 32 agricultural labourers*
*1 staymaker*
*1 shoemaker*
*1 baker*
*1 shop-keeper*
*1 woodman*
*1 gardener*
*3 masons*
*3 thatchers*
*8 carpenters*
*7 male & 7 female servants*
*1 rag gatherer*
*1 gatherer of ashes*

Clearly, apart from the farmers, Henry Farr and Thomas Cave were the largest employers in the village. The masons, carpenters and thatchers probably worked for the nearby Strangways Estate.

The rag gatherer and the gatherer of ashes are interesting. One would associate the former with paper making, and the latter, perhaps, with soap-boiling.

# Here and There

1680 Dorothy Willis to dyke her ditch and take in the water in her backside against Brake's house. s.p. 6s 8d
Sir George Strode to dike his ditch at his ground called Tark's Hill from Brake's house to the river. s.p. 6s 8d

This land lies between the present Melbury Road, Birch Lane and the river.

1618 Church Wardens' Presentments.
We present Margaret Gaste, wife of Thomas Gaste, for going away out of Leigh with Edmund Taunton in a very suspicious manner of incontinentcy.

1682 Surveyors of the Highway to raise the way at the east end of the bridge in Yetminster at the end of Watery Lane.

Watery Lane lies under the new housing estate at Brister End.

1682 Joseph Hodges to cleanse the water-course in his ground called Nether Mill from the river to Robert Bartlett's backside end. To be done before Christmas s.p. 10d. (This presentment was made three times).

1687 Samuel Keate of Leigh to remove the earth against the pound, it being a nuisance. To be done within a week. s.p. 3s 4d.

1700 Buried, William, aged 7 years, son of Robert Jenkins of Chetnole, drowned in a well.

1702 Buried, Mary, 6 years and Phillis, 2 years, daughters of John Hunt, both at one time drowned in a pitt on Leigh Common.

1796 The wife of Edward Harris of Yetminster, fell down-stairs and was killed. She left six children and was far gone with seventh. She was Mary, daughter of Joseph and Jane Cooper.
She married Edward Harris in 1779. Their children were Mary, Jenny, Elizabeth, Benjamin, George and Harriet.

1801 Died at Cerne Abbas, Mrs. Meech, relict of Mr. Meech, Surgeon and Apothecary, aged 95.

1801 Died at Harbour Grace, Newfoundland, Mrs. Garland, 118 years and daughter aged 86 years. The elder, mother to Charles Garland Esq., present Collector of Taxes at Harbour Grace.
The Garlands were wealthy Poole merchants trading with Newfoundland.

1804 Died at Dorchester, Miss Jane Smith, sister-in-law to Charles Cosens, Esq. of that place. The taking fire of her muslin dress, an accident extremely common and aften fatal, was the cause of this lady's much lamented death.

1807 Mr. Henry Sheppard of Yetminster returning from Stoford Fair, fell over a narrow bridge called Gallytram Bridge, lost his life in his 76th year. He had previously fallen and had cautioned people to be careful.
He was Churchwarden, 1805–1807 and died in office.
He was probably nephew to Mary Sheppard who married James Hayward, landlord of the "Blackamoor's Head".
Gallytram was off Coles Lane, a very wet area. Doubtless, poor Henry had climbed the hill from Stoford to Clifton Maybank and was making his way along the foot-paths from Clifton to Yetminster.

1810 John Dicker, aged 50 and boy, Thomas Patience, were found dead, thought to have been struck by lightning near Upcerne. They had been in the morning with their master's team from Batcombe to Dorchester with a load of potatoes.
Verdict at the Inquest: Found dead by the Visitation of God.

248

1811    Sale of prime oak, ash and elm timber at Stockwood and Yetminster. 17 Lots. Apply: Mr. Edmunds, Stockwood Mill or Mr Donne, cooper, Yetminster.

1812    Militia deserters include:
John Cooper of Yetminster, mason, 24 years, 5' 9", grey eyes, light hair.
James Pitman of Yetminster, mason, 23 years 5' 7" blue eyes, dark hair.

1809    To be auctioned at White Hart, Yetminster, 293 oak trees on divers lands at Stockwood. Particulars of White Hart or Farmer Brake, tenant. To be sold by Mr. James Male, timber surveyor and auctioneer.

*Stockwood* 19 February 1406                    *Dean Chandler's Register*

*William Hayward witholds 7 sheep and 6 bushels of oats from the Church and fails to provide a candle in Church yearly.*
*Penalty reserved because he is blind.*

These were gifts which had been made to the Church and which should have been sold and the proceeds devoted to the purchase of candles which would have burned for the intentions of the donors. Hayward was probably Church warden.

*30 March 1692*                    *Digby Manor Court*

*". . . we present John Gaste, tenant of customary cottage in Chetnole, who departed from Chetnole about fourteen years since declaring he would go beyond the seas, since which time he hath not been heard of, and, therefore, and for diverse other circumstances sworn in former Courts, we have good reason to present him to be dead. It is sworn that John Gaste did nominate his godson, Thomas Meech, to be Lord's next tenant of his cottage."*

## From the "Sherborne Mercury" c 1750

This is to give notice to all Gentleman, Traders and Others-That there will be a constant Flying Waggon set out from the Bell Inn in Wood

249

Street, London every Monday Morning at seven o'clock, and will be at Chard every Friday.

And, likewise, a Waggon will set out from the Cloughs in Chard every Tuesday morning and will be at London every Saturday and will carry Goods and Passsengers to and from the Places following (Where great care will be taken of them) viz.

Shaston, Stalbridge, Henstridge Ash, Milborne Port, Sherborne, Yeovil, Crewkerne, Chard, Axminster, Martock, South Petherton, Hinton St. George, Broadway, Thorncombe, Windsham, Beaminster, Melbury, Yetminster, Honiton, Ilminster, Taunton, Bridgewater, Uffcombe, Wellington, Wiveliscombe, Dulverton, Bampton, Tiverton, and Exeter and there lodge goods for all places in Cornwall and Places adjacent.

On 7 February 1803, at Lillington, Benjamin Watts had married his cousin, Elizabeth Watts. William Barrett was one of the Witnesses. Elizabeth's mother was born Elizabeth Barrett and married Joseph Watts in 1780. As well as Elizabeth, she had a daughter, Martha and a son, Joseph before dying prematurely from consumption in 1790, aged only 31.

So, Benjamin's bride had been motherless from the age of nine years. He, himself, was born in Chetnole in 1777, he grew up to be a butcher by trade, but, like many such, he was also farming.

In 1818, he appears to have been renting land from Mark Davis, the owner of the Holnest estate. One cannot help feeling that Davis might have given him time to pay off his arrears of rent instead of having him thrown into the debtors' prison. What a traumatic experience it must have been for Benjamin, the Dorset countryman, to have found himself, not only in London, but in one of the capital's largest gaols. No wonder he turned to his kinsman, William Barrett, for help, considering not only himself, but his wife and young children. Remembering, nevertheless, to instruct Barrett to hide some of his household goods to avoid distraint! How did he fare in the great metropolis, when, at last, the gates opened and he was free to find his own way home.

The next we hear of Benjamin is in July 1830. Joseph Barrett of Whitehall, Leigh had died without naming the Lord's next tenant to his property. William Barrett applied to the Manor Court to be admitted. Permission was granted on condition that he paid £60 to the Lord and

£200 equally between six of his relatives one of whom was Benjamin Watts.

A similar condition was placed upon 8 acres of land – £140 to the Lord and £400 to be divided between the six relatives. Benjamin Watts stood to receive well over £100, no mean sum at that time.

By 1834, Benjamin had moved to Sherborne. The Map of that date shows him renting a house and garden from one William Hull and part of a garden opposite from the Digby Estate. These properties were situated on the outskirts of Sherborne, just west of Castle Farm and north of the parish boundary of Castleton.

In 1851, he was still there, with wife, Elizabeth, Joseph and Sarah ("my little Joseph and Sarah") he had thought about in prison and a daughter, Elizabeth, born after his release.

## Letter written in 1818 by Benjamin Watts of Holnest to *William Barrett of Leigh*

November 6 1818 Kings Bench London Number 3 Mr Willm Barrett I hope that you received my last letter that I send to you that was this day wick on a Fryday but it make me afraid that you have not because I had No answer sence it is sence that I Receved the pasel and Letter from you that I send you a Letter but no answer from you It make me afraid that you had not a Got It be so Kind to write on the Next letter for to Convence me whether you Receve it or Not for I am unhappy about it becase I had no answer from It and I want answer a send to Me conserving the few things that is left, a chest of drows Nor No silver spoons nor Lucking glas nor Clock nor watch to be put on the a count you send me but if aney such thing in the way put it out of sight before it is praised. It must be dun emegetley for I want it you must not delay no time about it. And about the money Let that bide Quiet till call for and lett nobody now that you got aney and if they ask aney Qustens about it tell them the tuck all for rent. It is a bad job for me you can say and you dont now what I shall do. Be so kind to don it as Quick as posebel you can els it will be a great engerey to me in getting out. Please to Remember to My wife and lettel fameley and I hope thay are all well and my lettel Sarah and Joseph and I long to be with them. So no more at present I am your most humbel servant Benjn Watts.

An account of hay, etc. the property of Benjamin Watts formerly of Holnest farmer & now a prisoner for debt in the Kings Bench prison which was sold under a distress for rent due to Mark Davis Esq. amount to the sum of forty pounds on the 19 day of October 1818 the particulars of which hereunder:

| Lot | | | |
|-----|----|---------------------------|------|
| | 1 | *Hay rick in Calves Hay* | *£30* |
| | 2 | *Part of rick in Loaders Mead* | *23* |
| | 3 | *Part of ,, Calves Close* | *6* |
| | 4 | *Hay rick in Black Lion* | *23* |
| | 5 | *Part of ,, ,,* | *20* |
| | 6 | *Rick of hay in Cow Lane* | *18* |
| | | | *£120* |

Note in Watts's hand.

*Plese to go to Mr Tayler & have the hay put on a 2s 6d stamp that other papaer will not do for the Court that is send all redey & stated like that above. And you must get Mr Shering of Sherborne & value the rest things that is left and my wife & children's things bring in as low as he can and that must be on a 2s 6d stamp.*

## "Please to remember the Brief"

Nowadays, when asked to contribute to some charitable cause, we can be reasonably certain that our donation will benefit those for whom it was intended. This was not always so.

In earlier times, there was a system known as 'Briefs', i.e. royal mandates for collections towards some supposedly deserving object. The 'brief' was addressed to the Minister and Churchwardens of a Parish and read from the pulpit. At the close of the service, the Clerk stood at the Church door to take the collection, saying: "Please to remember the brief."

Briefs were issued for a variety of causes: for Church repair, for persons who had suffered loss by fire or flood and for the redemption of captives. The money was handed to an authorised travelling collector. After the Restoration, 'briefs' were often farmed out to professional collectors. The system was open to great abuse and much of the money collected failed to reach those for whom it was intended.

In the 17 c and 18 c an incumbent would sometimes enter in the back of his Register the amounts collected for 'briefs'. John Russell, Rector of Ryme Intrinseca, did just this.

Here is his record for the years 1666–1692

| | | | | |
|------|-----------------------------------------------------|-----|-----|------|
| 1666 | "for the late dreadful fire" of London paid to George Hill Constable of the Liberty of Ryme | | 11s | |
| 1669 | Thetford Norfolk paid to John Courtne | | 2s | |
| 1670 | Islham Cambridge paid to Joseph Wood | | 2s | |
| 1671 | Meere Wilts paid to James Piddle Constable | | 2s | |
| 1671 | Bradford Abbas paid to Thomas Creese | | 12s | |
| 1671 | Luton, Beds "lass by fire" paid to Lancelot Welsh | | 1s | 9½d |
| 1672 | Kingston upon Thames "loss by fire" paid to Lancelot Welsh | | 1s | |
| 1672 | Fordingbridge Hampshire "loss by fire" paid to John Bound | | 4s | |
| 1672 | Heston Middlesex paid to Lancelot Welsh | | 1s | 9d |
| 1673 | Russell St. St Martin in the fields "loss by fire paid to Lancelot Welsh | | 1s | 6d |
| 1673 | "Redemption of poor captives sometime of Poole from under their miserable slavery under the Turks in ?" Paid to Lancelot Welsh | £3 | 2s | 6d |
| 1673 | "loss by fire of Tho. Hewit, clothier, of Lawrence Waltham, Berks. Paid to Lancelot Walsh | | 1s | 3d |
| 1674 | "loss by fire in Nether Wallop, Hants" paid to William Knight | | 18s | 8d |

| 1674 | Repair of the Parish Church in Benenden, Kent | 1s | 5d |
|------|-----------------------------------------------|----|----|
|      | paid to Lancelot Welsh | | |
| 1675 | Redbourn, Herford | 1s | 0d |
|      | paid to Lancelot Welsh | | |
| 1676 | "loss by fire at Cerne Abbas" | 8s | 2d |
|      | paid to Francis Duferell | | |
| 1677 | "loss by fire in Borough of Southwark" | 4s | 0d |
|      | paid to John Savage | | |
| 1677 | "loss by fire at Blandford" | 1s | 4d |
|      | paid to Robert Crouch | | |
| 1680 | "loss by fire of the poor people of East Derham" | 3s | 0d |
|      | paid to John Tooker | | |
| 1680 | Poland brief | 1s | 6d |
|      | Stafford brief | | 6d |
|      | paid to Mr John Grateley | | |
| 1682 | East Budley, Devon | 2s | 3d |
|      | paid to Robert Coud | | |
| 1682 | "distressed French protestants" | 3s | 0d |
|      | paid to John Daggle | | |
| 1687 | "loss of Tho. Haggard alias Pinian of Melbourn | 2s | 0d |
|      | paid to William Perkins of the same | | |
| 1687 | the market town of Standly St Leonard, Glos. | 1s | 6d |
|      | paid to John Daggle | | |
| 1690 | brief for Southwark | 5s | 0d |
|      | brief for Estsmithfield | 1s | 6d |
|      | brief for Bishops Canington | 1s | 0d |
|      | paid to Will. Fletcher | | |
| 1691 | Morpeth | 1s | 6d |
|      | paid to Nicholas Daggle | | |
| 1692 | Teignmouth & Shasdon | 1s | 6d |
|      | paid to Abraham Laddimor | | |

How may we assess the generosity of the people of Ryme?

We might consider the Poor Rate, levied on all but the very poor. In Yetminster, the assessment ranged from 2s or 3s to as little as one farthing. It was probably much the same in Ryme.

A labourer's wage was about 8d to 10d per day.

254

The population of Ryme was, perhaps, about 130. In 1642, all males of 18 years and over were required to subscribe to the Protestation Oath. In Ryme, 46 men subscribed and it has been estimated that males over the age of 18 made up 31% of the population.

In 1676, Thomas Hayward of Ryme died leaving goods valued at £263. 4s. 5d.

*Four swine were valued at £6.*
*20 kine and a bull at £80.*
*4 plough steers at £17.*
*His stock of 900 cheeses was worth £9.*

It would seem that contributions were mostly for one or two pence, the value of one of Thomas's cheeses.

But, what happened in 1673 when the large sum of £3. 2s. 6d was collected to help redeem the men of Poole from the Turks? Doubtless, these unfortunate sailors had been captured by pirates and the successful outcome of a rescue attempt seems most improbable.

# Glossary

| | |
|---|---|
| Amory/aumbry . | a cupboard usually for food with doors pierced for ventilation. |
| andirons ....... | large fire-dogs with hooks at different levels which supported a spit for cooking in front of an open fire. |
| beavers ........ | a heavy woollen cloth. |
| cockloft ........ | space between ceiling and roof. |
| crock .......... | a metal pot with 3 short legs & 2 handles by which it can be hung over a fire by means of a pot-hook. |
| carpet ......... | a table-cover not a floor covering. |
| coffer ......... | wooden box or chest covered with leather. |
| desperate debts .. | those unlikely to be paid. |
| dicker ........ | 10 hides or skins. |
| dowlas ........ | a coarse linen. |
| drag .......... | a harrow. |
| dust-bed ....... | mattress filled with chaff. |
| fustian ........ | coarse, twilled cotton, inc. moleskin, velveteen, corduroy. |
| galloon ........ | narrow tape-like trimming. |
| gimp ......... | a trimming. |
| harness-girdle ... | a girdle made of chain-links, gold or silver. |
| holland ....... | coarse linen fabric, unbleached or dyed brown. |
| inkle .......... | small loom for weaving tape. |
| kerseymere ..... | twilled cloth of very fine wool. |
| kettle ......... | an open cooking-pot with a handle by which it is suspended over a fire. |
| kip ........... | skin of young animal (between calf & cow-hide). |
| lawn .......... | fine cotton or linen cloth. |
| mantel ........ | chimney. |
| pannell ........ | pad used as a rough saddle. |

| | |
|---|---|
| pot-hooks ....... | for suspending pots of varying sizes from adjustable hooks from bar in chimney. |
| pottinger ....... | a bowl for soup, porridge etc. |
| pillow-bier ...... | pillow-case. |
| putt .......... | heavy two-wheeled cart made to tip. |
| rodder/rother beasts ....... | oxen. |
| saucer ......... | container for sauce. |
| seed-lipp ....... | large pouch with shoulder strap for holding seed when sown broadcast by hand. |
| shift .......... | woman's loose undergarment, from shoulder to calf of cotton or linen (or dowlas if cheap e.g. for the poor). |
| skillet .......... | metal pan with long handle & 3 short legs for setting on open fire. |
| swansdown ..... | cloth brushed on one side. |
| tallet .......... | a loft. |
| trendle ........ | large round wooden tub with handles. |
| turn .......... | a spinning-wheel. |
| wain .......... | 4 wheeled cart, removeable 'gate-like' structures fore and aft to enable hay and corn-sheaves to be piled high. |
| wendling calves .. | newly-weaned calves. |
| whittle ........ | baby's long flannel petticoat/shawl. |
| zull ........... | plough (the implement) |
| plough ........ | the team of horses, as 'plough and dung-pot'. |

# Index

Abington 143, 144, 145, 146, 148
Addams 99
Allambridge 11, 13, 15, 18, 19, 24,
  61, 62, 101, 107, 108, 109, 110, 111,
  112, 113, 114, 115, 134, 135, 149,
  152, 175, 177, 179, 203, 214, 243
Allwood 23
Andrews 16, 20, 28, 29, 33, 34, 46,
  52, 70, 71, 101, 103, 138, 159, 160,
  167, 184, 230, 242
Antill 142
Applin 108
Armstrong 142
Arnold 21, 91, 92
Ashley 31
Axe 131
Ayers 55

Bailey 110, 126, 127, 128, 153
Baine 31, 32
Baker 15, 44, 115, 116, 184
Ball 5, 185
Banger 34
Barbe 18
Barber 28, 29, 205, 207, 208, 210
Barjew 147, 148
Barker 167
Barnswell 46, 161
Baron 181
Barrett 34, 43, 44, 52, 85, 149, 150,
  238, 241, 250
Barter 34
Bartholomew 151
Bartlett 8, 18, 25, 27, 34, 36, 39, 43,
  45, 49, 52, 53, 63, 88, 99, 103, 110,
  127, 133, 138, 166, 167, 168, 169,
  173, 176, 184, 193, 210, 247

Bastable 63
Batson 181
Batt 53, 62
Batten 115, 150
Baverstock 191, 192
Beard 203
Bearer 113
Beaty 62
Beer(e) 70, 112, 113, 116, 134, 179
Bellamy 120, 170
Bellringer 72
Besant 34, 168, 180, 184
Bestland 168
Bewsey/Bucey 23, 238
Bird/Burd 218, 219, 222, 232
Bishop 11, 28, 34, 45, 46, 49, 56, 57,
  89, 90, 132, 151, 160, 215, 232
Blackdon 28
Blake 34
Blanchard 116, 222
Blaydon 11
Bound 203
Bowdidge 71
Boyle 95
Bragg 213, 214
Brake 20, 22, 26, 33, 34, 45, 46, 56,
  58, 59, 60, 61, 62, 80, 84, 89, 102,
  139, 173, 185, 190, 192, 203, 204,
  212 to 228, 247, 249
Brassier 98
Brewer 11, 210, 21
Brinsome 116
Brooke 112
Brown 22, 32, 50, 167, 185
Bruorton 142
Bridle 62
Buchanan 167

259

Buck   26
Buckland   34, 55, 63, 142, 181
Budge   71
Bugler   16, 46
Bullen   149
Burbidge   56, 57
Burrows   226
Byrt   28

Cadie   131, 132
Caffe   11, 198
Cake   92
Carter   32, 177
Causier   82
Cave   63, 127, 246
Chaffey/Chaffie   63, 170, 177
Chadwick   33
Chainey   161
Channing   165
Chant   15, 89
Chapman   143, 188, 194, 226
Chaundler   116
Chedzoy   232, 236
Cheesman/Chisman   8, 25, 34, 54,
   62, 127, 128 139, 177, 215
Chilcott   66, 69
Child(s)   90, 134, 135
Chinnock/Chynock   55, 56, 63, 113,
   141
Chipp   46
Chubb   199
Clapcott   11, 105, 106, 113
Clark(e)   70, 71, 109, 179, 216
Clement   145
Clifton   146
Cobb   181
Cockeram   132, 214
Colbourne   225
Cole   27, 79, 185, 209
Colfox   167
Collins   33
Colson   145
Comb/Coombes   15, 16, 26, 27, 32,
   34, 46, 49, 53, 58, 62, 63, 99, 100,

101, 103, 112, 114, 119, 151
Compton   145
Conway   12, 27, 29, 53, 54, 55, 62, 63
Cook   62
Cooper   4, 11, 12, 28, 55, 139, 141,
   166, 169, 248, 249
Cooth   30, 31
Corfield   46
Cornick   102
Cornish   147
Corry   72, 76
Cosens   19, 30, 138, 143, 145, 148,
   163, 164, 165, 168, 169, 170, 171,
   172, 173, 174, 184, 209
Cox   173, 193
Crabb   229
Cranham   227
Critchell   188, 189
Crocker   223, 224
Cupper   34
Curtis   25, 33, 103
Custard   103
Cullen   142
Culliford   184

Daggle   23, 152, 185
Dampney   79, 83, 151
Davis   250, 252
Dawe(s)   34, 43, 44, 45, 46, 101, 208,
   226, 246
Deering   11, 15
Devenish   27, 72, 74, 76
Dicker   28, 204, 229, 230, 232, 233,
   235, 236, 248
Dingley   191, 192, 193, 209
Doddrell   80, 84, 204, 205
Dodge   55, 180, 181, 184
Dolberie   108
Donne   34, 58, 59, 60, 62, 190, 249
Douch   91
Douglas   56, 212, 213
Downton   11, 28, 116, 230
Dunham   110
Dun(s)ford   62, 79, 80, 86

260

Durden 63
Duris 61
Dyer 89

Eastman/Eastment 34, 61, 157, 158, 159
Edmonds/Edmunds 16, 57, 103, 135, 159, 173, 226, 249
Edwards 16, 34, 57, 58, 59, 60, 61, 62, 80, 102, 159, 161, 163, 177, 207
Elford 18, 37, 116
Ellary 62
Ellis 154
Everard 27, 108, 175, 176, 177, 178
Everett 208
Eyears 59, 60, 61, 123, 160, 161
Eynon 165

Farr 222, 246
Feaver 61, 112, 113, 114, 148, 177
Ferguson 239
Fiander 246
Field 223
Fisher 10, 203, 228
Fitzherbert 105, 184
Fitzjames 3, 154
Floyer 146, 147, 148, 149
Fluellen 207
Fooks 6, 76, 104, 134, 135, 155, 157, 158, 161, 178, 204
Foot(e) 104, 148, 166, 167, 178, 181
Forward 40
Fox 56, 63, 213
Foy 37, 39, 177
Foyle 109
Frampton 46, 139, 160
Freek 141
French 27
Fudge 25, 34, 62
Furber 177

Gale 216
Galpin 16, 34
Garland 167, 215, 248

Gast(e) 11, 28, 247, 249
Gaulton 222
Geard 103
Genge 71
Gibbons 95
Gilbert 80
Gill 157, 159
Gillard 190
Gillingham 177
Giner 34
Glyde 62, 67, 116, 207
Goffe 116
Goldring 11, 23
Goldwine 8
Gollop 28, 101, 122
Good(e) 72, 76, 77, 79, 161
Gordon 80
Gorge 50, 53, 54
Goring 34, 157
Gould 89, 132, 147, 148
Granger 34, 50, 140, 162, 237
Gray 13
Greenfield 109
Griffiths 159
Grimstead 30, 50, 124, 148, 163
Groves 20, 181
Grubbing 109
Gundry 11
Guppy 34, 139, 157
Guyer 13
Gylles 88

Hackwell 160
Haddock 177
Haines 113, 181, 184
Hallett 80
Hammond 132
Hann 234
Harben 145
Hardie/y 30, 119, 127
Harding 30, 198
Hare 63, 237, 238, 241, 242
Harris 8, 10, 13, 18, 22, 25, 79, 116, 177, 203, 248

261

Harrison 25
Harvey 145
Hart 185
Hawker 166
Hayes 8, 15, 16, 23, 34, 48, 49, 50, 51, 52, 63, 140, 184, 209
Hayward 11, 25, 33, 56, 57, 58, 59, 62, 63, 66 to 88, 95, 116, 119, 122, 137, 151, 159, 161, 162, 177, 184, 186, 190, 191, 193, 194, 202, 203, 204, 209, 210, 212, 248, 249, 255
Head 234
Helyar 20, 138, 165, 169
Henning 149
Hewlett 10, 11, 170, 200, 201, 214
Hill 116, 142
(H)illary 11, 13, 32
Hillier 34
Hobbs 227
Hodges 17, 19, 27, 43, 53, 56, 62, 120, 127, 144, 145, 152, 198, 247
Hole 71
Holloway 22
Holly 103
Holt 50
Hooper 63, 169
Horsey 118
Hosey 145
Hull 34, 116
Humber 13
Hume 158
Hunt 12, 13, 18, 19, 23, 226, 247
Hurcombe 116
Husday 14, 15, 116
Hussey 62
Hutchin(g)s 63, 44, 207
Hyde 167, 226, 227

Ilchester 21
Iliff 171
I(s)les 13

Jacob 103
Jeanes 41, 50, 160

Jeffrey 33, 58, 103, 172, 187
Jenkins 13, 15, 16, 50, 52, 60, 84, 92, 98, 201, 202, 246, 247
Jenner 155
Jenning(s) 13, 44, 101, 102, 108, 149
Jerrard 90
Jolliffe 89
Jones 184
Jukes 217

Ke(a)te 6, 28, 143, 144, 145, 146, 247
Keech 104
Kellow 18
Kelway 14, 116
Kente 45
King 18, 28, 172, 238, 241
Knight 143, 145, 146, 147, 164, 165, 170, 198

Lacy 11
Lane 145
Langdon 20, 33, 34, 45, 123, 161, 225
Lashbrooke 234
Latymer 202
Laver 34, 58
Leeman 41, 42
Legg-Bagg 45
Legge 109, 126
Lemon 58
Lester 215
Lillington 11, 62, 144, 145, 146, 147, 148, 149
Lisle 105, 106
Little 19, 116, 207
Loder 13, 22
Long 23
Longman 167
Loope 27
Lucas 150
Lumbard/Lumber 25, 26, 209
Luxford 78
Lydiat 3, 155, 157, 158, 159

Maber   24, 127, 133, 141
Maidman/Ment   25, 55, 152
Maie   27
Male   249
Marsh   79, 86, 119
Martin   188, 201
Masters   66, 69, 88, 109, 116
Matthews   202
McDowell   151
Mead   116
Meech   63, 142, 151, 173, 248, 249
Melmoth   146, 165, 170, 171
Miller   10, 11, 19, 27, 28, 58, 62, 63,
   66, 69, 102, 119, 122, 124, 125, 146,
   152, 164, 199, 243
Minchinton   181
Minterne   3, 11, 28, 29, 109, 119, 163
Mitchell   11, 34, 187, 229
Mohun   142
Moor(e)   34, 181
Moorhouse   79, 86
Morey   52
Mose   113, 152
Munden   11, 27, 67, 69, 99, 113, 116,
   135, 179
Murley   122, 161
Murton   207, 216

Nash   103
Neal   34, 61
Newman   103, 165
Norman   181, 184, 198
North   142
Notley   103, 155

Oke   113
Old   213
Oldis   27, 29, 177
Oliver   34
Orchard   187
Osment/Osmond   45, 72
Owen   40

Padbury   90

Page   82
Paine/Payne   12, 23, 176, 177
Painter   34, 46, 153, 225
Palmer   203
Paltock   73, 142
Panton   167
Park   221
Partridge   104, 139, 140, 141
Patience   248
Patten   103
Pauley   141, 232
Peach   122, 161
Pearce/Peirce   31, 97
Penistone   19, 20, 21
Penny   57, 62, 90, 156, 157, 177, 178
Perkins   202
Perrot   13, 23, 62
Petty   101, 102, 137
Phippard   167, 169
Phipps   155
Pickard   133
Piddle   116, 126
Pitcher   34
Pitman   141, 166, 249
Plowman   15, 116
Pointer   167
Pomeroy   116
Porter   103
Pounsett   156
Prankard   28
Prowse   144, 145
Purdue   116

Quilton   50, 51

Radford   128
Randall/Rendell   92, 142, 234, 236
Rawles   95, 165
Read   11, 13, 22, 45, 53, 56, 73, 103,
   115, 123, 140, 141, 155, 166, 178,
   181, 203, 204, 210, 211
Redway   104
Reynolds   10, 34, 169
Rheinhart   79, 86

263

Richardson   19, 33, 34, 55, 141, 152, 160
Ridout   46, 237
Ring   20, 33, 34, 46, 90, 134, 179, 198, 199, 200, 210, 211, 243
Rocke   107, 108
Rodber   127
Rogers   90
Roper   61
Roskelly   70, 71
Rowland   181
Russell   57, 67, 191, 192, 193, 253
Ryall   84, 181, 184, 186 to 196, 199

Sam(p)son   20, 43, 84, 136, 162, 201, 202, 237, 241
Samways   157, 160, 233
Sansome   120
Saunders   142, 153
Scott   209
Scutt   177
Shappick   216
Shave   25, 26
Shear   62, 63
Shepherd/Sheppard   46, 55, 56, 57, 73, 80, 85, 103, 115, 248
Sheering/Sherry   26, 31, 186, 188, 209, 252
Shirley   34, 140, 149
Shorey   139, 173, 234
Shuttleworth   187
Silk   72, 76
Slade   89, 207, 216, 217
Smith   60, 92, 98, 101, 108, 248
Smitheram   200, 201
Snook   18
Somers   146, 148
Soper   62
Southcombe   234
Southwell   33, 139, 141, 178
Spencer   63, 178, 179
Spooner   115
Stains   168
Steed   80, 82

Stephens/Stevens   26, 33, 45, 116, 142, 152, 173
Sterr   109
Stickland   23, 70
Stileman   177
Stone   13, 37, 38, 39, 40, 70, 92, 93, 151, 242
Stow   36
Strange   11
Stro(u)d(e)   30, 34, 37, 66, 116, 247
Stubbs   108, 109
Sturmey   62
Sutton   177
Symes   17, 18, 41, 42, 77, 127
Symonds   207

Taunton   10, 13, 27, 136, 165, 247
Taylor   62, 66, 69, 103, 207, 252
Templeman   103, 113, 141
Thomas   16, 115, 194
Thompson   86
Thorne   180
Tidcombe   122, 161
Tilley   49, 100
Tompkins   34, 56, 104, 105, 106
Topham   214
Toravil   216
Traske(r)   28, 119
Tribley   195
Truebridge   80, 82
Tuck   168
Tunneys   146
Turner   70, 71, 181

Udall   207
Upward   92
Uvedale   205, 207, 208

Vardy   46
Vincent   16, 18, 21, 34, 70, 71, 138, 165, 166, 168, 169, 172, 184
Vining   46
Vowles   181

264

Waddon   145
Wadman   72
Walbridge   34, 55
Walcombe   88
Walles   118
Walters   91
Wardle   154
Warr(e)   19, 95, 98, 107, 146
Warren   28, 116
Warry   15, 16, 17, 18, 19, 129, 130,
    131, 132, 133, 134, 135, 136, 137,
    155, 156, 179, 180, 181, 203, 214
Watts   10, 15, 16, 18, 34, 40, 59, 79,
    80, 83, 85, 122, 159, 160, 161, 198,
    208, 209, 210, 250, 251, 252
Webb   155, 156, 157, 184
Welsh   11, 26
West   103
Wheadon   11, 23, 34, 152, 153
Whiffen   11, 23, 62, 113, 187, 209
Whitby   46
White   22, 92, 158, 169

Whitehead   113
Whiting   72
Whittle   80, 92
Wickham   207
Williams   11, 18, 113, 116, 151
Willis   25, 98, 107, 232, 247
Wills   116
Wilson   132
Wiltshire   13, 170, 186
Wilton   41
Winch   63
Windridge   143
Winter   11, 34, 57
Winterhay   31
Wolfe   222
Wood   14
Woodforde   156, 157, 159
Wright   45, 56, 80, 89, 167, 243

Yeates   237, 242
Young   144, 146, 147, 201

265